# The Living Legacy

# The Living Legacy

*"the soul in paraphrase, the heart in pilgrimage"*

Ben Witherington, III
with
Julie Noelle Hare

WIPF & STOCK · Eugene, Oregon

THE LIVING LEGACY
"the soul in paraphrase, the heart in pilgrimage"

Copyright © 2009 Ben Witherington III. All rights reserved. Except for brief quotations in critical publications or reviews, no part of this book may be reproduced in any manner without prior written permission from the publisher. Write: Permissions, Wipf and Stock Publishers, 199 W. 8th Ave., Suite 3, Eugene, OR 97401.

Wipf & Stock
A Division of Wipf and Stock Publishers
199 W. 8th Ave., Suite 3
Eugene, OR 97401

www.wipfandstock.com

ISBN 13: 978-1-55635-895-1

Manufactured in the U.S.A.

*To my Bishop, Al Gwinn, and his wife Joyce.
To James and Ken, my Charlottean Methodist minister friends
and colleagues in ministry. This one's for ya'll
since you both have the souls of poets.
And to Christopher Armitage,
my favorite poetry teacher from UNC days.*

# Contents

*Preface* ix
*Foreword* xiii
*Lectio Divina* xvii
*Introduction* xix

Advent and Christmas: The Dawning of the Light  1

Epiphany: The Light Appears  39

Lent: The Lengthening of the Light  71

Holy Week and Easter: The Light Rises  113

Eastertide: The Light Rises  131

Pentecost: The Light Bursts into Flame  163

Kingdomtide: The Dimming of the Light  205

# Preface

## *Scholar on Knees, with Harp*

I OFTEN THANK GOD, both in my private prayers and in my public declarations, for the saints I knew in my boyhood. They were beautiful people and to the best of my memory they were all what one would call "simple folk." As I call their roll in the times when I give thanks for the favors of life, I realize that there was probably not one among them who had more than an eighth grade education. The eloquence of their prayers or their testimony was not in sentence structure or metaphors, but in some irresistible integrity of life that seemed to possess them. So it would never have occurred to me to expect that *saint* and *scholar* should be seen as compatible—yes, even synonymous — terms. All the saints I knew were simple folk who lived at the modest corners of life.

It wasn't until—while still a teenager—I had read the Bible through half a dozen times that I began to realize that the psalms were not only earnest prayers, they were also literature of the highest order. Later I came to know the poetry of Gerard Manley Hopkins and of John Donne, and then some of the devotional expressions of Blaise Pascal, and with all of this to appreciate that the command to "love the Lord your God with . . . all your mind" was not just a figure of speech. Indeed, that God desires our intelligence as well as our emotions, so that waiting upon God may be as much a stretching of the mind as a tuning of the spirit.

And yet, we rarely think of the tie between scholarship and piety. If I speak the word scholar, I doubt that the first picture that comes to your mind is that of someone on his or her knees in deep and passionate pursuit of God. Rather, "scholar" suggests a person in the lower bowels of a library, among books that have been untouched for at least a generation—

*Preface*

specifically, since the last specialist in some obscure field found his way there.

In a sense, there's logic and reason for this kind of thinking. By its nature, scholarly research inspires not passion but more research. I suspect that the biblical or theological scholar may easily lose the loving wonder of the Book in the pursuit of its finer controversies.

But it need not be so. I think of John Baillie, the premier twentieth century Scottish theologian. He is known among scholars for a wide variety of publications, but he is no doubt most loved for *A Diary of Private Prayer*. Brevard Childs taught at the Yale Divinity School for 41 years and may have had greater influence than any other biblical scholar of his generation in shaping biblical studies, but many of his students remember him best for the prayers with which he began each class. I knew him as friend rather than as teacher, and it was a friendship with a good deal of laughter and wide-ranging conversation, but I always sensed that the underlying quality in Brevard was his devotional life.

All of which brings us to this little book of devotion. Its author, Ben Witherington III, is a biblical scholar. This is his profession, and it has been for roughly a third of a century. He has been published widely, with specialized knowledge and research in several fields as well as some forays in areas of popular religious writing. But he is also a person of prayer and in this book he invites us to enter that sacred room with him.

Now I confess readily that I have no detailed knowledge of Ben's spiritual life. I have seen him on his knees often, but only in the process of his receiving holy communion. But I know that for some time he has wanted to share his devotional pilgrimage with his readers. This is consistent with the pattern of his personality, because Ben rarely has a thought without wondering how soon he can put it into writing. In this instance he has also sought the help of an excellent former student to provide structures that will help readers make their devotional time a learning time as well. The teacher doesn't cease to be a teacher because he has gone to his knees; he simply seeks to teach from that posture.

But Ben has gone a step further. He has built this book around a number of his poems. As I see it, he reasons that the poems belong here because they so often have come to birth in the times of his devotion. Since this is their origin, this is the setting in which they are likely to be best understood. So, too, the people who will appreciate them most are those persons who are in the place of prayer, since the author and the reader have the setting in common.

A great many years ago, during the final year of my seminary studies, our campus was visited by a man who had spent much of his life as a missionary to China. When the country was taken over by the new Communist government, he was arrested and put in prison. For several years he was in a solitary cell, with virtually nothing to read. He had always loved poetry; now he began to compose some. Unfortunately, he was without paper or any writing instrument. It occurs to me that he was reduced to the same situation as, perhaps, were some who have left us with certain of the psalms. He composed the poems in his mind, then memorized them, believing that someday—please, God!—he would be released from imprisonment and he would be able to transfer his collection to paper.

I bought his book, of course! I regret to say that I have lost it somewhere along the way, perhaps by loaning it to some friend or perhaps in a careless time of cutting my library to a more manageable, transportable size. I remember, at any rate, that the poetry was good, but not great. I suspect that there was never more than the initial press run. But what mattered most to me as I read this now-forgotten man's poems is that in their lines I could feel the stunning solitude of his meeting with God. Whatever the limits of the poems as literature, their devotional integrity drew me to God.

Obviously, Ben Witherington's poems have not come to us from a prison cell, but there is a connection with that writer I mentioned. I make the connection because Dr. Witherington has chosen to make a disclaimer about his own poetry. He doesn't profess that it is great art; it is, he tells us, "quite metrical and traditional in character—involving rhythm and rhyme, alliteration and assonance." He advises further that "those who prefer free verse of various sorts, or avant-garde poetry will perhaps need to be patient with what they find here." Ben's poetry is an expression of who he is, and more particularly of who he is in relationship to his God. The reader who desires to join another believer in the ceaseless pilgrimage is the reader who will be best served by this poetry. At times such a reader will find himself or herself reading some lines again, to see what nuances of both faith and beauty may be hidden away in what is, on the surface, a simple line or an easy metaphor. Often there is more to be found than a surface reading reveals.

*Preface*

But because we live in a period when poetry is suffering neglect, no doubt someone is asking why a person should bother to put their thoughts in this genre—or why, in turn, a reader should be expected to invest the extra effort that poetry demands of those who read it.

One might answer with the authority of scripture. That is, the Bible makes an unnerving case for poetry simply by the hundreds of pages of poetry that it contains. I speak of course not only of Job, Psalms, Proverbs, Ecclesiastes, and Song of Solomon, but of the preponderant portion of such Hebrew prophets as Isaiah, Jeremiah, Hosea, Joel, Amos and Micah. As one of my professor friends has said playfully, "If you believe that the Bible is inspired by God, you have to conclude that God likes poetry."

But there is also an argument from logic. Poetry treats words with more respect than any other form of communication. It depends for its existence on a love for words; or more precisely, for the *right* word, at the *right* time, in just the *right* place. Poetry is not for those who use words carelessly. Those of us who believe that God has chosen to be revealed to our human race through the medium of words must on that ground feel that words are inherently sacred, and that we honor God's word when we show respect for the integrity of all words. Poetry encourages and confirms such thinking. I do not, myself, seek to write poetry, but I try to exercise the poet's commitment to language in my writing of prose, and I honor those who choose to bring themselves under the discipline of poetry.

One more word must be said about this book. The writer is not only a scholar who chooses in this book to write on his knees, in the spirit of devotion, and he is not only a scholar who takes up his harp to put his feelings into rhyme and meter. He is also an evangelist. That is, he isn't content to know God unless he can hope that others too can know God; he isn't satisfied to enjoy the fruit of Zion's field without offering handfuls on purpose to those who might be spiritually and intellectually hungry. He doesn't impress his commitments upon us, but he wants terribly for us to experience what he himself has found in Jesus Christ. May it be so.

J. Ellsworth Kalas
President of Asbury Theological Seminary

# Foreword

IT IS NOT REALLY a surprise that poetry is making a comeback in a postmodern age where evocative images, ideas, phrases are seen and used as potent means of communication. Nor should we be surprised that a good deal of that poetry has spiritual, religious, and sometimes even more specifically Christian content. Poetry after all is the sound of the soul verbalized, and with the strong emphasis on spiritual formation in so many different Christian traditions these days, here is one way to encourage and nurture 'soul work' both in the poet and in those who read the poetry.

Having recently worked through Garrison Keillor's remarkable anthology entitled *Good Poems*[1] I was struck by how many of those poems were in fact profoundly spiritual in character and indeed often profoundly Christian as well. So much for the theory that the soul of America at the cusp of the 21rst century has become profoundly secular in character. No, these poems in Keillor's volume tell us something similar to what we learn from the most recent Gallup poll which tells us that over 65% of all Americans attend church or synagogue regularly, and over 80% believe profoundly that God is the creator of the universe we live in, whether they adhere to theistic evolution or creationism. America, as foreigners (going all the way back to Lafayette) are often prone to notice, remains a profoundly religious and spiritual country even in jaundiced and cynical times like these where the shadow of war and terrorism continues to hover as a dark cloud over the land.

It is then perhaps a propitious moment for a brief book of Christian poems coupled with theological reflection, and spiritual formation exercises. Our souls need something positive to contemplate, hopefully something nourishing for the human spirit. The subtitle of this volume "the soul in paraphrase, the heart in pilgrimage" is a line taken from George Herbert's wonderful poem entitled "Prayer (I)". It aptly sums up what is going on in poetry, if it is any good at all. Poetry shows what is on the

---

1. Garrison Keillor, *Good Poems*, N.Y. Penguin, 2002.

## Foreword

heart and in the heart, and shows its longings as well—where it is going, or at least would like to go were it able to do so.

I have been writing poetry since I was a child. It has always seemed a natural means of self-expression to me. This is not a surprise really since I have also been immersed in music all my life, and its lyrical patterns and imprints. Not surprisingly since the music I have been immersed in has been classical music, hymnology, but also popular music of my age (rock and roll and folk music), all of which follow very regular rhythms, my poetry tends to be quite metrical and traditional in character—involving rhythm and rhyme, alliteration and assonance. I am not a rap artist or a beat poet. I also have a degree in English literature and studied at length the sonnets of Shakespeare, and the metaphysical poets (Herbert, Donne, and others), and I have found that the quatrain, the four line stanza often works best with metered and rhyming verse.

I am a Methodist whose piety is deeply grounded in song, hymn, ode, anthem, oratorio, rock opera, folk ballad and the like. For this reason, those who prefer free verse of various sorts, or avant-garde poetry will perhaps need to be patient with what they find here. The test of any good poetry however is not so much its form, but whether the marriage of form and content works, and whether the marriage of self-expression and form is genuine, authentic.

I have accepted long ago that, as these poems show, I am a traditional Christian person who lives a full but orderly life, not one plagued with huge doubts or the tempests of the soul. My poems reflect the settled convictions by which I live, and they also reflect the fact that I always have some tune or rhythm in my head. I have been told this is one reason I find writing so easy, and it may be so. What I am clearer about is that I write poetry to find out what I am really thinking, feeling, believing, and it is in the articulation that the self-revelation is complete, or at least made clearer.

These poems are arranged according to the various seasons of the church year, beginning of course with Advent and working our way around to Kingdomtide in the fall. I say 'our' because I am especially pleased to have an Asbury Seminary graduate, Julie Hare, who has gifts in the area of spiritual formation writing to be providing the spiritual exercises that are found in part three of each of these expositions on the poems. Furthermore, Ellsworth Kalas, President of Asbury Seminary, has graciously agreed to write a brief introduction for this volume as he did for my sermon volume entitled. *Incandescence*, and J.D. Walt the chaplain

*Foreword*

of Estes Chapel here at Asbury has added his reflections. Finally, Rick Danielson, one of our Beeson pastor graduates of Asbury, who has been such a help in various of my books, has provided beautiful hand drawn illustrations for some of these poems. I owe them all a great deal.

The order of presentation, after the front matter, in each instance is: 1) the poem; 2) theological and spiritual reflections on the poem; 3) spiritual formation exercises based on the poem. In regard to 3) the astute reader will recognize that the spiritual formation exercises are basically following the format known as 'lectio divina' a practice used in reading the Scriptures and other sacred texts. There are four steps to this practice each of which were seen as spiritually nourishing: 1) recitation—the reading of the sacred text out loud; 2) meditation—reflecting for the first time on the meaning of the text, and ruminating on its substance; 3) prayer, based on the meditation and on the text. Sometimes, when Scripture is the text this would even include praying the text itself, especially if it resonated or exegeted the soul of the reader in the way it did the soul of the poet; 4) contemplation. This last act of the spiritual formation process goes beyond meditation. Here is where the real soul work is done and one asks one's self pointed questions about how this text speaks to or for or about one's own spiritual pilgrimage. I am so pleased to have the help of Julie Hare with this third part of each subsection of the book, applying her knowledge of spiritual formation literature and exercises to each poem.

It is my hope that this little book will provide some stimulus for Christian growth in the faith, and in one's relationship with God the Three in One. If it accomplishes even a little of this, I will be content.

BW3

# Lecto Divina

To help the reader with the spiritual formation exercises which come at the end of each segment of our book, we felt it would be good to include *a more thorough* explanation of 'Lectio Divina' at the very outset of the work. Here it is.

## LECTO DIVINA

Lectio divina literally means "divine reading." This is an ancient monastic practice that involves a prayerful and meditative approach to the Scriptures. With the resurgence of interest in the spiritual disciplines over the last decade has come a revival of interest in this ancient practice.

The practice of *lectio divina* historically involves four moments: lectio, meditatio, oratio, contemplatio. The first moment, **lectio**, involves a repeated reading of the selected passage. The reading should be done aloud and should be careful and unhurried. If done in a group, it might be beneficial for the leader to read the passage through at different paces at least three times. A modern adaptation of this moment might be to read it in varying translations, though this might diminish the next moment.

The second moment in *lectio divina* is **meditatio**. Involved in meditatio is focused reflection on the text of the passage. During this phase, the individual (or participants) is to reflect and determine if there is a specific word or phrase that seems to be of particular interest. In other words, are any key words or phrases playing over again in your mind as you hear/read the passage? Careful thought should be given as to how this word (and passage) apply to one's own life.

**Oratio** is the third phase in *lectio divina*. In this phase, the individual or participant is called to respond to the passage by opening the heart to God. This is not meant to be just an intellectual exercise. It should be more of a conversation with God about what has surfaced during the previous two moments. Spiritual journaling might be very beneficial during this phase.

*Lecto Divina*

 The final phase of *lectio divina is* **contemplatio**. All four moments demand a posture of listening, but this one demands a quiet listening. This phase is characterized by a letting go of one's own thoughts and feelings and allowing God to speak. Often what is discovered or felt during this phase is unexpected and unlike what we would think.

Julie Noelle Hare  
Pentecost 2008

# Introduction

## *On Poets, Professors and Methodist Confessors*

> *Poetry is a fragile craft and poets die a thousand deaths from timidity and discouragement. Poetry lives in the place of travail and thrives in the realm of mystery. We must call forth our poets and take time to declare their verse "alive."*
>
> —J. D. Walt

In 1862, Thomas Wentworth Higginson, a pastor, contributed an essay in the Atlantic Monthly magazine. He wrote a letter of encouragement and advice to the young writers of America. Shortly following, he received in the mail a letter containing four poems and a humble question.

"Mr. Higginson, —Are you too deeply occupied to say if my verse is alive? The mind is so near itself it cannot see distinctly, and I have none to ask. Should you think it breathed, and had you the leisure to tell me, I should feel quick gratitude."

The letter was postmarked from Amherst, Massachusetts. Containing scant punctuation, the author used dashes to delineate the ideas. There was no signature, only a small card with a name written lightly in pencil.

The name was Emily Dickinson.

Many speculate the initial correspondence between Higginson and Dickinson, which would continue consistently for years following, gave her the courage needed to become a real poet and write what she called her "letter to the world."

In their ensuing correspondence, which lasted throughout the next decade and included personal meetings, Higginson resisted the temptation to take her to task on the rules, traditions and conventions of poetry. He instead offered a reflective quality of encouragement, taking care to

## Introduction

nurture the relationship, often referring her to other great poets of the day. The signature of her letters henceforth read, "Your Scholar."

In one of her letters she writes, "If I read a book and it makes my whole body so cold no fire can ever warm me, I know that is poetry. If I feel physically as if the top of my head were taken off, I know that is poetry. These are the only ways I know it. Is there any other way?" (pp.19-20)

By the time of her death twenty-four years later, though unpublished and unknown, she penned 1,775 poems. Her work was largely anonymous. Over a century later Emily Dickinson ranks as one of the most prolific poets in American History. (Selected Poems & Letters of Emily Dickinson. Ed. Robert N. Linscott. Doubleday. New York. 1959. 1-24)

The time has come for pastors to once again call forth and encourage poets. Poetry is a fragile craft and poets die a thousand deaths from timidity and discouragement. Poetry lives in the place of travail and thrives in the realm of mystery. We must call forth our poets and take time to declare their verse "alive."

Though I have written poetry all my life, seasons of hardship most often birth new works. The first year of law school offered such a season. I remember sharing a fresh poem with an acquaintance who had abandoned the law for a masters in English. After a cursory glance, he excoriated my work, relegating me to the dungeon of hacks. It took years to regain the confidence to write and share again.

One of the all time greatest movie moments occurred in the film, *The Dead Poet's Society*. Everyone remembers it. Professor Keating requests a student to read the opening paragraph of the preface entitled, "Understanding Poetry." Nothing short of the script can do it justice.

> NEIL KEATING: Understanding Poetry, by Dr. J. Evans Pritchard, Ph.D. To fully understand poetry, we must first be fluent with its meter, rhyme, and figures of speech. Then ask two questions: One, how artfully has the objective of the poem been rendered, and two, how important is that objective. Question one rates the poem's perfection, question two rates its importance. And once these questions have been answered, determining a poem's greatness becomes a relatively simple matter.

Keating gets up from his desk and prepares to draw on the chalk board.

*Introduction*

> NEIL KEATING: If the poem's score for perfection is plotted along the horizontal of a graph, and its importance is plotted on the vertical, then calculating the total area of the poem yields the measure of its greatness.

Keating draws a corresponding graph on the board and the students dutifully copy it down.

> NEIL KEATING: A sonnet by Byron may score high on the vertical, but only average on the horizontal. A Shakespearean sonnet, on the other hand, would score high both horizontally and vertically, yielding a massive total area, thereby revealing the poem to be truly great. As you proceed through the poetry in this book, practice this rating method. As your ability to evaluate poems in this matter grows, so will your enjoyment and understanding of poetry. Neil sets the book down and takes off his glasses. The student sitting across from him is discretely trying to eat.

Keating turns away from the chalkboard with a smile.

> NEIL KEATING: Excrement. That's what I think of Mr. J. Evans Pritchard. We're not laying pipe, we're talking about poetry.

Cameron looks down at the graph he copied into his notes and quickly scribbles it out.

> NEIL KEATING: I mean, how can you describe poetry like American Bandstand? I like Byron, I give him a 42, but I can't dance to it.

Charlie suddenly appears to become interested in the class.

> NEIL KEATING: Now I want you to rip out that page. The students look at Keating as if he has just gone mad.

> NEIL KEATING: Go on, rip out the entire page. You heard me, rip it out. Rip it out!

Charlie looks around at the others. He then looks down at his own notes, which consists of drawing breasts.

> NEIL KEATING: Go on, rip it out.

Charlie rips the page out and holds it up.

*Introduction*

> NEIL KEATING: Thank you Mr. Dalton. Gentlemen, tell you what, don't just tear out that page, tear out the entire introduction. I want it gone, history. Leave nothing of it. Rip it out. Rip! Begone J. Evans Pritchard, Ph.D. Rip, shred, tear. Rip it out. I want to hear nothing but ripping of Mr.Pritchard.

Meeks looks around reluctantly and then finally begins tearing out pages.

> NEIL KEATING: We'll perforate it, put it on a roll.

> NEIL KEATING: Keep ripping gentlemen. This is a battle, a war. And the casualties could be your hearts and souls.

Keating holds out the basket to Charlie who spits out a wad of paper.

> NEIL KEATING: Thank you Mr. Dalton. Armies of academics going forward, measuring poetry. No, we will not have that here. No more of Mr. J. Evans Pritchard. Now in my class you will learn to think for yourselves again. You will learn to savor words and language. No matter what anybody tells you, words and ideas can change the world. I see that look in Mr. Pitt's eye, like nineteenth century literature has nothing to do with going to business school or medical school. Right? Maybe. Mr. Hopkins, you may agree with him, thinking "Yes, we should simply study our Mr. Pritchard and learn our rhyme and meter and go quietly about the business of achieving other ambitions." I have a little secret for ya. Huddle up. Huddle up!

The boys get up from their seats and gather around Keating in the center of the class.

> NEIL KEATING: We don't read and write poetry because it's cute. We read and write poetry because we are members of the human race. And the human race is filled with passion. Medicine, law, business, engineering, these are all noble pursuits, and necessary to sustain life. But poetry, beauty, romance, love, these are what we stay alive for. To quote from Whitman: "O me, o life of the questions of these

*Introduction*

recurring, of the endless trains of the faithless, of cities filled with the foolish. What good amid these, o me, o life? Answer: that you are here. That life exists, and identity. That the powerful play goes on, and you may contribute a verse. That the powerful play goes on and you may contribute a verse.

Keating looks up at Todd.

NEIL KEATING: What will your verse be?

Poets must be encouraged, for with a mere handful of words they subvert the world order. Is it any wonder our poets are the most dangerous ambassadors of the Kingdom? Poets take words to their highest power. Like chemists experimenting in the lab, poets combine words into combustible compositions. Theologians laboriously wrestle with words to describe, define and delineate the qualities and character of God. Poets train words to dance in the declaration of God's glory. They craft cathedrals with words. And when poems burst into song the world joins the dance.

As a general rule, academics tend to scorn poets, but scholars who study in the theological tradition of John and Charles Wesley remember our roots live in songs. In this volume of poems comes such a scholar. This is Ben Witherington. Though he be part New Testament scholar, part preacher, part pastor, part archaeologist, and part guitar hero, he is all poet. Ponder this piece from the poem he calls "The Secret."

> For too much information
> Obscures the revelation
> Prevents a clear reception
> May even cause deception
> Instead of some advance.
>
> So let us treasure mystery
> And truths that unveil history
> Spoken in due season
> Reflecting divine reason,
> And never left to chance.

Now watch this playful turn from the one called "Creatures of Habit."

*Introduction*

> What if we found
> That ordering our sphere,
> Is just a misnomer
> For controlling our fear?
> Through all the words, Ben artfully writes the wonder of redemption. Behold this verse from "Shade Tree."

> The cross a tree on which he hung
> Bore the curse of which they sung
> 'His ways are not ours, our eyes can not see,
> The logic of love nailed to a tree.'

    This odyssey of words promises to transform tourists into pilgrims. This collection shows more than tells and demonstrates the processional movement of words into the winepress of poetry. From the whimsical to the wondrous, Ben gently weaves words together into the dangerous verse of the Kingdom, making us see realities yet to be, while inspiring us to walk into them as though they were. May their fruit be to sow the seed of this question,
    "What will your verse be?"

John David (J.D.) Walt, Jr.
Asbury Theological Seminary
Dean of the Chapel
KingdomTide 2008

# Advent and Christmas

*The Dawning of the Light*

## THE BONDING

A cold and listless season,
And full of cheerless cheer,
When hopes are raised and dashed again
And joy dissolves in tears.

The search for endless family
The search for one true Friend
Leaves questers tired, disconsolate
With questions without end.

Best find some potent pleasure quick
Some superficial thrill
Than search for everlasting love
When none can fill that bill.

So hide yourselves in shopping
And eating 'til you burst,
Use endless entertainment
As shelter from the worst.

And hope at least for truce on earth,
Though warlords rattle swords
As if to kill could solve our ills
We seize our 'just' rewards.

Mistake some rest for lasting peace
And calm for 'all is well'
And absence of activity
As year end's victory bell.

But what if Advent is no quest
Despite the wise men's star
What if Advent isn't reached
By traveling from afar?

# The Living Legacy

What if Good News comes to us
From well beyond our reach?
What if love and peace on earth
Are more than things we preach?

What if a restless peace
Is what He did intend
Until we open up our lives
And let the stranger in?

**What if a peaceless rest**
Is not the Christmas hope
What if nothing we could do
Helps us truly cope?

What if there is a bonding
With one who rules above
Who came to us in beggar's rags
And brought the gift of love?

The God shaped hole in every heart
Is healed by just one source
When Jesus comes to claim his own
Who are without recourse.

So give up endless seeking
Surrender is required
The one who is the Lord of all
Cannot be bought or hired,

He's not conjured into life
By pomp and circumstance
By Yuletide carols boldly sung
By fun or drunken trance.

He comes unbidden, unawares
Fills crevices of souls
He comes on his own timely terms
And makes the sinner whole.

'We shall be restless' said the saint
'Until we rest in thee'
And find that we have been reborn,
Our own nativity.

How silently, how silently
The precious truth is given
And God imparts to human hearts
The blessings of his heaven.

## THEOLOGICAL MUSINGS

This poem was written when I was quite fed up with the commercialization of Christmas. I felt that we were getting it all wrong, as Christmas was supposed to be about giving not getting, about relating not acquiring, about a spiritual transaction not a monetary one. But there is another side to this, namely that Christmas is a time of questing, not just requesting. It can be the most hideously lonely time of year if one does not have close family or friends to spend it with, or if one's nearest or dearest has recently passed away. This is of course one reason why alcohol flows so freely at this time of year—for some it's a matter of surviving Christmas, and obliterating the bitter memories or pain that the season causes to surface in one's soul. Some drink to remember, but more drink to forget and block out the pain.

It is a strange thing nevertheless, that Christmas should become something of a litmus test on the state of one's unions or relationships. That first Christmas was surely not experienced as a condemnation or inquisition. It was rather a time of awe and wonder and celebration by various orders of beings from the angelic to the bucolic, from the questers to the sequestered family. And we should note that the gifts brought by the star gazers were not gifts they exchanged with each other or with the Holy family. They were gifts given to the new born king. The primal question these stories raise is not the question of one relative to another hinting "what have you done for me lately"? Rather the primal question raised is—in light of the gift of the Son, what of yourself are you prepared to lay at his feet? Indeed, what about your life do you need to lay at his feet and subject to his inspection? For the King that has everything, ultimately all we have to offer is our selves, or some token thereof. And in the end, Christmas is not about seeking, it is about allowing yourself to be found, to be loved, to be treated as a person of sacred worth, just like the Christ child.

The peace that passes understanding does not refer to the absence of activity of any sort, but rather to the presence of a sense of well being which comes from the encounter with the Presence. No amount of revelry, however joyful, 'produces' revival—personal or corporate. Christmas is not something one can conjure into life by activities. Christmas comes when the Christ enters in once more into our life, and fills up the crevices of our souls with the divine presence and love.

I have often wondered why the Incarnation happened as it did. The Son of God could surely have come as a full adult if God had so willed it. Is there something to the notion that Jesus came as he did: 1) to make clear every age and stage of life is of sacred worth; and 2) he came in the humble condition he did to make clear that no one on earth is beneath his dignity—not even the least, the last, and the lost?

And there is more to contemplate. If there really was an Incarnation of the divine pre-existent Son who took on human flesh and dwelt amongst us, then surely this required remarkable condescension on God's part. If there is to be a corporate merger between the divine and the human, then surely the divine must accept some limits, lest the human side of the equation be obliterated. Human beings have limitations of time, space, knowledge, and power and Jesus reflects all these limitations in the Gospels if we read them closely. His life was a real human life, while not ceasing to be divine. His life was not a charade or a play where he pretended to be human.

The Christmas story then is indeed about the goodness of being human, and how human nature can even be hallowed and embraced by God, and it is about God's great love and desire to renew, restore, redeem human beings so they might better reflect the image of God within us. But there is more. The Christmas story, involving as it does the story of a miraculous virginal conception, reminds us that Jesus could not come simply as we are—fallen creatures, if he wished to redeem us. He did not come simply to identify with the fallen human condition as if that in itself would make us better persons or at least feel better about ourselves. Jesus came as we ought to be, and modeled how we ought to be. His entire life "tempted like us in all respects, save without sin" is a reminder that sin is not an inherent and necessary feature of human nature as it was originally created. It is however endemic of all fallen humans, which is to say all of us except Jesus. So Jesus did not come to simple identify with us, he came to redeem us, since we had fallen and could not get up on our own. Perhaps one reason Christmas time seems like a condemnation to many is that it reminds us that we are not light, or in the light, unless we are in Christ, and yet we so badly long to be in the light, and to have the light within us.

So then Christmas does indeed reveal the human face of the Christ, but it also reveals the all too human face of us all, and so it becomes a time for taking stock, contemplation, re-evaluation. It is then the perfect time for some spiritual reflection of the first order.

In his poem "He Wishes for the Cloths of Heaven" W. B. Yeats says "but I being poor have only my dreams; I have spread my dreams under your feet; tread softly because you tread on my dreams."[1] What would it mean to lay your dreams before God, and submit your plans to Christ? Do you, like Yeats, find this a daunting prospect, something you would be afraid to do, and so you must ask God to tred lightly?

A brief story is in order. For a long time in my life I assumed my mission was to get a job at a United Methodist seminary and help with the renewal of my own denomination. This was my dream and my mission, or so I thought. I went through a gut-wrenching interview process at one U. M. seminary and was told after the fact that I did a better job than the other finalist, but the other finalist "met a certain quota we needed to fill." It was this experience that led me to go back to God and submit my dreams to him, and ask—'What is it that you want of me?' not merely "What is it that I would like to do for you?' I realized that if one loves one's dreams more than one loves one's God, God will require that dream of you, however salutary or noble the dream is. It is never easy to lay what is on and in your heart before God, hoping he will not smash your dreams to pieces.

Dreams are a good litmus test of where one's heart is, or what is on your wish list, much like the saying of Jesus about how our hearts are where our treasure is. Ask yourself the question—what do I treasure the most, about what do I most often dream and hope for? Then, say to yourself—Am I prepared to offer this up to God and see what God will do with it?

---

1. Keillor, G. *Good Poems*, (N.Y.: Penguin Press, 2002), 96.

### The Living Legacy

## Spiritual Mediations

### "The Bonding"

- Lectio Divina: John 1:1–15
- Spend some time journaling about "The Bonding" and the theological musings that follow. What thoughts or feelings did this evoke? How did this change your view of the Advent Season? How might you respond in the coming weeks?
- Over the next several days, make use of the "little solitudes" that fill your day or carve out an extended period of solitude (minutes to hours, depending on what your life situation permits). During this time, spend time simply listening and allow yourself to be still. Bring a journal or a sketchpad along to write down reflections near the end of your time(s) of solitude.

### Thoughts for Further Reflection

*"Christmas is not about seeking, it as about allowing yourself to be found, to be loved, to be treated as a person of sacred worth . . . "*

Ben Witherington III

*"Advent is the beginning of the end of all that is in us that is not Christ."*

Thomas Merton

*"Life from the Center is a life of unhurried peace and power. It is simple. It is serene. We need not get frantic. He is at the helm. And when our little day is done we lie down quietly in peace, for all is well.*

Thomas Kelly

*"Come Thou Long Expected Jesus,
Born to set Thy people free:
From our fears and sins release us;*

Charles Wesley

*Advent and Christmas*

### Personal Ponderings on "The Bonding"

The words of Saint Augustine referenced in this poem have long haunted me: "Thou hast made us for Thyself and our hearts are restless until they find their rest in Thee." This is the heart of the matter. Anything short of absolute rest in Him leaves us restless and empty, constantly seeking and searching for something to fill the void in our hearts. There is but One who can fill that hole in each of our hearts. This poem and the musings that follow speak to this so beautifully and plainly. Christmas shows us that it is not so much about seeking as it is about allowing ourselves to be found by a God who has come to us. "The Word became flesh," the Gospel of John states, "and made his dwelling among us." This love that would live among us is ours to receive. This is the only true antidote to our restlessness and our emptiness.

I have found no greater human illustration of this than a brief story told by one of the great missionaries of our day. Vincent Donovan tells a beautiful story in his book *Christianity Rediscovered* about his days as a missionary to the Masai people in Tanzania. In his early interactions with the people, the people indicated a belief in a God who was remote and far away, unknown. Through a long period of time Donovan committed himself to search for this "unknown God" with the Masai people. Many months later, an elder in the tribe relayed to him what belief looked like and how he was coming to know God. He talked about how real belief was not unlike a lion going after his prey. The entire body of a lion is involved from start to finish. Once the prey is caught, the lion draws it into himself and makes it a part of himself. This is the way a lion kills its prey and this is, in the eyes of the Masai elder, what true belief and faith are. Donovan found this description of faith stunning and incredible, but the elder was far from finished.

"We did not search you out, Padri," he said to [Donovan]. "We did not even want you to come to us. You searched us out. You followed us away from your house into the bush, into the plains, into the steppes where are cattle are, into the hills where we take our cattle for water, into our villages, into our homes. You told us of the High God, how we must search for him, even leave our land and our people to find him. But we have not done this. We have not left our land. We have not searched for him. He has searched for us. He has searched us out and found us. All the time we think we are the lion. In the end, the lion is God."²

This Advent Season, I pray that the Lord, the Lion, will find you anew and bring rest and wholeness to your heart.

(JNH)

---

2. Donovan, Vincent J. *Christianity Rediscovered*. New York: Orbis Books, 2003, 48.

*Advent and Christmas*

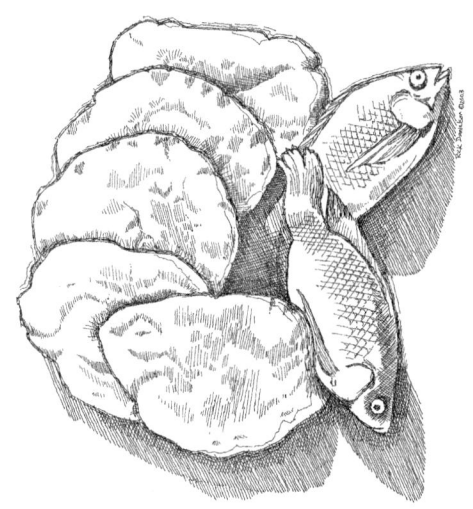

### CREATURES OF HABIT

Creatures of habit,
Day after day
Go about life,
The same old way.

Nothing disturbs
Their orderly routine
All must be neat,
And all must be clean.

They're making their lists
And checking them twice,
Trying to make sure
Their work will suffice.

Impatient by nature
They don't suffer fools
Gladly or otherwise
Because of the rules.

## The Living Legacy

A place for everything
For all there's a place
Don't touch the guest towels
But please wash your face.

They insist on living
Orderly lives,
And of course only marry
Orderly wives.

Their homes antiseptic
Their cars always clean,
Their food always healthy
Their meat always lean.

Like ants in an ant hill,
Repeating their tasks
Rest in repetition
Ignore the masks.

Chaos is forbidden
Experiment absurd
Don't ask for creative
Don't mention the word.

Creatures of habit,
By whose design?
Is this just human,
Or is it divine?

What if we found
That ordering our sphere,
Is just a misnomer
For controlling our fear?

Fear of the truth,
Fear of falling
Fear of the unknown,
Fear of our calling

## Advent and Christmas

Fearing to let go,
Fearing to try,
Fearing to live,
And fearing to die.

Perhaps if we surrender
Control of our lives,
And offer ourselves
To all seeing eyes

We'd find a new freedom
Though not out of bounds
For when he controls us
The order's profound.

Let go of the death grip,
You have on your life
Inhibit your habits
Without artifice.

Accept serendipity,
Free by design
Eat the new manna
Drink the new wine.

Come to the manger
Kneel at the throne
Realize your ruler
Won't leave you alone.

Celebrate Christmas
Deliverance declare
You're freed to inhabit
A creature's full share.

December 1, 2005

## THEOLOGICAL MUSINGS

"For God is not a God of chaos, but of peace as in all the churches" (1 Cor. 14:33), says Paul, and we can understand his concern. Things can get pretty chaotic if self-centered human beings are all allowed to do their own thing, as seems to have been happening in Corinth. But in fact, we are as likely if not more likely to see over-organization over-controlled situations in the life of individual Christians and indeed in the life of the church, including its worship life and all the more so at Christmas time.

Of course it is true that orderliness in itself is not a bad thing, nor an ungodly thing. But there is an ordering of things that sometimes comes from a deep sense of insecurity in the soul. That insecurity, and its accompanying feeling of chaos or things being out of order, is compensated for by an attempt to control every eventuality. Some people even are obsessive-compulsive about it. Unfortunately this sort of over-compensation often characterizes holiday seasons where one is trying too hard to do things in a way that feeds that nostalgic need for one's good old days, one's childhood, and the like. The end result is that we celebrate the greatest creative miracle of God, the Incarnation, in the least creative or innovative ways possible! What is wrong with this picture?

I take it as a Christian axiom that faith, not fear should be the basis of our decision-making in life. When we allow ourselves to be simply creatures of habit who stifle our fears and insecurities by over ordering things, rather than dealing with them we are at the same time quenching the Spirit and renouncing the freedom we have in Christ to be all that we were meant to be. A Christmas celebration without some serendipity is not in the spirit of real Christian celebration. Freedom, even an 'orderly' and ordering freedom, like freedom in Christ, is of course a scary concept and prospect, at least to many. And yet they also deplore the deadening effect of mere repetition because "we've always done it that way."

But what would happen if we really took holidays as holy days—times to rest in the Lord, times to turn off the alarm clock, times to get caught up in love, wonder and praise, times to 'turn and become as a child' so that we might really enter into the kingdom and royal spirit of the season? I once wrote a poem in which I said:

*Advent and Christmas*

"Holidays are hollow
Unless they're hallowed well,
For holidays are holy days
The time for truth to tell.

There's time to spare
Time to waste
Time to make amends
Time to do most anything
Even make new friends

Holidays, a good time
For writing poetry
A silent, subtle indolence
Inspires creativity."

My point is simply this. Holy days are prime time, when one needs to allow the land to go fallow, to allow the things that normally order our days to disappear. We need to lose track of all time, except prime time—the creative celebration and worship of the Christ child. Space, silence, rest and worship are in fact the soil from which creative responses to God come forth. At such seasons of the year as Christmas, worship should especially be the primary thing, and all other activities pushed further down the 'to do' list, even family celebrations. Worship, whether we realize it or not, restores our souls, renews our hope, redefines our vision, reorients our priorities, and restores order to the created world. And it is in that all-important dialectic between worship and rest that we begin to see the rest of our habits in proper perspective. Once we have seen the vision glorious, once we have experienced the peace that passes understanding (not to be confused with the rest that comes after exhaustion) then perhaps we can release the death grip we tend to have on our lives and the tendency we all have to try and control those lives by ordering activities of various sorts. Sometimes losing or at least loosening one's grip on one's life is precisely what needs to happen so that the door is left ajar for renewal, rejuvenation, rebirth, re-creation, and recreation.

The Living Legacy

# Spiritual Meditations

## "Creatures of Habit"

- Lectio Divina: Psalm 27; Matthew 6:24–26
- Conversation can be a rich spiritual discipline. Grab a friend and a cup of coffee and reflect on the poem "Creatures of Habit" and the theological musings. Pray with each other at the end of your time together.
- Worship of God should be at the top of our priority list as Christians. More than just an experience on Sunday mornings and special occasions, worship should permeate our existence. Spend time today in concentrated worship by responding to God's love for you in whatever form you find most natural (singing, reading, reflecting, drawing, etc.). Also try to take time each day this week to prepare yourself for the experience of gathered worship. Both corporate and private worship are essential parts of our life as Christians and neither should be neglected.

### Thoughts for Further Reflection

*" Worship, whether we realize it or not, restores our souls, renews our hope, redefines our vision, reorients our priorities."*

Ben Witherington III

*"Sometimes losing, or at least loosening one's grip on one's life is precisely what needs to happen so that the door is left ajar for renewal, rejuvenation, rebirth, re-creation, and recreation."*

Ben Witherington III

*"We need to gather together to worship this King. That's the point. We need it, not to escape reality, but to find it. Not to avoid the world out there, but to keep our heads screwed on straight about Whose world it is. And to Whom we belong. Forever."*

Stan Gaede

*Advent and Christmas*

*"Rest. Rest. Rest in God's love. The only work you are required to do now is to give your most intense attention to His still small voice within."*

Madame Guyon

*"In commanding us to glorify Him, God is inviting us to enjoy Him."*

Oswald Chambers

### Personal Ponderings on "Creatures of Habit"

What a blessed thought to consider worship an act of rest! Oh that it would truly cause us to loosen our grip that we might be renewed, revived, reborn, recreated, and rejuvenated! It is for this we were created and we settle for so much less. We approach worship in anything but an attitude of absolute surrender and rest. We are not a restful people. We abandoned the idea of Sabbath long ago and with it went our sense of rest and our sense of recreation. This should not be.

A few years ago I stumbled upon a book of letters penned by François de Salignac de la Mothe Fénelon entitled *Let Go*. The contents of this book have challenged, blessed, and encouraged me time and again, especially as I've pondered what a life of worship should look like. The poem "Creatures of Habit" and the theological musings that followed immediately brought to mind this little book by Fénelon. The letters in it are written to a small group of people to whom Fénelon was a spiritual advisor, each one containing inspiration for a life abandoned to God and his purposes. "Let me tell you what real surrender is," Fénelon states. "It is simply resting in the love of God, as a little baby rests in its mother's arms. A perfect surrender must even be willing to quit surrendering if that is what God wants!"[3]

Our task as Christians seeking a lifestyle of worship is simple to let go and acknowledge that God is God and we are not and that is a good thing. To borrow once more from Fénelon, "Full surrender is full peace. If we are restless and concerned about things . . . we have not genuinely

---

3. Fénelon, François de Salignac de la Mothe. *Let Go*. Pennsylvania: Whitaker House, 1973, 76–77.

surrendered. Surrender is the source of true peace."[4] May this rest be ours as we seek to worship God with our lives.

(JNH)

---

4. Ibid.

*Advent and Christmas*

## INCOGNITO

He came in incognito,
A thinly veiled disguise
The not so subtle son of man,
A human with God's eyes.

The messianic secret,
Left many unawares
A God had walked upon the earth
And shared our human cares.

We did not see his glory,
At least not at first glimpse,
It took an Easter wake up call,
Before it all made sense.

The truth of Incarnation,
Of dwelling within flesh,
Shows goodness in creation,
And Word of God made fresh.

Standing on the boundary
Twixt earth and heaven above
A Jew who hailed from Nazareth
But came from God's great love.

Born of humble parents,
Installed inside a stall
This king required no entourage
No pomp or falderal

No person was beneath him
No angel o'er his head,
He came to serve the human race
To raise it from the dead.

His death a great conundrum,
How can the Deathless die?
But if he had not bowed his head,
Life would have passed us by.

## The Living Legacy

Though we are dying to be loved,
And long for endless life,
He was dying in his love,
And thereby ending strife.

Perhaps the incognito
Belongs instead to us,
Who play at being human,
And fail to be gold dust.

But there was once a God-man
Who played the human's part
And lived and died and rose again
Made sin and death depart.

Now through a glass dimly,
We see the visage royal
And feebly honor his great worth
And his atoning toil.

We cannot see his Spirit,
But moved by its effects
We are inspired to praise his worth
And pay our last respects.

Yet that too brings him glory
That too makes a start,
The journey of a million miles
Begins within one's heart.

And someday we shall see him
And fully praise his grace,
Someday when heaven and earth collide
And we see face to face.

He comes in blinding brilliance,
A not so veiled disguise
The not so subtle Son of God,
A God with human eyes.

       May Day 2005

*Advent and Christmas*

## THEOLOGICAL MUSINGS

How many times do we hear these days—'just make it simple,' or 'put the cookies on the bottom shelf' or even 'dumb it down'? I am just waiting and wincing for the day when someone produces 'The Gospel for Dummies.' Whatever you may think of this sort of approach to pedagogy, it certainly does not comport with Jesus' approach to self-revelation, or for that matter the Gospel writers' approaches. They were all about teasing one's mind into active thought, rather than over-simplifying things. They were all about forcing the audience to reach for it, so that their reach would extend further than their grasp. They were all about forcing us to concentrate, or as Jesus put it "let those with two good ears, hear." Revelation of profound things, as it turns out involves mystery, incognito, and secrets revealed at great cost and in amazing ways. It requires boiling up the people, not boiling down the revelation if it is to be understood.

It is doubtful that there was a widespread expectation in early Judaism for a messianic figure who would call himself 'the Son of Man', and almost certainly no one was expecting a crucified and risen Son of Man. Jesus, it would seem did not come to meet people's expectations, but rather their needs, and in so doing he decided to reveal his real nature and God's real plan in his own way, on his own terms, without conforming to pre-set or simple formulas. Indeed, one NT scholar, Eduard Schweizer once said Jesus is the man who fits no one formula, the man who can't be stereotyped or pigeon-holed. It is thus not surprising that Jesus is not always, or in every way easy to understand. In fact one can say that while many profound theological ideas and truths can be stated clearly, this does not mean that they are easily understood.

There is a further problem as well, of which Paul is cognizant and refers to in 2 Cor. 3. He speaks of the veil over the human heart which prevents people from seeing Christ as he is, seeing his glory. But not only do we have to deal with our own spiritual obtuseness, there is the further problem that we, as fallen creatures, often are not 'ourselves' or better put not our best and authentic selves. We play at being human, we pretend to be honest and forthcoming, but much of the time we are actually hiding behind one persona or another, one incognito or another. We have a hard time letting people see our real 'face' indeed we have a hard time facing it ourselves.

In this sort of darkness, and dealing with truths that take us clearly out of our depths, Karl Barth's wisdom becomes all the more clear when he said that God, even God in Christ, can only be known as he reveals himself. Even then, there must be a transformation and indeed conversion of our imagination and understanding if we are to understand the revelation as well. In other words revelation without transformation of our understanding and our hearts avails for nothing. One more thing. While we clearly understand Jesus better now with the benefit of hindsight than at least some of the disciples did before Easter, it is also true that even we only know in part. There will come a day when faith will become sight, but for now only believing leads to seeing, not the other way around, when it comes to the divine incognito.

## Spiritual Meditations

### "Incognito"

- Lectio Divina: Isaiah 53; 1 Corinthians 13
- The mystery of God's love in Jesus Christ ought to spill over in our lives in joy and gratitude. Times of celebration and joy bring us strength for the everyday. Celebrate the mystery made manifest in Jesus Christ in some creative way this week. Turn a corporate meal into a celebration of God's activity in your life. Gather a few others for a party to simply celebrate life and enjoy the fellowship of other believers and friends.
- Participating in the discipline of service is the perfect way to reveal the mystery of Jesus Christ to another. Explore the various avenues of service and find a way to reach out to others for the sake of the kingdom on a regular basis. This can range from the everyday (encouragement, listening, hospitality, etc.) to the more project-oriented forms (donations, trips, outreach, etc.).

*Advent and Christmas*

## Thoughts for Further Reflection

"Revelation of profound things, as it turns out, involves mystery, incognity, and secrets revealed at great cost and in amazing ways."

Ben Witherington III

"The grace of heaven is everywhere."

Thomas Merton

"It is in Jesus, of course, and in people whose lives have been deeply touched by Jesus, and in our selves at those moments when we also are deeply touched by him that we see another way of being human in this world, which is the way of holiness."

Frederick Buechner

## Personal Ponderings on "Incognito"

There are opportunities for us to see and to say God in our everyday. We fail to see Him because we are looking too hard or not hard enough. We fail to say His name to others because we cannot see past ourselves or because we distance ourselves from those He called us to serve. We find it difficult to see Him and serve Him because we have forgotten that He has seen us and served us first. We have distanced ourselves from the God of Exodus 3 who has seen us, heard us, and come down to us. Because of this, we fail in our attempts to share Him with a world of people desperate for a God like that.

We are here for no more reason than simply to say God to other people. We are here to tell people of how he came to us in our need and saved us. We are not here to do the saving, but simply to point others to the Savior. We are God's ambassadors, a people called not to bring God to people, but to point him out in the everyday. God is already there, our task is simply to say His name to others.

Eugene Peterson speaks poignantly of this in his book *Subversive Spirituality*. I leave you with his words. May they encourage and challenge you as they have me.

## The Living Legacy

"Why are we [here]? We are [here] to say God. We are [here] for one reason and one reason only: to pray. We are [here] to focus the brimming, overflowing, cascading energies of joy, sorrow, delight, or appreciation, if only for a moment but for as long as we are able, on God. We are [here] to say God personally, to say his name clearly, distinctly, unapologetically, in prayer. We are there to say it without hemming and hawing, without throat clearing and without shuffling, without propagandizing, proselytizing, or manipulating. We have no other task... We are not needed to add to what is there; there is already more than anyone can take in. We are required only to say the Name: Father, Son, and Holy Ghost."[5]

(JNH)

---

5. Peterson, Eugene. *Subversive Spirituality.* Grand Rapids: Eerdmans Publishing, 1997, 150.

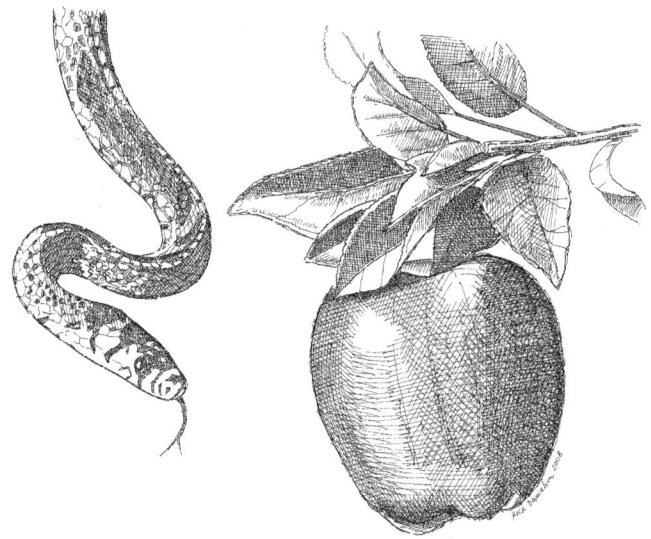

## MOTHER LOAD

From the very beginning
The burden was clear
Sometimes bearable
Sometimes severe

Ate from the apple
Shared it with him
Disobeyed the order
Indulged the whim.

What was the outcome?
The fruit of the act?
She 'knew' good and evil?
She experienced it in fact?

Did the earth creature join her?
Did he crumble into dust?
Did he die in an instant?
Or just tumble into lust?

## The Living Legacy

To love and to cherish
Becomes 'desire and dominate'
Objectify the 'other'
So you can subjugate.

Suddenly self conscious
Instantly aware
There are no coverings
Only nakedness there.

Hiding in the garden,
The creature in shame
Running from her Maker
Like some kind of game.

Passing the blame on
From God to the wife,
From the wife to the snake
'The' creator of strife.

Banished from the garden,
But clothed by their God
Not allowed to live forever
Find a living from the sod

Pain in her labor
Shortness of breath
The mother of all living
Gives birth near to death

And would she be able
To raise Cain at all?
Or will her next offspring
Be first to fall?

And how to redeem this?
Set the process in reverse
Put a stop to the death toll
Undoing the curse?

*Advent and Christmas*

## II

From the very beginning
The burden was clear
"Be it unto me as you said,
The Lord's servant is here."

A virginal conception
Had a child without a man
Which no one expected
And few would understand.

She received a word of warning
A sword would pierce her soul
But the death of her first born
Would make the race whole.

There beneath a crooked tree
Stood that woman and a man
Neither disobeyed the orders
Each accepting the plan.

Then He rose in the garden
Reopened its gate
To the tree for the living
To the Adam without mate.

And there in the Scriptures
Was a promise true and sure
"She'll be saved through the childbearing"
That Mary did endure.

The story revisited
The human tale revised
Motherlode now delivered
Curse reversed before our eyes.

      December 20, 2005
      For Brian, Lawson, Sandy, Bill, Joel, and David

# The Living Legacy

## THEOLOGICAL MUSINGS

It has long been the case that Christians, including theologians have compared and contrasted the stories of Eve and Mary, just as they have contrasted the stories of the first and the last Adams, Jesus being the last one. No descendants could come into the world without Eve, the mother of all living, and no one could come into the world to come without Mary, the mother of the messiah. Sometimes even the church fathers resorted to typology or allegory to find connections between the stories of Eve and Mary. For example Eve beneath the tree with the fruit and the snake, is seen as like Mary beneath the cross, only Eve listened to the serpent and disobeyed God, while Mary listened to her Son and obeyed his words. There is then considerable precedent for the kind of comparisons and contrasts that are going on in this poem.

One of the things I was exploring and trying to probe in this poem is the burden that women have always borne since the beginning of humankind, and by this I do not just mean bearing the burden of childbearing, though that is no small task in itself. I referring to the fact that women have tended to be viewed as either like Eve or Mary, with nothing much in between. From deceived by a serpent to believing an angel, women have been seen as either sirens or saints. This has been quite a burden to bear, to say the least, and it is unfair. But there is more. Mary had the additional burden of not only being the mother of a controversial messianic figure who came into this world in an irregular manner, but she was warned as well that Jesus would leave the world in a shocking manner as well.

The correspondences between these stories underline a few dominant Scriptural themes: 1) God is a God of second chances but 2) on the second go around it is none other than his Son that makes sure that the human tale is set right and will have a happy ending. In other words, God takes matters into his own hands, and yet all hangs on a Jewish maiden saying "be it unto to me as you have said, I am the handmaiden of the Lord." Human response to the divine initiative is neither pre-empted nor pre-determined. The curse was reversed through an obedient woman just as the curse was initiated by a disobedient one. The human drama involves both divine and human decisions, and women have as much to do with salvation as they do with fallenness. In fact, the author of 1 Tim. 2.8–15 is prepared to remind us that "women shall be saved through the Childbearing," an oblique reference to the birth of Jesus. But none of this story would have turned out well if God had not raised Jesus from the dead. All the obedience in the world cannot produce divine grace or salvation. Only the divine activity itself can produce such an outcome. Resurrection is not the outcome of a human self-help program. One then must give God the glory, while still giving Mary her due.

## Spiritual Meditations

### "Mother Load"

- Lectio Divina: Luke 1:46–56
- Choose one of the key women in the Bible to study over the next several weeks (i.e.—Ruth, Esther, Hannah, Mary, Martha, etc.). Gather resources and do an in-depth character study. Journal your findings and reflections so that you may return to them again and again.
- Spend some time this week in complete silence. If you can, schedule extended time of silence at a monastery or a spiritual retreat center. If your life does not lend itself to such, consider abstaining from music in your car and/or during your daily walk/jog. We all long for the joyful surrender we see in Mary. We need times of quietness and stillness to hear what God might be asking us to joyfully surrender in our own lives. Spend your time reflecting on "Mary's Song" in Luke 1:46–56 or Psalm 143.

### Thoughts for Further Reflection

*"All the obedience in the world cannot produce divine grace or salvation. Only the divine activity itself can produce such an outcome."*

Ben Witherington III

*"The world does not need more of you; it needs more of God. Your friends do not need more of you; they need more of God. And you don't need more of you; you need more of God."*

Eugene Peterson

# The Living Legacy

*"Father, I abandon myself into Your hands; do with me what You will. Whatever You may do, I thank You; I am ready for all, I accept all. Let only Your will be done in me, and in all Your creatures. I wish no more than this, O Lord."*

Henri Nouwen

## Personal Ponderings on "Mother Load"

I was introduced to Thomas Kelly's *A Testament of Devotion* during one of my first semesters in seminary. A beloved professor of mine began each class with a reading from this remarkable book. With each reading I found myself challenged and moved in such a way that I assumed that this was wisdom from the distant past. The discovery that this was a modern work written by a Quaker Missionary from Ohio (1893–1941) made the words carry even more weight. That such words could come from the not-so-distant-past brought me immeasurable hope.

The excerpt below is from this modern classic. It speaks of the "overwhelming experience" of complete surrender and utter abandon to God's purposes. Mary must have experienced something of this when she surrendered to God's purposes that led to that first Christmas. It is to this that the Season of Advent calls us.

> "It is an overwhelming experience to fall into the hands of the living God, to be invaded to the depths of one's being by His presence, to be, without warning, wholly uprooted from all earth-born securities and assurances, and to be blown by a tempest of unbelievable power which leaves ones' old proud self utterly, utterly defenseless... Then the soul is swept into a Loving Center of ineffable sweetness, where calm and unspeakable peace and ravishing joy steal over one."[6]

(JNH)

---

6. Kelly, Thomas R., *A Testament of Devotion*. San Francisco: Harper Collins Publishing, 1992, 30.

### THE SECRET

Hidden reality
Like life in the womb
Hidden reality
Like death in the tomb
Hidden away
For the appropriate day

Wrapped in enigma, cloaked in secrecy,
Awaiting a wake up call with urgency.
But how shall such a song be sung?

A tale that's never told,
A trail that's long gone cold,
A mystery unrevealed,
A truth that is concealed,
Seems useless on first glance.

Who said there was a secret,
Who told us we must keep it
Who set the search in motion
And stirred up our devotion
If 'clueless' was our stance?

## The Living Legacy

Call forth the revelator,
Who hinted something greater
A light that has been hidden
A thought that comes unbidden
And is not mere romance.

Go to the old gate keeper,
And wake the guardian sleeper,
Arouse the story teller
Seek out the boundary dweller
Lulled into tragic trance.

For sometimes revelation
Awaits the new creation
Propitious point in time
When insight is sublime
And we're prepared to dance.
The time may fully come

The race be fully run,
The truth could then be heard,
And taken at its word,
As happy happenstance.

Thus mystery has a point
When times are out of joint
And no one wants to hear
About the truth they fear
Because of circumstance.

In one sense all of history
Apocalyptic mystery
With secrets kept and told
By prophets young or old
Who speak, suggest, recant.

For too much information
Obscures the revelation
Prevents a clear reception
May even cause deception
Instead of some advance.

## Advent and Christmas

So let us treasure mystery
And truths that unveil history
Spoken in due season
Reflecting divine reason,
And never left to chance.

## THEOLOGICAL MUSINGS

THERE IS A FAMOUS saying attributed to Julius Caesar by Shakespeare which stresses that there is a tide in the affairs of humankind which if taken at the flood leads on to great things. There can be no doubt that this is a Biblical idea. We see it for example in Gal. 4.4—"But when the time had fully come, God sent forth his Son . . . " There is a sense in which there are certain propitious moments in history which, when something happens it really matters. One way people express this concept is when they say "timing is everything." For example, the invention of the automobile would not have amounted to much if it had not been preceded by several other inventions, such as the internal combustion engine, and various sorts of technology first used with trains.

In this Christmas season, one of the things most worth contemplating is why it was that Jesus came when he did. In what sense had the time fully come? We might even ask—Why wouldn't God have waited until an era of mass communication if Jesus was to be the savior of the world in all generations? Several things come to mind.

Firstly, it has been widely recognized that Jesus was born at a time when there was something of a unified culture in the known world, with a language all could use, and roads and government that reach from far east of Israel to the western most part of Spain to Scotland in the north, and to Africa in the south. Thanks to the spread of Hellenism and Greek by Alexander the Great and his successors even Israelites could speak Greek and relate well in the Greco-Roman world. Thanks to Roman engineering there were durable roads in all directions, and thanks to the Roman military might the seas had largely been swept clean of pirates and brigands. Even just a little before the birth of Jesus in the time of Julius Caesar, Rome was just a Republic, and there were many competing forces in the Mediterranean world. Jesus could hardly have come at a time more propitious for starting a new world religion if we were to evaluate the previous 2,000 years before Jesus' birth. Then too he was borne in the land that was the land bridge between three continents—Asia, Africa, and the regions in the north that led to what we call Europe. Suppose, for example, Jesus had been borne while the Jews were in the Babylonian exile. It would have been far more difficult for a Jewish messianic movement to start then and in such a locale.

Of course our author thinks as well that it isn't just natural factors we should consider, but also the divine plan, as promised and predicted in the OT. When Paul says the time had fully come, he is thinking of the fulfillment of prophecy, and of the divine time table for things. He believes as well that God has a sense of timing, and that there is such a thing as a timely truth. Many things are kept secret until just the right moment when they need to be revealed. Sometimes God waits until we are prepared to receive a certain truth or message or revelation.

We in our age of 'freedom of information' and all access passes to the Internet have difficulty with the concept of information being revealed on a need to know basis, or secrets needing to be kept, until the timing is right for their revelation. We simply assume that all information should be available to us at all times, because "the people have a right to know." This assumption is of course rather naïve. It assumes a lot about our powers to comprehend most anything if we study it long enough. But in fact it is sometimes the case that "we can't handle the truth," and God knows this. God knows our weaknesses, and God also knows when the time is ripe and right to share new revelation. There is another factor as well.

T. S. Eliot famously asked where is the wisdom we have lost in knowledge and where is the knowledge we have lost in the sea of information. One of the problems with living in the age of Google and the Internet, is that there is frankly too much information available and much of it unreliable or even untrue. I have this problem all the time with my students who take ideas or articles or information off the Internet assuming that it must be true since someone made it publicly available, but alas much of it is what the Rolling Stones once called "useless information supposed to fire my imagination."

We may live in the information age, but it would surely be better to live in the revelation or even the wisdom age. It is not only possible to get lost in the forest looking for the right tree of knowledge, but it is also the case that we may well mistake pulp fiction for a cedar of Lebanon, so to speak. One needs some criteria, some guidance, some wisdom, some kind of road map to recognize the truth when we see it. And sometimes it is not a matter of finding the right wise man or expert. Sometimes it's just a matter of being patient and waiting until God chooses to make the truth known, and the light finally dawns on us. Some realities and truths need to be hidden away, like a baby in a womb, "until the time had fully come." We must come to terms with the fact that some times we must wait until the truth "comes to full term" and then is brought forth into the world. Patience is not a virtue much practiced in the information and Internet age. Sometimes a secret needs to be 'kept' until the appropriate time for it to be revealed.

One of my favorite Christmas stories is O'Henry's famous tale "The Gift of the Magi." O' Henry was one of my childhood favorites as he grew up in the town right next to my home town—High Point N.C. The story hangs on two things—the great love a couple has for each other and their willingness to sacrifice much to get the other a precious Christmas gift, but it also hangs on the fact that the truth about the gifts must be kept secret until the appropriate day comes. Thus, unbeknownst to his girl, the young man pawns his precious heirloom pocket watch to buy beautiful combs for his beloved's beautiful long hair, and unbeknownst to the young man the girl has cut off and sold her hair so she could buy him a beautiful gold chain for the pocket watch. Imagine their surprise when Christmas comes and both unwrap gifts they cannot at the present moment use, but which demonstrate the great love they have for each other. The Christmas story in our Gospels goes this story one better, as it not only reveals God's sacrificial love, but it offers a timely and timeless truth that is always helpful and useful to anyone from the very minute it is unveiled. Indeed, there is a tide in human affairs, and God has a perfect sense of timing when it comes to revealing and healing, saving and restoring, reconciling and justifying us all.

## Spiritual Meditations

### "The Secret"

- Lectio Divina: Psalm 40; Matthew 1
- When you fast, the "what" is less important than the "why." Fasting is abstaining from food or something else for spiritual reasons. First spend some time in prayer, asking God what he might be asking you

to abstain from and for how long (hours, days, etc.). Spend some time in concentrated prayer during your fast talking to and listening to God, asking him to reveal to you the things that keep you from receiving his truth.

- Meditate further on Psalm 40. Allow God to speak to you through specific words or phrases in this Psalm. Write out your response in the form of a letter or prayer to God. Seal it in an envelope and place it in your Bible or somewhere else where you'll be sure to see it. Read your response again a few months from now.

## Thoughts for Further Reflection

*"Many things are kept secret until just the right moment when they need be revealed. Sometimes God waits until we are prepared to receive a certain truth or message or revelation."*

Ben Witherington III

*"Indeed, there is a tide in human affairs, and God has a perfect sense of timing when it comes to revealing and healing, saving and restoring, reconciling and justifying us all."*

Ben Witherington III

*"God's timing is rarely our timing. But far better than we do, He numbers our days and knows our moments and hours. Our task is to trust."*

Os Guiness

*"God has several ways of drawing us to Him; sometimes He hides Himself from us, but faith, which alone never fails us in our need, should be our support and the foundation of our trust which should be completely in God."*

Brother Lawrence

## Personal Ponderings on "The Secret"

This poem is the perfect way to end the section on the Seasons of Advent and Christmas. Advent is a season of holy expectation and Christmas a reminder of God's perfect timing and creativity. God has a history of meeting and surpassing our expectations, and yet we struggle to trust him with our lives. Enter prayer. It is only in daily prayer that our hope is renewed and our eyes opened to the God who reveals and heal, saves and restores, reconciles and justifies.

Henri Nouwen once said that "every prayer is an expression of hope" and we, as Christians, are nothing if not a people of hope and holy confidence. When we live in hope we can wait in anticipation of what God will do. And our hope is not hollow; it understands the goodwill of the Giver. Prayer is the avenue of such hope.

"When you pray with hope," Nouwen says, "you might still ask for many things: you might ask for everything . . . . Whenever we pray with hope, we put our lives in the hands of God. Fear and anxiety fade away and everything we are given and everything we are deprived of is nothing but a finger pointing out the direction of God's hidden promise which one day we shall taste in full."[7]

(JNH)

---

7. Nouwen, Henri J. M. *With Open Hands.* New York: Ballantine Books, 1987, 37, 46.

# Epiphany

*The Light Appears*

## THE REBIRTH OF WONDER

Jaded, Jaundiced
Left out in the cold,
Cynical, clinical
Tired of getting old
Looking for something,
More glittering than gold . . .
The rebirth of wonder.

Seeking, searching
Coming from afar
Reaching, lurching
Wishing on a star
Wise guys, shepherds
Bordering on bizarre
Where's the boy wonder?

## The Living Legacy

Child-like, crawling
Wide-eyed, on his knees
Compact, contact
With everything he sees
Babbling, bobbling
Hoping to believe
Wandering towards wonder.

Silence, science
Analysis complete
Seeing, being
Honest but discrete
Empirical evidence
Incarnation's feat
Makes you wonder.

Believing's seeing
Not blinded by the light
Seeing's believing
Leaves one in the night
Longing, aching,
Couldn't love be right?
Wonderfully contrite.

Unveiled, unabashed
Breaks into the world
Shattering the smatterings
Of reasons we have heard
'Why it could never be,
Of course it is absurd'
Until she bore the Word.

Child birth, new birth
Coming from the womb
Fine wine, wonderbread
Placed upon the plate,
Revelation, consummation
Never out of date,
The rebirth of wonder.

        Dec. 2, 2004

*Epiphany*

## THEOLOGICAL MUSINGS

THE WORD EPIPHANY MEANS appearing, and in this case refers in particular to the appearing of Jesus on the public stage of human history, recognized even by foreign dignitaries. Though most Christians do not realize this, the story of the wise men is about something that happened after Christmas, not on Christmas. The wise men come to visit Jesus from some distant place bringing gifts and we are not told how many of them there were, all we know is that they bring three gifts—gold, frankincense, and myrrh. These are indeed gifts fit for a king, but the wise men themselves are not kings, but rather sages or star gazers—the Greek word **magi** from which we get the word magician does not refer to a royal person. These are the king's advisors, the court astrologers or wise men. They are not recorded as having given any advice however to the Holy family. They simply come, give their gifts and slip back off the stage of history into oblivion.

The focus of this particular poem is on wonder and of course the Boy Wonder, Jesus. More particularly the focus is on wonder during a cold and often cynical time of year as the New Year dawns. But what is wonder? It's more than just musing or being impressed. It has to do with seeing, hearing, sensing, feeling something that is more than what one expected, and indeed different than what one expected. It has a sense of recognizing that one is in the presence of the Presence, and that something special has and is likely to happen. It is like being present when someone discovers a new star, or a new cure, or new information that suddenly explains the meaning of something which was long puzzling. In this case 'wonder' has to do less with the miracle of child-birth, although that is a wonder in itself, and more to do with the wonder of how, and how much God loves us, caring enough to send the very best—not merely a message, not merely a prophet, not merely an angelic messenger, but his very and only Son.

The coming of Jesus can be said to be a paradigm buster, shattering numerous false assumptions about how life works, how God interacts with his people, and about the very nature of reality. If the divine can be contracted into the size of an infant, then all sorts of things must be possible. Just his appearing leads to thoughts like—perhaps love will triumph over all the hate and violence of our world? Perhaps good will triumph over evil?

There is of course a sense in which the appearing of Jesus is the point at which faith becomes sight. Previously the true God had been believed in but no one had seen this God. Well no one except perhaps Moses who saw him in passing. Paul it will be remembered famously says that now we see through a glass darkly, which is true enough, but there was a time during the life of Jesus when we saw God in flesh, physically present with us and tangible, touchable, viewable by wise men and others. This is indeed a wonder since it is a fundamental tenet of Jewish and Christian monotheism that God is spirit, and so is not just like one of us. No wonder that that great cleric and poet John Donne once said that while our being born in the image of God is much, God's being born in our image is much more. Talk about value added to human life!

The Incarnation and appearing of Jesus says something fundamental to us about how God views human life, namely that it is inherently a good thing, so good that God was prepared to take part in it for our sake. Divine condescension into the form of a human being required divine self-limitation, putting the 'omnis' on hold as I like to put it. By this I mean that God's Son had to accept the limitations of time, space, knowledge, and power that all human beings have in order to be truly and fully human. Notice however that he did not have to assume the limitation of fallenness. The author of Hebrews rightly says of Jesus he was tempted like us in all respects, save without sin (Heb. 4.15). What this means is something wonderful—while sinning is now a congenital problem for human beings, it is not how God made us, nor is it what God made us for. Jesus is the living proof of this. He was not a sinner, though he lived and died with and for sinners. This in turn means that while it is true that "to err is human" as Alexander Pope once said, the converse of that statement is not true—one need not err or sin in order to be truly human. God did not send his Son down to us so he could merely identify with us in our sinful condition. He sent him so that we could be like his Son, and cease to be sinners. There is a difference between salvation and total identification, and Jesus came for the former purpose, not merely to be 'one of us' in all that phrase might entail. And yet, he knew what he was getting himself into when he came. Jesus says "The Son of Man did not come to be served, but to serve and give his life a ransom for the many" (Mk. 10.45).

It was C. S. Lewis who said that when the author of the play steps out on the stage, the play is over. There is truth in this, but it is at best a half truth. When Jesus came, it signaled the beginning of the end, the final act of the play. It signaled that God had come in flesh, in person, to finish what he had started with us so long ago in the garden. This indeed did and should

*Epiphany*

cause the rebirth of wonder—indeed it should cause it over and over again, for there is a sense in which every time someone receives this truth Christ is born again—in one person or another, in one group of believers or another, in one place or another. It is a wonder, and it is wonderful.

## Spiritual Meditations

### "The Rebirth of Wonder"

- Lectio Divina: Isaiah 9:3–7; Philippians 2:1–11
- Take a reflective walk, jog, or hike and meditate on the wonder of God's creation. If weather (or life!) does not permit an extended time outdoors, consider meditating on the creation story in Genesis 1. Spend some time journaling (through any medium: words, art, etc.) your thoughts and thanksgiving.
- Rediscovering wonder ought to create in us a desire to celebrate. Find a creative way to celebrate the rebirth of wonder in your own life. Plant a seasonal flower or grab a new indoor plant. Write out a Bible verse that reminds you of the wonder of it all and place it somewhere you'll see it and be reminded of God's activity in your everyday. Create or do something to celebrate wonder today . . . be creative!

### Thoughts for Further Reflection

*"The incarnation and appearing of Jesus says something fundamental to us about how God views human life, namely that it is inherently a good thing, so good that God was prepared to take part in it for our sake."*

Ben Witherington III

*"God did not send his Son down to us so he could merely identify with us in our sinful condition. He sent him so that we could be like his Son, and cease to be sinners."*

Ben Witherington III

*"A Christian should be an alleluia from head to foot."*

St. Augustine

# The Living Legacy

*"God made us, redeems us, provides for us. The natural, honest, healthy, logical response to that is praise to God."*

Eugene Peterson

*"Wherever you are, be all there.
Live to the hilt every situation you believe to be the will of God."*

Jim Elliot

## Personal Ponderings on "The Rebirth of Wonder"

We have all but lost the sense of wonder in our lives. We are so preoccupied with our own expectations that we fail to recognize how God is displaying his majesty all around us. We rarely see, hear, sense, and feel something greater than ourselves because we are so inwardly focused that we cannot see the overflowing beauty outside of us. We fail to recognize that we are in the presence of the Presence because we are not present. We are somewhere else entirely.

Stan Gaede talks about this sense of wonder in his incredible book *An Incomplete Guide to the Rest of Your Life*. His words are both inspiring and challenging. In a chapter exploring the deeper meaning of love and grace, he writes the following:

> "That we don't regularly wake up feeling stunned by the morning in all its beauty and majesty and wonder is an abomination, I think. That we don't lie down at night seeing the foggy dew on the trees or hearing the sounds of night critters or seeing the stars as thick as sugar against a jet black sky—that we don't see and hear all of that and weep for joy—is just amazing. That we don't regularly marvel at how our bodies work, what our eyes take in, the music our ears hear, the various tastes our tongues can hardly describe they're so varied, the things we can learn and enjoy—that we can do all these things, every day, and not drop down on our knees in worship and wonder—well that is the wonder! That is the wonder!"[1]

We will never experience what the wise men experienced that first epiphany until we recapture our own sense of wonder. It is only when we look

---

1. Gaede, Stan D. *An Incomplete Guide to the Rest of Your Life*. Downers Grove, IL: InterVarsity Press, 2002, 78–79.

outside of ourselves to the world around us—no matter how familiar—that we can truly see God. As we allow ourselves to be present in our everyday, we will find ourselves in the presence of the Presence more than we could ever imagine.

(JNH)

## The Living Legacy

## IF ONLY

### I

I would have dressed up,
Only it was too much trouble.

I would have gone out,
Only it cost too much.

I would have driven,
Only travel's dangerous.

I would have eaten,
Only I weigh too much.

I would have danced,
Only I didn't have a partner.

I would have returned,
Only it brought back bad memories.

### II

I would have gone,
Only I didn't have time.

I would have visited,
Only I wasn't wanted.

I would have tried,
Only it was a waste of energy.

I would have helped,
Only they didn't need me.

I would have cared,
Only I didn't feel like it.

I would have cried,
Only I wasn't sorry.

*Epiphany*

## III

I would have volunteered,
Only I had better things to do.

I would have voted,
Only it wouldn't have changed things.

I would have donated,
Only they'd made their quota.

I would have spoken up,
Only I was afraid to.

I would have acted,
Only others got there first.

I would have felt sorry,
Only I didn't feel guilty.

## IV

I would have prepared,
Only it was too much work.

I would have studied,
Only I wouldn't have passed.

I would have corrected it,
Only it was too late.

I would have told the truth,
Only it would have offended.

I would have graduated,
Only life intervened.

I would have gotten the job,
Only they didn't like me.

## V

I would have prayed,
Only God only knows.

I would have worshipped,
Only I hate to sing.

I would have fellowshipped
Only I didn't know them.

I would have served,
Only I didn't have the calling.

I would have loved,
Only it hurt too much.

I would have lived,
If only.

    January 20, 2006

## THEOLOGICAL MUSINGS

HERE IS THE OTHER end of the spectrum from the pilgrimage of the wise men. Here is a poem about someone who is afraid to even try, afraid of his own shadow, and quite prepared to say that other things in life prevented him from doing what he or she might like to have done. This is a sad poem, and I have known lives that embodied this posture towards life. It is like the words of the poet "the saddest words of tongue or pen, what might have been, what might have been." In a sense then this poem is about the opposite of 'carpe diem.' This poem is about a person who never seized the moment, never went on pilgrimage, never dared to try, and instead just made excuses.

 The coming of the New Year brings us often to the point of making New Year's Resolutions, but one has to have the personal resolve to do that. For some people the fear factor is so strong in their lives that they simply cannot commit to much of anything. They are paralyzed by paranoia. How very different this is from the orientation of faith, which is quintessentially defined as "the assurance of things hoped for, the conviction about things not seen" (Heb. 11.1).

## Epiphany

A person of real Christian faith is a person brave enough to venture forth into life, to be willing to try, and even to fail sometimes in the process. A Christian sets off on the pilgrimage of life believing that "the future is as bright as the promises of God" as Adoniram Judson the missionary once put it. They are essentially forward looking and hopeful persons. They believe in, indeed are profoundly convicted about, what they cannot see, and they feel assured God is with them even to the close of their lives. This leads to all sort of ventures and adventures.

I once knew a man who was an alcoholic. He was a quiet and even gentle man but he had allowed his whole life to be consumed in drink, and life had certainly passed him by. He blamed his father for all of this, because his father had forbad him to go and play professional baseball, which he was so good at as a teenager and had been offered a pro contract. His father had forced him to stay at home and work on the farm. According to this man, this had crushed his spirit and he was never the same there after, driven to drink. Now I have no desire to belittle the terrible thing that this man's father did, destroying a child's hopes and dreams of playing professional baseball, but as a Christian I have to say that while we cannot control the various and varied circumstances of life, we can, by the grace of God control how we will respond to them. We can either let these circumstances make us bitter or better. We have a choice about how we respond to life's opportunities and life's depredations and disappointments.

There is a New Testament promise that "greater is he who is in us, than any of these forces in the world" and it is a truth so profound that it is sometimes hard to plumb its depths. There is the further promise in 1 Cor. 10 that no temptation has overcome us that is not common to humanity such that with the temptation God will provide an adequate means of escape. If Christ is both in us (the hope of glory) and with us, we should be able to realize that God is bigger than our circumstances. We should as well be able to take St. Paul at his word that God is able to provide escape hatches to get out of situations that try our souls. Whether we succumb to such temptations, whether we give in to the assault of human wickedness is up to us, but the grace to stand and withstand is available to the Christian person.

There is a difference between existing and really living. The person who fails to try may indeed be trying to fail, or just too afraid to try, but whatever else one can say that kind of person is just existing, not living. Jesus says that he came that we might have abundant life, a life that propels us forward even into the darkness, even against heavy odds, even when we don't 'feel like it', and even when we are afraid. The two words I would hope would never characterize a Christian life are—'if only.'

## Spiritual Meditations

### "If Only"

- Lectio Divina: Psalm 121; John 6:35–40
- Confession is more than just a time to air our outward failings. Spend some time confessing where you struggle with fear, faith, and self-sufficiency. Ask God to conquer your fears, strengthen your faith, and make you more dependent on Him. Depending on your struggle, you might write a short prayer (one or two words or a short sentence from a Psalm, etc.) to repeat throughout the day/week.
- Guidance is an oft-overlooked corporate discipline. It is difficult for us to ask for the help and accountability of others. However, developing such a group can provide strength and encouragement that we cannot find on our own. Gather a group of people to meet regularly (weekly, monthly, etc.) for accountability and encouragement.

### Thoughts for Further Reflection

*"A person of real Christian faith is a person brave enough to venture forth into life, to be willing to try, and even to fail sometimes in the process."*

Ben Witherington III

*"Jesus says that he came that we might have abundant life, a life that propels us forward even into the darkness, even against heavy odds . . . and even when we are afraid."*

Ben Witherington III

*"Be not afraid of growing slowly, be afraid only of standing still."*

Chinese Proverb

*Epiphany*

*"Hope begins in the dark.*
*You wait and watch and work. You don't give up."*

Anne Lamott

*"I have learned to live each day as it comes,*
*and not to borrow trouble by dreading tomorrow.*
*It is the dark menace of the future that makes cowards of us."*

Dorothy Day

## Personal Ponderings on "If Only"

Inside the small collection of Peter Marshall's sermons that sits on my shelf, there are countless words of wisdom. This book, yellowed by years and worn by use, is a priceless treasure to me. As with many of my favorite books, I just happened upon this book. I knew of Peter Marshall, but had never read any of his sermons. What I found inside this little book was a treasure-trove of wisdom and inspiration. Many of his words seem to follow me, challenging and inspiring me as I walk along the Way.

One such sermon is the one entitled *The Problem of Falling Rocks*. The inspiration for this particular sermon is the sign that often appears on highways nestled in the mountains that says, "Beware of Falling Rocks." Marshall questions what exactly a person can do about rocks that are already in the process of falling. He likens worrying over the danger of falling rocks to allowing fear to run our lives. Worry is destructive and debilitating. It keeps us from experiencing all that God longs to give us in the now and prevents us from walking in faith and freedom. Marshall challenges "if you are a Christian, if you are a child of God, then your worrying is not only futile, it is sinful."[2] Faith alone can free us from fear and allow us to truly live and experience the abundant life promised to us in the now and forevermore.

"The rocks will fall," Marshall states. "We don't know when, and we cannot find out for sure. Worrying about it, fearing it, does not help. Life must go on, and so must we."[3] We must choose to walk, holding

---

2. Catherine Marshall, ed. *Mr. Jones, Meet the Master: The Sermons and Prayers of Peter Marshall.* New York: Dell Publishing, 1950, 214.

3. Ibid., 216.

confidently and unswervingly to a God who has a history of helping his people through it all. In this is our hope, not that we will avoid all danger, but that God will sustain us through it all. He has promised that "there is a loving purpose in it all . . . even though our tear-filled eyes cannot see it" at first.[4] Let us not let fear and worry rob us of our joy and steal the song from our hearts. For the Promised Land is there, up ahead in the distance, and it is glorious!

(JNH)

---

4. Ibid., 219.

*Epiphany*

## SOMETHING DEEP INSIDE

Between living and dead
Between heart and head
Between flesh and blood
Between soul and spirit,
Something deep inside.

Between thought and action
Between image and reflection
Between act and being
Between sight and seeing,
Something deep inside.

Between silence and speech
Between grasp and reach
Between alone and lonely
Between singular and only,
Something deep inside.

Between begotten and made
Between art and artifice
Between lost and mislaid
Between offering and sacrifice,
Something deep inside.

Between parent and child
Between Father and Son
Between many and one
Between finished and done,
Something deep inside.

Between union and communion
Between friendship and family
Between sister and brother
Between One and the other,
Something deep inside.

Between loosed and bound
Between circular and round
Between labyrinth and maze
Between fog and haze,
Something deep inside.

Between Spirit and spirit
Between breath and life
Between time and eternity
Between image and identity,
Someone deep inside.

Between appearing and being
Between thought and meaning
Between revery and reverence
Between wholeness and holiness,
Worship deep inside.

January 24, 2005

## THEOLOGICAL MUSINGS

This poem is trying to get at something elusive, get at the gaps in life. One of the things that I have come to be convicted about is that there is a large gap between our experience and our ability to articulate it. As wonderful as words are, they fall far short of actually encapsulating or capturing human experience. And this is all the more the case when we are talking about profound religious or spiritual experience. Let me give you an illustration.

My grandmother was not a well educated woman. She never got beyond high school, indeed I am not even sure she finished high school. She had a limited vocabulary, but it was colorful, nevertheless. She used to talk about her husband "carrying her to the store." That conjured up quite an image since I only remember my grandmother as an adult, indeed an elderly one, and my grandfather, though once the town fire chief could not have 'carried' her to the store. Of course this was just her way of saying 'take me to the store.' My grandmother was a deeply Christian person, but if you had asked her to articulate her faith, say, give a brief definition of the Trinity, she really could not have done it. Her experience of God was far more profound than her ability to conceptualize and articulate what

## Epiphany

she was experiencing. When I got older and wiser I realized that this was true not merely of those of limited education, but of us all. There is a gap between the knowing of experience and the putting of that experience into words. This poem tries to get at that indefinable something.

But as it turns out, there is not just a gap within us between experience and conceptualization. There are actually gaps in reality itself. Blueprints are one thing, the actual construction of the house is quite another. There is no 'perfect' house, 'perfect' vacation, 'perfect' job, 'perfect' partner, and so on. There are just varying degrees of approximation to the design or mental image we have conjured up. Have you ever wondered why this is? I suspect it has to do not merely with ordinary human failings but with human fallenness itself, and indeed the fallenness of all creation.

Lions are not lying down with lambs just yet, or if they are, they are licking their chops or thinking of lamb chops. Fallen creation is intractable and will not conform to our design of what it ought to be. It is malleable to be sure, but there are always knots in the pine planks, so to speak. No wonder Paul in Romans 8 speaks of all of creation groaning, longing for the day of liberation. There are gaps in reality even when we manage to make it useful for our purposes. But there is also another truth that is touched on at the end of this poem.

Notice that the last two verses speak of someone deep inside, and of worship deep inside. The biggest gap of all in reality is the divine-human one, the broken character of our relationship with God. Martin Buber used to talk about the longing for an I-Thou relationship with God instead of an I-It relationship. The Good News is that God has fixed this part of the problem by bridging the gap in person. God has come to dwell amongst his people permanently, Emmanuel, and also within individual Christians as well.

Now if God is within us, then not only do we have a hope and anticipation and foretaste of glory, we also have something else. We have the stimulus and the enabling for worship, for a true I-thou personal relationship with God in Christ. This is not to be confused with some sort of narcissistic relationship with our 'inner child' or anything of the like, because we are not God, and even when God bridges the gap in our relationship we neither become God nor does God melt into the mass of our identity. Even when Christ is within us, there is still a distinction between the Creator and creature which is maintained, so that we do not end up worshipping ourselves, but rather are enabled to worship the one who is

Wholly Other, but who longs to be in intimate relationship with us. This is what produces worship deep inside—an Other oriented activity which confirms in our own souls both the gap between ourselves and God, and also the fact that God has blessedly bridged that gap in Christ.

## Spiritual Meditations

### "Something Deep Inside"

- Lectio Divina: Jeremiah 31:10–14 (or Jeremiah 32:37–44); Romans 8:1–11
- Spend some time in concentrated worship. Using any medium (music, arts, divine reading, etc.), praise our God who bridges the gap, creates and recreates, redeems and restores.
- Write an original prayer of praise to God for his creativity and his provision in your life. For inspiration, look to the Psalms. Use some of the thanksgiving and praise psalms to guide your own writing or simply use your life as the inspiration.

### Thoughts for Further Reflection

*"The Good News is that God has . . . bridg[ed] the gap in person. God has come to dwell amongst his people permanently, Emmanuel, and also within individual Christians as well."*

Ben Witherington III

*"Expect unexpected things."*

Andrew Murray

*"God is God. If he is God, he is worthy of my worship and my service. I will find rest nowhere but in his will and that will is infinitely, immeasurably, unspeakably beyond my largest notions of what he is up to."*

Elisabeth Elliot

*Epiphany*

*[Epiphany] is something that surprises us from behind, from the hidden and personal part of our being; like that which can sometimes take us off our guard . . . It is rather as if a man had found an inner room in the very heart of his own house, which he had never suspected; and seen a light from within."*

G. K. Chesterton

### Personal Ponderings on "Something Deep Inside"

You might know that the word "Gospel" literally means "good news" or "glad tidings." But while you know that the Gospel is the Good News, do you really know that to be true in your life? It is a difficult thing to grasp, but it is of utmost importance. I have found no better description of this than the one Frederick Buechner gives in his delightful book *Wishful Thinking: A Theological ABC*. Buechner captures the radical nature of the Gospel with his words. He calls to mind the wildness of the idea that God in Jesus loves us in spite of us. He reminds the reader that not only does the Gospel claim this, but also that, if we will let him, God will actually transform our hearts himself, enabling us to love him and love others. He concludes with the thoughts below.

> "What is both Good and New about the Good News is the mad insistence that Jesus lives on among us not just as another haunting memory, but as the outlandish, holy, and invisible power of God working . . . in countless hidden ways to make even slobs like us loving and whole beyond anything we could conceivably pull off by ourselves."[5]

That God not only loves us but also likes us and longs to accomplish great things through us is difficult for us to fathom. The truth of the matter is that this is the truth. The Good News of the Gospel is alive in us when we allow God to work through our very lives. God is greater than our limited view of ourselves and his dreams for what he can do with a life are far beyond what we could ever imagine. For proof of this one need not look any further than the Incarnate One, Jesus Christ.

(JNH)

5. Buechner, Frederick. *Wishful Thinking: A Theological ABC*. New York: Harper & Row Publishers, 1973, 33.

## The Living Legacy

### TRAVELING MERCIES

They really weren't wise
To travel that far
But then pregnant Mary
Didn't follow a star.

Unlike the sages
Stargazers not kings,
Whose journey to Herod
Led to horrific things.

The shepherds had visitors
Who traveled the most
Their singing was moving,
The heavenly host.

It's quite unlikely
Luke meant an inn,
For elsewhere in Greek
It's a guest room for kin.

So not in a barn
But the ancestral home
Twas a short trip for Jesus
Who was not left alone.

Surrounded by animals,
Family and friends
He left quickly for Egypt
Lest Herod do him in.

The longest journey
Is the one in our hearts
When Jesus comes calling
His love to impart.

Between hearing and believing
Between doubt and trust
Lies a deep valley,
And cross it we must.

*Epiphany*

His traveling mercies
Can make a way
If we walk in the light,
He'll be our day.

Epiphany 2000

## THEOLOGICAL MUSINGS

WHILE I AM NOT one of those who think that life is all about journeying rather than 'getting there' (because in my view there is not much point in journeying unless you are going somewhere, or are at least open to arriving at some destination), I am persuaded that something happens when we go on pilgrimage. I am also persuaded that we certainly need traveling mercies along the way—since many journeys are perilous.

Some journeys are not pilgrimages, they are just wanderings, like the Israelites in the wilderness, and this could be said to characterize some lives as well—they are in motion but they really aren't going anywhere. This is because the most profound journeys are the ones of the heart and some people are never prepared to go on a pilgrimage of the heart. Carson McCullers once spoke of the heart being a lonely hunter, and this is true enough, but sometimes the heart is so battered that it is like an old hunting dog that just refuses to hunt anymore. And when the heart gives up on pilgrimages then life's external journeys can never become pilgrimages. They are just wanderings in the wilderness.

This is a poem I wrote with a child's rhyme scheme. It is meant to be simple and it is meant to be heard, as in fact all poetry is. Poetry is an aural art operating on borrowed time in a visually oriented and computer screen culture, where one can go on journeys of the mind just by turning on the computer. I wanted to encapsulate the fact that there were a variety of journeys that ended in Bethlehem, but none of them were nearly as long or arduous and the one God made to be reconciled with us, and the one we must make to be reconciled with God. A pilgrimage is a journey with a purpose, indeed with a divine purpose. I would distinguish it from a crusade, which in fact was and is sometimes not a holy journey. Some Christians live as though their lives are crusades—crusades against this or that evil, and I am not saying there is not a place for some kinds of crusades, for example a crusade against pornography and sexual abuse of children. The problem with crusades is that they can often degenerate into something unholy, unloving, unkind, intolerant, and the like.

A pilgrimage however is a different sort of journey. It is a journey through a fallen world to God. It always has a divine purpose, and it always first and foremost involves a journey of the heart. Henri Nouwen talks about living lives with open hands. I am talking about living lives with 'happy' feet even, or as the psalmist puts it 'beautiful' feet, moving towards God, or conversely down from the mountain top experience to share the Good News with others. This is the dialectic of the Christian life upward towards God, and downward and outward towards others. It is not an accident that the two great commandments are about loving God with all we are and all we have, and loving neighbor as our selves. These commandments were not in the first instance about feelings. They are about actions, about feet set in motion, about doing something, about going on pilgrimage towards God or towards others. The question then becomes not merely will we travel wisely, but will we travel well and in a godly fashion.

The ancient Jews had a word for ethics—they called it walking. One could be walking in the way of sinners, or walking in the paths of righteousness for God's name sake. Paul talks about walking according to the flesh or walking according to the Spirit's guidance, promptings, fruit (Gal. 5). The New Year is a time for us to reflect on such pilgrimages, and indeed to begin a new one. Perhaps the bumper sticker cliché is one worth pondering as we choose our path—"wise men still seek him."

## Spiritual Meditations

### "Traveling Mercies"

- Lectio Divina: Isaiah 43; Galatians 5:22–25
- Henri Nouwen once said, "Writing can be a true spiritual discipline." It can help to center our thoughts and get at the heart of things. Writing can be a great tool to help us reflect on pilgrimages—past, present and future. Spend some time in written reflection. Grab a notebook and pen and simply write what comes to mind. You might find, to borrow from Nouwen once more, that "a difficult, painful, or frustrating day can be 'redeemed' by writing about it."[6] Even our best days are better when we take time to notice where God met us in it.

6. Nouwen, Henri. *Bread for the Journey: A Daybook of Wisdom and Faith.* New York: Harper Collins Publishers, 1997.

*Epiphany*

- Study is an important part of who we are as Christians. Time spent studying the pilgrimage of another can inform our own journey through life. Choose a person from the Bible (i.e.—Esther, Jonah, Daniel, etc.) or one from the communion of saints (i.e.—Corrie ten Boom, Thomas Merton, Dietrich Bonhoeffer, Thomas Aquinas, etc.). Study their pilgrimage and reflect on how it informs your own.

### Thoughts for Further Reflection

*"A pilgrimage is a journey with a purpose, indeed with a divine purpose."*

Ben Witherington III

*"The feeling remains that God is on the journey [with us], too."*

Saint Teresa of Avila

*"Show me your ways, O Lord, teach me your paths; guide me in your truth and teach me, for you are God my Savior, and my hope is in you all day long."*

Psalm 25:4–5

*"The Lord Himself goes before you and will be with you."*

Deuteronomy 31:8

*"Never be afraid to trust an unknown future to a known God."*

Corrie ten Boom

### Personal Ponderings on "Traveling Mercies"

Adventure. Journey. Walk. Pilgrimage. These words resonate with us as Christians. We hear them and are immediately transported to places of significance in our history: Eden, Red Sea, Sinai, Bethlehem, Golgotha, and countless others in-between and all along the way. We know that we are on a pilgrimage to a place of promise. Ours is a journey with a divine purpose, a daily walk that brings us face-to-face with God.

The concept of life with Christ as a walk has long informed my life. It paints for me a vivid picture of constancy, companionship, and commitment. I must choose to walk and know that I do not walk alone on my journey. There are countless people who walk with me on this journey—past and present. In my love affair with the saints, I have found many who have encouraged and challenged me along the way. One such person is a contemporary on the journey—Eugene Peterson. Thought I have not met him personally, I am constantly challenged by his life and his words. In his book *A Long Obedience in the Same Direction*, he explores the Psalms of Ascents and what it means to take the pilgrimage with God. I leave you with his words.

> "The Christian life is going to God. In going to God, Christians travel the same ground that everyone else walks on, breathe the same air, drink the same water . . . fear the same dangers, are subject to the same pressures, get the same distresses, are buried in the same ground.
>
> The difference is that each step we walk, each breath we breathe, we know we are preserved by God, we know we are accompanied by god, we know we are ruled by God; and therefore no matter what doubts we endure or what accidents we experience, the Lord will guard us from every evil, he guards our very life.
>
> We Christians believe that life is created and shaped by God and that the life of faith is a daily exploration of the constant and countless ways in which God's grace and love are experienced."[7]

(JNH)

---

7. Peterson, Eugene. *A Long Obedience in the Same Direction.* Downer's Grove, IL: InterVarsity Press, 2000, 45.

*Epiphany*

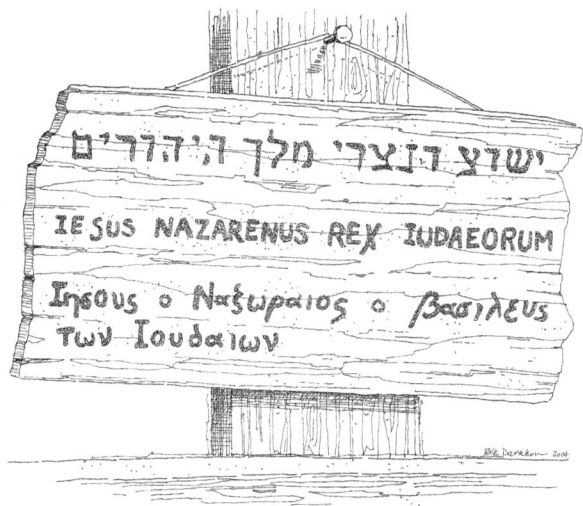

## PILGRIM'S PAEAN

The heaven's open, the clouds do part
To give a glimpse of heavenly art,
The light which shines upon our earth
Reveals his will, his work, his worth.

The highest priest lifts up his hands
The Father gives what he commands
The prayer of priest who intercedes
And speaks of all our human needs.

Now sacrifice of lips and hands
Is what of us our God demands
Since Christ did end in death our need
To offer others that may bleed.

A pilgrim people on their way
Should travel light, in light of day
And keep their eyes fixed on the goal
On One above who saves the soul.

The vision of above, below

Will guide us where we ought to go,
And faith shall grasp what hands cannot
And journey on to unseen spot.

For shepherd shall return one day
And bring his host in bright array
The heavenly city shall descend
And gather all the sheep within.

The priest whose death did here below
Begin his priestly work we know
And above in Holy Space
Offered his life blood in our place.

This priest comes forth from Holy Place
And brings his gifts to his own race
The benefits of death and life
That binds our wounds and ends our strife.

· This priest, this Son whom God did raise
We offer now our prayer and praise
And look upon horizon's bend
As Son comes down and night does end.

December 28, 1988

## THEOLOGICAL MUSINGS

THIS IS ANOTHER PILGRIMAGE poem, only this one is not based in the Christmas story, it is grounded in the remarkable book of Hebrews. It is a good one to end this Epiphany section of poems with, as it points us towards the Lent and Easter seasons. One of the most remarkable things about the heavenly high priest Christology of the book of Hebrews is not only that we find it nowhere else in the NT really, but that Christ is said to be both priest and sacrifice, both offering and offerer, both atoner and atonement, and these roles are said to span both his career on earth and his post ascension work in heaven. It seems that Jesus did not merely sit down at the right hand of God after his earthly ministry, and settle in for a long winter's nap, called the church age. It seems that he is constantly busy interceding, praying, entreating God the Father on our behalf, and pleading on the basis of his bleeding and death.

*Epiphany*

What is perhaps most striking about this Christology is that it reveals a Christ who in his own person bridges the gap between earth and heaven, doing ministerial work on both sides of the divide. If we think we will be exchanging earthly activities for heavenly boredom and rest, I suspect we have another think coming. To judge from Jesus' career, heaven is a haven of fervent activity. It is also, according to Rev. 6, a place of impatience, with the saints asking how long before God will conclude the tale of judgment and redemption on the earth. Heaven is not viewed as the final destination of the saints, only an interim condition until heaven comes down and there is a new heaven and earth. Read through the latter half of Hebrews 12 sometime. The final theophany takes place on earth, after the second coming of Jesus. It is thus an odd fact that the most heavenly oriented and minded books of the NT (Hebrews and Revelation) both stress that the end of the story will transpire on earth. This is certainly not heavenly mindedness that is no earthly good. The pilgrimage, as it turns out, ends up back down here after the parousia and resurrection and the last judgment. Thus the book of Hebrews teaches us to look forward while also looking upward. Perhaps better said we are to look forward *by* looking upward. But the author of Hebrews is just as concerned with the sacral journey of Jesus as the human pilgrimage towards the eschaton.

Jesus goes from being the sacrifice that makes purification (see Heb. 1) to being the high priest who enters the inner sanctum in the Holy of Holies and applies the blood to the horns of the altar. He has the all-access pass into God's presence, and he has it perpetually having made the once for all time perfect sacrifice. When he intercedes for sinners he is heard. His sacrifice and interceding should lead to our sacrifice of praise and our prayers. Jesus' sacral journey into the inner sanctuary should lead to our making the same sacral journey—"I was glad when they said unto me, let us go into the house of the Lord." Indeed there is a sense in which the journey into worship is the one which prepares us for the journey into life and onto the eschaton. It is not enough to see the epiphany, the appearing of the Christ child. The question then becomes—where do we go from here. One answer is down on our knees to worship. The other is on into the Kingdom, on to the final epiphany, the final theophany.

## The Living Legacy

# Spiritual Meditations

### "Pilgrim's Paean"

- Lectio Divina; Psalm 122 or 128; Hebrews 4:14–16
- Meditate on the kingdom of heaven. Search the Scriptures for passages that talk about the kingdom of heaven and meditate on the descriptions there. Journal in words or perhaps artistically what you envision in your times of meditation.
- The season of epiphany and all that it encompasses ought to bring us to our knees in worship and prayer. Spend some time in prayer, praising God for revealing Himself to us in Jesus Christ. Take time to confess where you have lost sight of all that Jesus' life, death, and resurrection represents for you. Ask God to renew your vision and remind you of your need for Him. You might also spend time praying for those in your life who have not seen the true light of epiphany, Jesus Christ.

### Thoughts for Further Reflection

*"It is not enough to see the epiphany, the appearing of the Christ child. The question then becomes—where do we go from here? One answer is down on our knees to worship. The other is on into the Kingdom, on to the final epiphany, the final theophany."*

Ben Witherington III

*"[T]here is a sense in which the journey into worship is the one which prepares us for the journey into life . . . "*

Ben Witherington III

*"Lord Jesus Christ, fill us, we pray, with Your light and love, that we may reflect Your wondrous glory. So fill us with Your love that we may count nothing too small to do for You, nothing too much to give, and nothing too much to bear. Amen."*

Saint Ignatius of Loyola

## Epiphany

*"Light, when suddenly let in, dazzles and hurts and almost blinds us: but this soon passes away, and it seems to become the only element we can exist in."*

Julius C. Hare

### Personal Ponderings on "Pilgrim's Paean"

It is a wonderful and convicting thought to consider worship the preparation for the journey of life. It is wonderful because worship of God is just that. It is convicting, because we too seldom stop to honor God in worship. Even our times of regular worship are crowded with thoughts of a thousand other things. And because we have lost the sacredness and necessity of corporate and daily worship, we walk through the journey of life unprepared and ill-equipped.

In his book, *Invitation to a Journey*, M. Robert Mulholland speaks clearly and beautifully about the necessity of corporate and individual worship. He describes worship as "the practice of regularly seeking to bring the complete focus of our being upon God." What a glorious thought! If our whole being is focused upon God, the circumstances of our everyday fall under His care. Nothing can overtake us but His love and grace and freedom if we will make Him our center.

> "[Worship] is the discipline of returning to the true center of our individual and corporate existence as God's people. The pressures of life and the assaults of the fallen world constantly blur our focus and tend to shift us away from our center in God. Worship is the means by which we recover our focus and return to our center. The quality and consistency of our worship will determine how well we are able to live Christ-Centered lives in the world."[8]

(JNH)

---

8. Mulholland, M. Robert. *Invitation to a Journey: A Road Map for Spiritual Formation.* Downer's Grove, IL: InterVarsity Press, 1993, 118.

# Lent

*The Lengthening of the Light*

## SHADE TREE

A tree always a tree,
That shadows forth his shade to me.

The tree of Eden long before
Tempting those who longed for more
Knowledge, power, experience,
But lacking trust, lacking sense.

A tree, always a tree
That shadows forth his shade to me.

The burning bush
Could Moses see
More than curiosity
Ablaze with all infinity.

# The Living Legacy

A tree always a tree
That shadows forth his shade to me.

That terrible Terebinth
Oh Absalom, a tithing tenth
Ensnared in branches as he went,
The royal robe of David rent.

A tree, always a tree,
That shadows forth his shade to me.

Elijah lost and on the run
A broom tree shading from the sun
He prayed to die but fell asleep
And angel's food his soul did keep.

A tree always a tree
That shadows forth his shade to me.

Ezekiel's cedar of Lebanon
Which once was here but now is gone
Cut down by ruthless foreign foes
A symbol of the chosen's woes.

A tree always a tree
That shadows forth his shade to me.

Moaning Jonah could not see
In a tree-like vine, God's mercy
And so it withered and it died,
And Jonah sulked and Yahweh cried.

A tree always a tree
That shadows forth his shade to me.

Isaiah saw Eden's door
Fertile fig trees, no more war
But exiles failed to take the hint
Returned to fight, hope misspent.

A tree always a tree
That shadows forth his shade to me.

*Lent*

The cursed fig of Jesus' day
Sign of judgment on the way
Blighted when it bore no fruit
Unplanted souls without a root

A tree always a tree
That shadows forth its shade to me.

The cross a tree on which he hung
Bore the curse of which they sung
'His ways are not ours, our eyes can not see,
The logic of love nailed to a tree.'

A tree always a tree
That shadows forth his shade to me.

And then at last Jerusalem
Where rivers flow and kingdoms come
The tree of life, twelve fruits it bears
Medicinal leaves that heal the cares.

A tree always a tree
That shadows forth his shade to me.

## THEOLOGICAL MUSINGS

THE WORD LENTEN COMES from the English word lengthen referring to the time of the year when we experience the lengthening of the days. Theologically speaking it is the season of repentance, prayer, fasting, and various other spiritual disciplines as we take up our crosses and follow Jesus to Golgotha. I have chosen to begin this section with a salvation historical poem which reflects on the fact that trees, or in some cases bushes, seem to be vehicles of or symbols of spiritual encounters, or even of the people of God.

Trees were certainly important to Israel, not least because they didn't have a lot of them in Judea at least. The really good trees were in Lebanon and even Solomon imported some of these cedars when he final built the Temple and his palace. Trees always signified something precious, valuable, and in some cases even expensive. The tree was especially valued for its shade and fruit in a land that was often incredibly hot, a land where rain only came in certain seasons of the year, and not in the summer at all. It became an apt symbol for God's protection and provision.

By salvation historical, I mean a poem that focuses on moments throughout the history of God's people where significant and spiritually determinative encounters happened at trees or bushes. We need to remember that Israelites, and early Christians as well, were not nature worshippers. They did not see trees as somehow inherently a locus of the divine. We certainly do not find in Scripture what we later find in the Gospel of Thomas sayings like "cleave the wood and I am there" as if pan-entheism were a legitimate option—the worship of God in nature, in this case particularly in a tree.

This makes the numerous Biblical encounters at the various bushes or trees all the more remarkable.

Notice in the examples I have recited in this poem that only one of them is really negative—the cursing of the fig tree, which is the only negative miracle Jesus performed, though I suppose one could point to the story of Absalom's encounter with the tree that hung him as well, bearing in mind the OT phrase "cursed be he who hangs upon a tree" (Deut. 21.23). Jesus' wrath however tells us that he fully expected the fig tree to bear fruit. He looked for good things from trees. This of course doesn't prevent trees from becoming instruments of death in the wrong hands, whether they be the hands of Satan or the hands of Pilate. But again this goes counter to the normal function and purpose of a tree.

What all these tree stories do is remind us to ask ourselves—what do we expect of a God of history, who is also the God of nature? Where do we look for God's presence? Do we know to look for it in unexpected places, at unexpected times, in unexpected ways? Do we learn from these stories that God continues to seek encounter with us even through death on a cross? And of course there is the message that we should seek God not just for or in his protection and provision, but for the sake of relationship with God, for the sake of knowing God, for the sake of loving God.

Lent begins with Ash Wednesday and then heads for Golgotha. Its 40 days can be likened to Jesus' forty days in the wilderness. And notice that the 40 days take a rest once a week—the Sundays of Lent don't count in that number. Lent is a time for being apart, and setting one's self apart and for the testing of one's Christian metal. During this season it would be well to go and sit in the shade of the presence of God and think about these things and where one's life is going.

*Lent*

# Spiritual Meditations

## "Shade Tree"

- Lectio Divina: Exodus 3:1–15; Ezekiel 17:22–24
- Thomas à Kempis viewed silence as the "discipline of remembering." He believed that practicing this discipline brought calmness and clarity. Silence is key to living a centered life and truly knowing God. Set aside pockets of time this week to simply sit still and be silent. If you cannot block out a significant amount of time, take advantage of whatever silences fill your day, even if they are brief.
- Fasting has been a mainstay in the season of Lent across the centuries, though it seems we have lost sight of the reasoning behind it. We are to fast to know God and identify with Jesus Christ with the help of the Holy Spirit. Often times our fasting is hollow because it is not centered on the things of God. As you enter this Lenten Season, ask God to give you a fresh understanding of fasting and a clear vision of what you need to fast from during these forty days.

## Thoughts for Further Reflection

*"[W]e should seek God not just for or in his protection and provision, but for the sake of a relationship with God, for the sake of knowing God, for the sake of loving God."*

Ben Witherington III

*"To cling always to God and to the things of God—this must be our major effort, this must be the road that the heart follows unswervingly."*

John Cassian

*"The sovereign God wants to be loved for Himself and honored for Himself, but that is only part of what He wants. The other part is that He wants us to know that when we have Him we have everything . . . "*

A. W. Tozer

## The Living Legacy

*"How splendid the cross of Christ! It brings life and not death; light, not darkness; paradise, not its loss. A tree had destroyed us, a tree now brought us life."*

Theodore of Studios

### Personal Ponderings on "Shade Tree"

William Law's writing stemmed from his profession as an Anglican priest which emphasized spiritual direction and formation. His best known work is *A Serious Call to a Devout and Holy Life*, a book that offers uncompromising principles of a life fully devoted to God. Unwavering in his conviction that the holy life is a life of union with God in the everyday, Law gives practical help for attaining such union. Though Law lived more than two hundred years ago, his words continue to bring insight even today.

A spiritual classic remains applicable through the ages only insofar as it first informed the life of its writer. Such is the case with William Law. It is abundantly clear from the beginning that Law writes from a wealth of experience. The principles arrived at come from his own life, both personal and professional. It is for this reason that I thought of Law as I reflected on the above poem and theological musings.

Law considers devotion to God a "state of the heart." What a blessed, freeing thought! Union and devotion to God is nothing less than letting go of self and reorienting the heart toward God. Devotion understood as such should be God-centered, and not self-centered. Devotion to God often takes the form of compartmentalization rather than integration. Law warns against this at every turn. He believes that the devout "consider God in everything, serve God in everything, and make every aspect of their lives holy by doing everything in the name of God and in a way that conforms to God's glory." Holiness is happiness in the midst of the everyday as we surrender all to God. Law writes, "If we are to be new people in Christ, then we must show our newness to the world. If we are to follow Christ, in must be in the way that we spend each day." May it be so with you.[1]

(JNH)

---

1. Foster, Richard J. and James Bryan Smith. *Devotional Classics: Selected Readings for Individuals and Groups*. New York: Harper Collins Publishers, 2005, 157.

*Lent*

### RSVP

To move from fast to feast,
From ashes to riding an ass,
From wilderness wandering
God's willingness wondering
To follow the way of the cross
To find what was utterly lost
    All this was Lent to us.

The cup not passed over
By our Passover
The vinegar he willingly drank—
But through gift divine
New covenant wine
Came forth from his side as he sank
    All this was given to us

## The Living Legacy

Through breaking of bread
They knew their head
The joy of new life begun
From out of the depths,
From out of his death
His people one loaf had become
        All this was food for us.

Lent leads to Easter
The faster turns feaster
A foretaste for those in the dust
A bread with new leaven
The manna from heaven
        All this has risen for us.

God's ways are not our ways,
Our eyes cannot see,
The logic of love,
Nailed to a tree.
Come now to the dinner
Come saint and come sinner,
        The meal is now served to us.

        Lent 1982

### THEOLOGICAL MUSINGS

THIS IS A EUCHARISTIC poem, meant to reinforce the importance of the Lord's Supper during Lent. Traditionally during Lent some church activities have been suspended as this is intended to be a time of mourning for sin, introspection, fasting, prayer and the like. For example, traditionally in the Roman Catholic church there are no weddings during Lent. And in some other traditions there are no baptisms either. The one constant however is that the Lord's Supper continues to be served throughout the period.

There is of course a logic to this. In most Christian traditions there is a prayer of repentance that one is supposed to pray before coming to the Lord's table. "We do not presume to come to this thy table, presuming on your mercy . . . " it begins. Repentance, a staple of Lenten devotion is built into the celebration of the Lord's Supper, and rightly so. It could be stressed that one needs the grace of God, one needs the 'real presence' of Christ as much or more during Lent as during any season of the church year. So the Lord's Supper continues to be served.[2]

Recently Asbury sponsored some fine lectures by Mark Allen Powell. One of these lectures was on the absence of Christ. By this he was referring to the fact that during the church age and since the Ascension Christ has been physically absent from his people and will remain physically absent from his people until the parousia. There is then a sense in which, since we do not have the bridegroom with us in the flesh, it is appropriate for us to fast, as Jesus said it was (see Mk. 2.19–20). Powell is right that while Jesus is present with his church even now, there is a sense in which he is absent as well, and since we are supposed to be the church expectant, awaiting the bridegroom, there has to be a sense in which Jesus' full presence with us is something to be celebrating in a way that we are not celebrating now. He reminded us as well that the language of the Lord's Supper is all about remembrance and 'until he comes' underlining that he was once here with his people and that he will return to celebrate with us again in a bolder way. The Lord's Supper language then, paradoxically enough reminds us of the current absence of the physical presence of the Christ. Clearly God's ways are not our ways.

In this poem I have tried to stress a few different Lenten themes, including 'the logic of love nailed to a tree.' In one sense it is not difficult to see this logic. If you really love someone you will be willing to make sacrifices for them, even the ultimate sacrifice of one's life if one truly loves that person. But there is another side to this equation that makes less sense on the surface of things. It was not just the case that Jesus voluntarily gave up his life. The tradition is clear that he asked for the cup of God's wrath and it turned out to be God's will that he should drink it. Now we have this image of God demanding payment for sin.

For some this image of the Father, as one who demands that things be set right, and that justice be done for sin, is an image that is forbidding and forboding. Is this really the character of God? And one could ask a pointed question—What sort of Father would demand that his Son undergo this sort of death, unless of course it was absolutely necessary for our salvation? But if it is both the necessary atonement for sin, and the essential means by which we all may be saved, then indeed Jesus' volun-

---

2. See Witherington, *Making a Meal of It*, (Waco: Baylor Univ. Press, 2007).

tary submission to this death is the greatest example of self-sacrificial love imaginable. It shows us that God's mercy found a way to be both just and the justifier of sinful human beings. God's love is a holy love. Not holiness without love, and not love without holiness. Holiness without love is judgment without mercy. Love without holiness not only has no definite shape or character, it become infinite indulgence of things which destroy human life, human character, human nature. In Jesus' death God found a way to be righteous and loving in the same event, dealing with sin but saving the sinner. This is at the very heart of the Lenten message. It is why Golgotha is the goal of this season, its termination and resting point.

## Spiritual Meditations

### "RSVP"

- Lectio Divina:Romans 3:21–26

- While confession can be deeply personal, it is also a discipline to be practiced within fellowship. Dallas Willard reminds us that sharing our flaws and failures will "nourish our faith . . . and our humility before our brothers and sisters."[3] Allowing trusted others to see us fully and transparently brings us strength in our weakness and a deep sense of fellowship with other Christians on the journey. If you already have trusted others to whom you confess, meet with them regularly during the Lenten season. If you do not already have people to whom you go for confession and accountability, seek a few trusted others to meet with on a regular basis.

- Spend some time today meditating on the love of God. If weather permits, do this somewhere outdoors. If you have difficulty centering your thoughts, consider using a passage of Scripture such as Ephesians 3:14–21 or Exodus 3:4–9 as a guide for your thoughts and meditations. You might take a journal or a sketch pad with you to record your thoughts.

---

3. Willard, Dallas. *The Spirit of the Disciplines: Understanding How God Changes Lives.* San Francisco: Harper Collins Publishers, 1988, 187.

*Lent*

## Thoughts for Further Reflection

*"In Jesus' death God found a way to be righteous and loving in the same event, dealing with sin but saving the sinner. This is at the very heart of the Lenten message."*

Ben Witherington III

*The task of the heart is self-preservation, holding together what is its own. The pierced heart of Jesus has . . . truly overturned this definition. This heart is not concerned with self-preservation but with self-surrender. It saves the world by opening itself. The collapse of the opened Heart is the content of the Easter mystery. The Heart saves, indeed, but it saves by giving itself away."*

Pope Benedict XVI

*"Gracious Father, whose blessed Son Jesus Christ came down from heaven to be the true bread which gives life to the world: Evermore give us this bread, that he may live in us, and we in him; who lives and reigns with you and the Holy Spirit, one God, now and for ever. Amen."*

BCP (219)[4]

## Personal Ponderings on "RSVP":

Henri Nouwen has a way with words. Time and again I have found his writings to be both convicting and inspiring, haunting and exhilarating. His writings are raw and honest, dealing with the struggles and the triumphs of following Jesus at all costs. In *Can You Drink the Cup?*, Nouwen begs the ultimate question. It is the question that Jesus asked James and John and the one that we must ask ourselves. For Nouwen, though drinking the cup is not easy, it is a doorway to freedom for us to live as God's sons and daughters.

> "The cup that Jesus speaks about is neither a symbol of victory nor a symbol of death. It is a symbol of life, filled with sorrows and joys that we can hold, lift, and drink as a blessing and a way to salvation. 'Can you drink the cup that I am going to drink?' Jesus asks us. It is the question that will have a different meaning every

---

4. Book of Common Prayer.

day of our lives. Can we embrace fully the sorrows and joys that come to us da*y after day?*

Drinking the cup that Jesus drank is living a life in and with the spirit of Jesus, which is the spirit of unconditional love. The intimacy between Jesus and his Father is an intimacy of complete trust . . . it is only love—pure, unrestrained, and unltimate love. That intimacy gave Jesus the strength to drink the cup. That same intimacy Jesus wants to give us so we can drink ours."[5]

(JNH)

---

5. Nouwen, Henri J. M. *Can You Drink the Cup?* Notre Dame, IN: Ave Maria Press, 2001, p. 107.

*Lent*

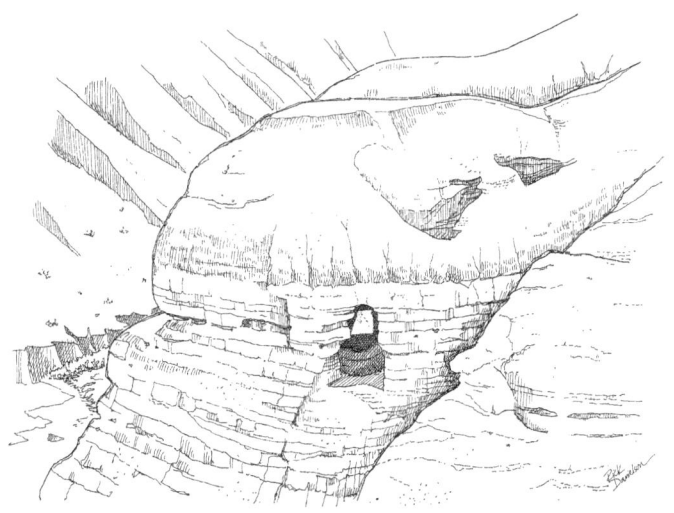

## THE ALCOVE

A niche,
A hideaway
A retreat
A sanctuary

For prayer
Communion
Contact
Reunion

Like the horns on the altar
Like the hem of his robe
Like the songs in the psalter
Like his hand on the globe

Like a vault for safekeeping
Like a treasury found
Like a library of answers
Like a truth that's profound

# The Living Legacy

One God
One sinner
One entreaty One answer

Forgiveness
For peace
For wisdom
Release

A secret space
A closet
A meeting place
An alcove.

"But when you pray, go into your closet, close the door and pray to your Father, who is unseen. Then your Father, who sees what is done in secret, will reward you. Do not keep babbling on like pagans, for they think they will be heard because of their many words. Do not be like them, for your Father knows what you need before you ask Him. This then is how you should pray: 'Our Father . . . .'

December 19, 2005

## THEOLOGICAL MUSINGS

THE SUBTITLE OF OUR volume, 'the heart in pilgrimage, the soul in paraphrase' is a line from a poem by George Herbert on prayer. Prayer is certainly one of the most central themes of Lent and this poems tries to undergird its importance, especially during this season. Public prayer too often becomes sermonizing with one's eyes closed. But prayer should be direct toward, and spoken to God—always and everywhere. Spiritual showmanship should be avoided at all costs. This is no doubt why Jesus urged on the one hand that we avoid praying like pagans who wish to be seen and on the other hand we seek out an alcove, a quiet or secret place to pray. There can be no pretense or pretending in one's prayer closet where it is just you and the Lord doing business together.

There are a lot of reasons to pray, and they cannot all be neatly summed up under the heading of 'things I would really like God to do for others and myself', although the prayer of petition is an important form of prayer. But in the first instance prayer is the indicator that we have a

*Lent*

personal relationship with God and in order to nurture that relationship we need to talk with one another. Yes prayer is both about speaking and silence, not just about our speaking. It is about listening as well as vocalizing what is in one's heart.

Of course to a considerable extent your theology of prayer will be determined by your theology of God. If you believe God has predetermined all things in advance, including what you will say in prayer, then prayer at most is about getting in touch with what God's will has always been about, and perhaps participating in that. It certainly is not about changing the mind of God, or changing the course of history for that matter, if by change one means altering something in a way that God did not originally will. If on the other hand, God is not viewed as having predetermined all things, then prayer looks very different indeed. As Maxie Dunnam has said, what if God has so set up the universe so that your prayers do matter? What if God, though he could have done otherwise, has chosen not to do certain things unless we pray and seek the face and will of God? What if we are in fact junior partners with God in the realization of the Kingdom of God on earth? As I have said, much hinges on one's theology of God.

And a few things need to be stressed. There is no such thing as unanswered prayer. It is just that God says no sometimes. Of course no is an answer we seldom want to hear, but it is in fact an answer. Secondly, perhaps the first and foremost kind of prayer we should offer is the prayer of praise to God. Notice that in the model prayer, the Lord's Prayer, we begin by hallowing God's name. We pray not for the realization of our kingdom and our will on earth, but for God's. Prayers of thanksgiving should also be high on our list of kinds of prayer and frequency of things to pray about. Thirdly, we are to pray for the forgiveness of sins, but only in such a fashion that it enables and requires of us that we be willing to forgive others who have deliberately sinned against us.

Then there comes the most amazing part of the Lord's prayer—praying that God himself will not put us to the test or perhaps it should be translated 'do not allow us to be led into temptation.' On the whole I think the translation ought to be 'do not put us to the test, but rather deliver us from the Evil One.' God of course knows our weaknesses, but this form of praying suggests that we know it as well, admit it, and thus pray not to be tested past our power to endure. This is the prayer of a wise person. You will notice as well in the Lord's prayer that there is nothing about praying for answers, though that does not make it illegitimate to do so. It would appear that this sort of praying is of a lower priority in Jesus' mind than prayers of praise, petition, confession and the like.

One of the things that happens in prayer is that one has communion with God, and a renewal of union with God, and this in itself gives a sense of peace and release, even if one does not discover an answer to one's questions. Sometimes in any case a solution to the problem is much preferable to just an answer to a question.

Sometimes people treat prayer like it was a visit to ye Olde Curiosity shop. They enter, they inspect the things they find there, they ask lots of questions, and then they leave without either getting the answers they want or without buying anything. They are simply window shopping, not really engaging with the owner of the shop or entering into an agreement with the owner. But what if prayer is plugging into the power source that runs the universe? What if prayer is a form of empowerment, and not just a game of twenty questions? George Herbert once famously said that prayer was reversed thunder and even called it Christ's side piercing spear! While these are bold images, they do remind us that we have a responsive God, not just an initiator God. And so it was with good reason that Jesus urged us to find the alcove, go into it, and seek the face of God alone.

## Spiritual Meditations

### "The Alcove"

- Lectio Divina: Matthew 6:9–15
- Sir Thomas More once said, "I have resolved to pray more and pray always, to pray all places where quietness invites . . . " Even the Scriptures urge us to "pray without ceasing" (1 Thessalonians 5:17). We know of and long for the communion that comes only with daily prayer and conversation with God. And yet many of us find prayer a difficult task. This is due in large part to the fact that we have not found our "alcove" or "closet" for praying. Create a space for prayer in your home and resolve to spend at least 15 minutes a day there in concentrated prayer (talking and listening). Finding your "upper room" will help you in your efforts to pray at all times. The greatest prayers will tell you that we must come to God somewhere some of the time before we can talk to him everywhere all of the time.

*Lent*

- Silence must be a regular part of our prayer life. Often our prayer time is crowded with words, leaving little time for the art of listening. Take time this week to pray without words at least once. As the Scriptures urge us, simply "be still" before the Lord (Psalm 46:10).

## Thoughts for Further Reflection

*"There can be no pretense or pretending in one's prayer closet . . . it is just you and the Lord doing business together."*

Ben Witherington III

*"One of the things that happens in prayer is that one has communion with God, and a renewal of union with God, and this in itself gives a sense of peace and release, even if one does not discover an answer to one's questions."*

Ben Witherington III

*"Pray alone. Let prayer be the key of the morning and the bolt at night."*

Philip Henry

*"Prayer is an all-efficient panoply, a treasure undiminished, a mine which is never exhausted, a sky unobscured by the clouds, a heaven unruffled by the storm. It is the root, the fountain, the mother of a thousand blessings."*

John Chrysostom

## Personal Ponderings on "The Alcove"

As with many of my (now) favorite books, I stumbled upon *The Meaning of Prayer* by Harry Emerson Fosdick almost by accident. I found it browsing through a shelf of bargain books in a cozy coffee shop in the tiny town where I attended seminary. I remembered the author from some sermons I was required to read for preaching class. I bought it on a whim and quickly fell in love with its contents. Rich with principles of prayer as well as prayers from saints through the ages, this book has breathed new life into my prayer life.

Fosdick writes,

> "Prayer is... not a burden to be borne, an obligation to be fulfilled, something that is due to God and must be paid. Prayer is a privilege; like friendship and family love and laughter... it is one of life's opportunities to be grasped thankfully and used gladly. The man who misses the deep meanings of prayer has not so much refused an obligation; he has robbed himself of life's supreme privilege—friendship with God."[6]

Prayer as a privilege rather than an obligation is a wonderful thought. If we were to view prayer more like Jesus did the whole of our lives would be opened for God's use. For Jesus, prayer was "not a monologue, but a dialogue; not soliloquy, but friendship." Viewed as such, prayer becomes nothing less than communion—walking and talking—with God. "The great gift of God in prayer," Fosdick writes, "is Himself, and whatever else He gives is incidental and secondary."[7] If we would begin to see it this way, I daresay we would all pray much more and always.

(JNH)

---

6. Fosdick, Harry Emerrson. *The Meaning of Prayer*. Nashville: Abingdon Press, 1981, 24.

7. Ibid., 30.

*Lent*

## TRIVIAL PURSUIT?

Trivial,
Tiny,
Miniscule,
Small.

'Unimportant',
Ignored,
Neglected
By all.

Overlooked
Out of sight
Out of mind
Yet real

Atoms,
Molecules
Quarks
A big deal.

Why would
We assume
Small's
Insignificant?

Why would
We assume
Tall's
Magnificent?

Humans
Miniscule
Compared
To the earth.

But this is
Hardly
A measure
Of our worth.

## The Living Legacy

Small
Holds
Together,
Much of the rest.

Details
Matter
History
Suggests:

"For want of a nail,
The horse was lost,
For want of the horse,
The message was lost
For want of the message
The battle was lost,
For want of the battle,
The war was lost,
And all for the want of a nail."

Minutiae
Matters
As it all
Turns out.

Attention
To detail
Helps things
Work out.

Study
The small things
Get down
To the root.

God's
In the details
So not
Trivial pursuit.

    December 7, 2005

*Lent*

## THEOLOGICAL MUSINGS

I MUST CONFESS AT the outset that I am not a detail person. Not surprisingly I married one, and this aspect of my personality tends to irritate my long suffering wife. In a sense this poem is a confessional one, as I am admitting that details, small things do often matter, indeed they can be the determining factor in various crucial things in life. Part of my Lenten confession is admitting this truth.

I suspect that I have been caught up in the general ethos of our consumer culture that assumes that bigger is both better and more important (super-size me!), that the newest is the truest, and that the latest is the greatest. Unfortunately, all too often all these things are false. But let's consider the first of these, which is the focus of this poem.

Consider for a moment the story of David and Goliath. What undergirds that story is the assumption that bigger is necessarily better and will prevail. Everyone is shocked when David wins the honor challenge with Goliath by one well placed shot. Sometimes one gets the feeling that God loves siding with the underdog, the smaller person, the less fortunate soul. In fact this is not just a feeling it is a fact. Look at the ministry of Jesus. He keeps talking about how the least, the last and the lost will become the first, the most, and the found. He speaks at length warning about not causing the little ones to stumble. In his famous parable about the sheep and the goats he reminds that inasmuch as one has done things to the least of these, one has in fact done it unto him. Small obviously is beautiful in God's eyes. Small does not equal insignificant in God's eyes.

But thus far I have been speaking mostly about persons. What about attention to details? What about small things? Do they really matter that much. Again Jesus seemed to think so. He even famously says that not one jot or tittle of the Law will pass away until all has been fulfilled. Now what he is referring to is probably diacritical marks, the equivalent to what we might call accent marks on some foreign words or an umlaut on a German vowel. Jesus thinks these small details are far from a trivial matter.

We still in English have a cliché phrase—'not one iota' of difference. It is interesting where this phrase comes from. It comes from the Christological debates of the 4th century A.D. at the council of Nicaea. The debate was raging on as to whether the Greek word **homo-ousios** best describes the relationship of the divine nature of the Son to the divine nature of the Father, or whether **homoi-ousios** best described it. The difference was the tiny Greek letter iota, the Greek equivalent of the letter

'I.' **Homo-ousios** means of the same substance, while **homoi-ousios** means of similar or like substance. There is a big difference between the two things. In the former case it would mean that the Father and the Son shared one divine nature, and so the doctrine of the Trinity would be preserved. If the little iota is added to the word, then it would mean that the Father and the Son were not of one nature or divine essence, but merely had like natures or substances. This would amount to Bi-theism, a belief in the existence of at least two Gods of similar substance, essence or nature. In short, monotheism hangs in the balance with this one little letter iota. The church fathers came to the conclusion that the iota should be left out in the middle of this word, because it made a huge difference. This in turn shows how ironic it is that the phrase today 'not one iota of difference' has the sense of making no difference at all, or at least making only a trivial difference. As it turns out, even one iota can make a huge difference in one's theology.

Lent is not just about fasting and becoming smaller. It is also about slowing down enough to appreciate the tiny miracles in life, the small things that matter enormously. In this poem I have sought to express this truth by sticking mainly to monosyllabic terms. Sometimes, as we like to say—less is actually more.

## Spiritual Meditations

### "Trivial Pursuit"

- Lectio Divina: 1 Samuel 17:32–50; Luke 9:46–48

- The discipline of service often calls to mind mission trips and ministry projects. While these are most certainly included in acts of service, often the most life-changing acts of service are done in the everyday. Find creative ways to serve the people in your life in small ways this week. Write a note of encouragement, Prepare a special breakfast. Surprise them with a favorite treat. Whether it is a friend, a family member, or a complete stranger, find ways to creatively serve others this week.

- Journal this week about how God has used small things in your own life to accomplish his great purposes. If you find it difficult to recall such experiences, simply begin writing. Use your writing as a prayer, thanking God and asking him to help you call to mind those times when he has used you in big and small ways.

## Thoughts for Further Reflection

*"Look at the ministry of Jesus. He keeps talking about how the least, the last and the lost will become the first, the most, and the found. Small is obviously beautiful in God's eyes."*

Ben Witherington III

*"Let your life—your heart, your words, your body—be an offering of praise to God."*

Joni Eareckson Tada

*"He asks all, but He gives all."*

Thomas R. Kelly

*"It makes no matter where He places me, or how. That is rather for Him to consider than for me; for in the easiest position He must give me His grace, and in the most difficult His grace is sufficient . . . No fear that His resources will prove unequal to the emergency! And His resources are mine, for He is mine, and is with me and dwells in me."*

Hudson Taylor

## Personal Ponderings on "Trivial Pursuit"

Though far too brief, the impact of Dietrich Bonhoeffer's life has been anything but trivial. His contribution to Christian thought and discipleship continues to be felt today and promises to do so for years to come. Bonhoeffer's writings challenge readers to a simplicity of life and fellowship while at the same time recounting the costs of truly following Jesus Christ. When you consider the legacy of his words through the lens of his martyrdom, it all carries more weight. Knowing that Bonhoeffer learned these lessons in the darkest and most unlikely circumstances makes his principles seem much more livable today.

In *The Cost of Discipleship*, Bonhoeffer challenges preconceived ideas about what it means to accept the call to discipleship and truly follow Jesus. Our vision of it is often limited by our own understanding of the call. We see it as difficult, impossible, and shudder at the idea that following Jesus means walking the way of the cross. Bonhoeffer acknowledges that the cruciform way is "hard, unutterably hard" for those that fight it. But for those that submit "single-mindedly" and" unresistingly" to Jesus Christ and cling to him, "the yoke is easy, and the burden is light." It is those that submit that find everything—large and small—an opportunity to know and serve the God who stopped at nothing for them.

> "And if we answer the call to discipleship, where will it lead us? What decisions and partings will it demand? To answer this question we shall have to go to him, for only he knows the answer. Only Jesus Christ, who bids us follow him, knows the journey's end. But we do know that it will be a road to boundless mercy."

Not many of us are prepared for the martyrdom Bonhoeffer faced in his life. But if we will surrender as Bonhoeffer did, God will use our seemingly insignificant, small lives to impact a world desperate for the boundless mercy and grace God offers. Answer the call today and let it lead you on a pursuit that is anything but trivial.[8]

(JNH)

---

8. Bonhoeffer, Dietrich. *The Cost of Discipleship*. New York: Touchstone, 1995.

*Lent*

## THE SOUND OF THE SOUL

The sound of the soul
At the speed of light
Passed through my brain
And into the night.

Stifling silence
Sensing the sigh
Feeling the longing
Wanting to cry.

The sound of the soul,
Like a get away train
Doppler effect
Plaintive refrain.

Listening intently
Longing to know
Who am I really?
And does it show?

The sound of the soul
Like a voice in a well
Echoing always
Clear as a bell.

Tuning the instrument
Assessing the tone
Looking for harmony
Searching alone.

The sound of the soul
Out of the depths
Heart cry towards heaven
Wordless precepts.

"By him we cry Abba . . .
Groaning within
Awaiting adoption
Release from all sin"

## The Living Legacy

> "The Spirit assists us
> With sighs double deep
> Interceding with Abba
> My soul to keep."
>
> Jan. 7, 2006

### THEOLOGICAL MUSINGS

THIS POEM, SOMEWHAT LIKE 'Something Deep Inside' is an attempt to express the search for the ever illusive inner or true self. Beyond all the facades, charades, and personas, there is a real self, created in the image of God. The Greek philosophers of course urged 'Know Thyself', but from a Christian point of view this is a difficult task, not least because sin and self-centeredness impede the search. Occasionally one gets a glimpse of the inner self, but it is fleeting, like the sound of a train going by, or the glimpse of the back of someone as they run by in haste. One of the things I am suggesting in this poem is that the Holy Spirit who dwells within knows us better than we know ourselves, and not only can illuminate us on this and other subjects, but also can articulate for us what is really down deep inside, what our real heart's cry is.

I am also suggesting in this poem that there is an art or craft to getting to know one's self, and that beyond progressive sanctification and illumination by the Spirit there is also the need for us to hone our craft, be intentional about the odyssey of self discovery. It is not as if we should be like Narcissus staring into the pool at our own reflection, but rather we should be seeking out the particular shape the image of God takes in us.

C. S. Lewis in his last, and some would say greatest literary work *Until We Have Faces* explores in depth what it means to become a whole self, and so to know one's self without posturing or personas. He intimates it is a painful journey to take off the masks and see ourselves as we really are. And since we are complex beings we may well ask, which self. Is it the public or the private self? Is the best self actually the real self, or only a pretender? And since personality grows and develops, at least in its self-expression we may well realize that we are talking about a moving target here. Indeed the New Testament suggests this very thing. In texts like Romans 8.28–30 or 2 Cor. 3–4 it suggests we are gradually being transformed and conformed to the image of God's Son, a process that will not be completed until we reach the eschaton and we get our resurrection bodies. Until then, we are always a work in progress. Notice that according to Rev. 6 this is even true in heaven. The saints under the altar are cranky, crying out—How long? They are given robes and the implication is they need to hush and be patient. As Lewis would put it, we do not fully have faces until we face Christ in person. Short of that we need to regularly take stock, to face ourselves, realizing we see in a glass darkly at this juncture.

## Spiritual Meditations

### "The Sound of the Soul"

- Lectio Divina: 2 Corinthians 3:4–18
- Conversation can be a glorious spiritual discipline. Schedule time to grab coffee or a meal with a friend (or friends) and talk in broad strokes about your life and God's presence in it and allow your friend(s) to do the same. You might need to do this a handful of times to be sure that you get the opportunity to truly reflect and respond to each other.
- Confession can really free us to discover our true selves. By releasing our false selves through confession, we are better able to live freely and joyfully in this life. Carve out some time this week to confess (privately or with others) where you have not been true to the image of God within you. Ask God to give you strength to see yourself as he sees you and to live into his plans for your life.

### Thoughts for Further Reflection

*"[T]he Holy Spirit who dwells within knows us better than we know ourselves, and not only can illuminate us on this and other subjects, but also can articulate for us what is really down deep inside, what our real heart's cry is."*

Ben Witherington III

*"We are dead without Him. He must give us life. If we are trying to please Him with our own hard work and good intentions, we will fail. God is pleased and we are saved only when we let Him do the work inside of us."*

Dennis Kinlaw

## The Living Legacy

*"We have the choice of two identities: the external mask which seems to be real and which lives by a shadowy autonomy for the brief moment of earthly existence, and the hidden, inner person who seems to us to be nothing, but who can give himself eternally to the truth in whom he subsists. It is this inner self that is taken up into the mystery of Christ, by His love, by the Holy Spirit, so that in secret we live 'in Christ.'"*

Thomas Merton

### Personal Ponderings on "The Sound of the Soul"

No modern writer has written more honestly, openly, and beautifully about the interior life that the late Trappist monk, Thomas Merton. A modern day mystic, Merton's brief life was a contemplative one. The whole of his life was a quest for peace within himself and throughout the world.

In *New Seeds of Contemplation*, Merton speaks of the necessity of silence, solitude, and prayer. He purports that it is only in these practices that we discover our true selves. This meant life as a monk for Merton, but he believes that the discovery of self through the contemplative is not only possible for others, but also vital for abundant life in the here and now. Merton writes,

> "Our discovery of God is, in a way, God's discovery of us. We cannot go to heaven to find Him because we have no way of knowing where heaven is or what it is. He comes down from heaven and finds us. He looks at us from the depth of His own infinite actuality, which is everywhere, and His seeing us gives us a new being and a new mind in which we also discover Him. We only know Him in so far as we are known by Him, and our contemplation of Him is a participation in His contemplation of Himself. We become contemplatives when God discovers Himself in us."

This journey to discovering what Merton calls the "true inner self" can only be reached when we dig deep within, listening for the voice of God within. It is an awakening of sorts, but one we cannot attain on our own. We only discover God when we lose ourselves and allow God to find us.[9]

(JNH)

---

9. Merton, Thomas. *New Seeds of Contemplation*. New York: New Directions, 1962, 37–39.

*Lent*

## CRACKS IN THE WALL

    Cracks in the wall,
There by design,
    Prayers on plain paper
One of them mine
    Rabbis are chanting,
Torah held high,
    Sunlight is fading,
In the blue sky.
    Guards are watching,
Passing the time,
    Nodding acquaintance
With the sublime.

## The Living Legacy

     Herod's temple,
All that remains
     Limestone platform,
Withstands the strain,
     Mosque's gold dome
Shines in the light,
     Whose God is honored
By what's in sight?
     Prayers of the righteous
Meant to be heard,
     But the papers are silent,
Say not a word.

     "We want messiah"
Yeshiva boy cries,
     The irony is thick,
And darkens the skies
     Christians with kepas
Stand by the shrine,
     Praying to Jesus,
As someone divine.
     The wailing wall,
Heard Jesus' lament
     That he would have gathered,
If Zion'd repent.

     Cracks in the wall,
Filled up with our prayers,
     Perhaps it is this,
Which keeps God right there
     Perhaps when Messiah
Comes (once again),
     Perhaps then the Spirit
Will descend through the air,
     Perhaps then true monotheists
Will kneel at God's feet,
     Be filled with his Spirit,
The Father's Son greet.

*Lent*

>True children of Abram
>>Meet at the wall
>>>And confess Trinity,
>>The One for us all.
>>>Is this a dream—we three could be one?
>Just as God is,
>>Whose plan is not done.
>"Something there is
>That doesn't like a wall"
>>But this one unites
>The One with us all.

>>September 11, 2005

## THEOLOGICAL MUSINGS

WHAT A BUNDLE OF contradictions and outrageous extremes Jerusalem is. And yet what a wonderful place it is as well. In some ways it is the most inviting city of all, in some ways the most forbidding. If you have spent any time there you can see why on the one hand Jesus longed to embrace the city, but on the other hand why he was unable to do so when he first walked this earth.

Going to the Wailing Wall is going to the ultimate meeting place for monotheists—whether Jews, Christians, or Moslems. Everyone is praying in their own way as close together as space will allow, and some, perhaps hoping God will pay more attention to words written and left in the wall, write little prayers, roll them up, and stick them between the massive Herodian stones in the retaining wall of the Temple mount, the so called Western or wailing wall. Does God hear the prayers of all three sorts of monotheistic prayers launched from this spot? Perhaps this is not the right question. Perhaps the better question would be, what does God do with all these prayers, besides listen to them? How does he answer them and why and when?

Some of this poem is simply chronicling some of the things I have actually experienced at that wall, some of the things I have heard—like Orthodox Jews chanting that they want the messiah to come. But some of this poem is a reflection on whether when Jesus returns, there might be a turning to him by monotheists of all three of these religions.

I remember the comment of the rabbi in Chapel Hill N.C. when he had a conversation with Dr. Bernard Boyd my college Bible professor at Carolina. Dr. Boyd said he finally was brave enough to ask the rabbi who he thought Is. 53 referred to. The rabbi got a smile on his face and said "If, when messiah comes, he has the face of Jesus, we will accept it. He was after all a Jew like us." This seems to comport with what Paul says in Rom. 11.25–26 when he speaks of all Israel being saved when the Redeemer comes forth from heavenly Zion and turns back the impiety of Jacob. It led me to wonder if C. S. Lewis was right when he conjectured that someday true monotheists from all three of these faiths who pray to the one God of the Bible will recognize their savior and become part of one people. Is this what Jesus meant when he said that many from all points of the compass, from all races and clans, will sit down together at the messianic banquet with Abraham some day? I do not know the answer to this, but it is worth pondering. If God is indeed like Jesus, and wants no one to perish but all to have everlasting life as John 3.16 suggests, these sorts of questions should not be lightly dismissed out of hand.

One thing I know for sure. God is a God who answers prayer, and no one is a perfect pray-er. I also know that none of us have perfect theology either. Within the parameters and perimeters of Holy Writ, it is not wrong to ponder what God's people will look like in the end. What does it mean to say that in Christ there is no Jew or Gentile, but all are one? What does it mean when Paul affirms in Romans that God is impartial, and all have sinned and fallen short of God's glory? Whatever else it means, it means that we had best have a bit of humility when it comes to giving answers to these sort of ultimate eschatological and final questions. For now we see through a glass darkly, and it does not yet appear what we shall be.

## Spiritual Meditations

### "Cracks in the Wall"

- Lectio Divina: Psalm 86
- Prayer is simply quality time in conversation with God. Armed with that knowledge, we ought to talk to God throughout each day. Set aside at least fifteen minutes each day this week to talk to and listen

*Lent*

to God. As you do this faithfully, you will find continual conversation much more natural.

- There is no substitute for learning to pray but to pray. However, spending time studying others whose lives were informed by prayer can encourage our own prayer lives. Consider reading *Purpose in Prayer* by E. M. Bounds or *The Meaning of Prayer* by Harry Emerson Fosdick or another from the endless collection of books on prayer. Many of these books are quite small and lend themselves to in-depth study. Choose one and study its contents over the next several weeks and seek to put into practice what you learn.

### THOUGHTS FOR FURTHER REFLECTION

*"God is a God who answers prayer . . . "*
Ben Witherington III

*"Teach me to pray, Lord; pray yourself in me.*
Fénelon

*"If you would pray in faith, be sure to walk every day with God.*
*If you do, He will tell you what to pray for. Be filled with His spirit,*
*and He will give you things enough to prayer for.*
*He will give you as much of the spirit of prayer*
*as you have strength of body to bear."*
Charles Finney

*"Bear up the hands that hang down, by faith and prayer;*
*support the tottering knees.*
*Have you any days of fasting and prayer?*
*Storm the throne of grace and persevere therein*
*and mercy will come down."*
John Wesley

# The Living Legacy

## Personal Ponderings on "Cracks in the Wall"

Prayer is not optional for the Christian. It is like breathing. It must be done in order for us to have a real relationship with God and with others. We cannot expect to know God and walk with Him in the everyday unless we spend time in conversation with Him. We cannot expect to know others and walk with them in the everyday unless we spend time praying for them. William Law once said, "There is nothing that makes us love someone so much as praying for them." Only in prayer—for ourselves and for others—do we understand God, ourselves, and others. It is vital and yet we scarce set aside time to engage in this discipline!

Browsing through the wonderful devotional *This Day with the Master* by Dennis Kinlaw, I stumbled upon these thoughts on prayer and our Lectio Divina passage for this selection (Psalm 86).

> "Psalm 86 is written as David's plea for God to remove the rebels who are harassing him. The psalm begins to change its focus, however, as the psalmist comes into the presence of God. He admits that his heart is divided, that he has a division in his being. He prays to God, 'Unite my heart,' so he can give thanks to him with a whole heart and not with a divided heart.
>
> God desires that each follower of Christ make this pilgrimage: to move from praying for changed circumstances to praying for a united heart. Of all the human aspirations and dreams, I suspect that longing for inner unity is the deepest hunger of the human soul—to have a heart completely united in commitment to God."[10]

This is at the core of our resistance to prayer: a divided heart. We fail to come to God in prayer because we do not want to admit this to ourselves or to God. This admission is the first step to freedom, to an undivided heart, and to a life rich with prayer.

(JNH)

---

10. Kinlaw, Dennis. *This Day with the Master*. Grand Rapids: Zondervan, 2002, August 2: *Get the Rebel out of My Heart*.

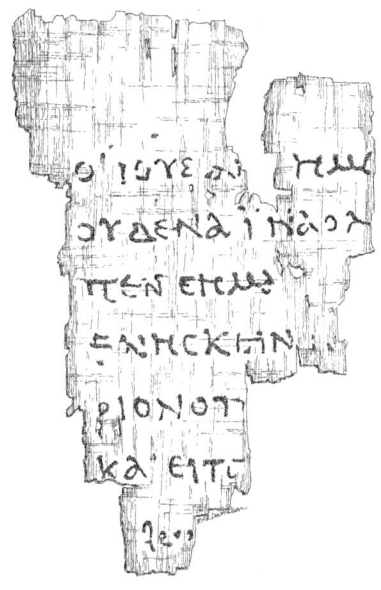

## WORDSHAPED

Partial and piecemeal, here and there
Vowels omitted, consonants square
No jots or tittles, not one iota
As if there was, some sort of quota.

Line upon line, word for word
Nopunctuationseparationabsurd
Scriptum continuum without an end
Space is so precious, conventions must bend

Fair hand copy, stylus in hand
Awaiting dictation, write on demand
Line length is even, no letters odd
So it must be—the Word of God.

## The Living Legacy

Written revelation, unveiled truth
Put on papyrus, sold from a booth
Unroll the scroll, unseal the seal
Meant to inform, not to conceal.

Nomina sacra, the Holy Name
In abbreviation, meaning the same
IX, XC, IHS too
Jehovah combines, God's name times two.

Inspired authors, inspiring text
God breathed words, soul resurrects
Let it be written, let it be done
Fulfilling fulfillment, victory won.

In the beginning, God chose to speak
Creation created, in under a week
Even the last Word, God will have too
Alpha-Omega, indwelling you.

March 26, 2006

## THEOLOGICAL MUSINGS

ONE OF THE MORE fascinating subjects to reflect on Biblically speaking is the theology of the Word. We are apt to see words as just combinations of letters or ciphers or symbols, but this is not how the ancients, living in an overwhelming oral culture, saw words. Words spoke things into existence if they came from God. Genesis 1 is quite explicit about this. But the Word could not only create reality, it could become a human being as John 1 says—'and the Word took on flesh.' Clearly the ancients saw words in a different light than moderns tend to do. Even in Rev. 19.13 when John of Patmos wants to unveil the final mystery he tells us that the Word of God will leap forth from heaven once more to bring closure to the drama of history. It's not just the Author stepping out on the stage at the end of the play, though that is true, it is that the author becomes the last Word, the last act of the play, bringing it to its proper conclusion.

In this poem I have tried to share some of the things about how the Word came to us through the hands of the ancient scribes, who had as their tools, a stylus, some water made black with soot (as ink), a papyrus roll, and a very steady hand and ability to take dictation on the fly. It is hard to even imagine how laborious it was where every single copy of every single page had to be hand-copied—word for word. If it was possible the scribe would use a wax tablet to copy the words first there, and then make a fair hand copy on a scroll since papyrus was quite expensive (as was hiring a scribe). Words took on almost a magical quality, especially religious or sacred ones, and especially the name of a Deity in such an oral culture.

It is all the more interesting then that Christian scribes chose to use abbreviations for the divine names—XC—Christos kurios; IX Iesous Christos; IHS the first three letters of the Greek word for Jesus (**Insous**), though later it was used in Latin to stand for 'in hoc signo'—in this Name. Experienced scribes knew that God's names would be mentioned more than all others, and so they developed these sacred abbreviations, called nomina sacra. But it was the Christian theology that the sacred Word not only could create reality or come in person, it could also indwell and thus inspire ordinary mortals like me and you. In the end, there is no last word on the Word. There is far too much to unveil and to ponder

## Spiritual Meditations

### "Word-Shaped"

- Lectio Divina: Proverbs 4
- Fast from words. It might not be feasible for you to spend your entire day(s) in silence, but a simple fast from words is possible for everyone once-in-a-while. As a spiritual discipline, set aside some time to listen more than speak. Begin your day(s) of fasting with prayer, asking God to give you ears to hear what he might be saying to you *and* what others need for you to hear. At the end of your day(s), journal about your experience.
- Silence before God and before others is key to our relationship with both. Our worlds are saturated with words and noise. To be silent and still is a necessity. It reminds us that God's Word is still alive and active. It also reminds us that our words carry weight and we would do well to choose them wisely. Spending some time in concentrated silence will help us to hear God and speak a word in season.

# The Living Legacy

## Thoughts for Further Reflection

*"The sacred Word not only [can] create reality or come in person, it [can] also indwell and thus inspire ordinary mortals like me and you."*

Ben Witherington III

*"The whole dance, or drama, or pattern of this three-Personal life is to be played out in each one of us; or (putting it the other way round) each one of us has got to enter that pattern, take his place in the dance. Good things as well as bad, you know, are caught by a kind of infection. If you want to get warm you must stand near the fire; if you want to be wet you must get into the water. If you want joy, power, peace, eternal life, you must get close to, or even into, the thing that has them. If you are close to it, the spray will wet you: if you are not, you will remain dry."*

C. S. Lewis

*"Every creature is a word of God."*

Meister Eckhart

*"The Word we study has to be the Word we pray. My personal experience of the relentless tenderness of God came not from exegetes, theologians, and spiritual writers, but from sitting still in the presence of the living Word and beseeching him to help me understand with my head and heart his written Word."*

Brennan Manning

*"Every word of God is flawless;
he is a shield to those who take refuge in him."*

Proverbs 30:5

## Personal Ponderings on "Word-Shaped"

Word is a powerful concept for the Christian to grasp. Creation began with a conversation, God said 'Let us make humankind . . . ' and all was created. Salvation is available to us because the Word became flesh in Jesus Christ. God puts great value and power in words. A Word from God has

*Lent*

the power to create and save. Thirteenth century mystic Meister Eckhart tells us, "Every creature is a word of God." We are a part of the divine conversation.

We long for the word that is our life to join with the voices before us and tell of God. We want our word to be God's Word spoken through us. Meister Eckhart speaks of this very thing repeatedly in his works. He writes of detachment and allowing our lives to be so fully consumed into God's that we radiate Him in all things. Read and reflect on these words from Eckhart:

> "[I]f a man really has God, and has only God, then no one can hinder him. Why? Because he has only God and his intention is toward God alone, and all things become for him nothing but God. That man carries God in his every work and in every place, and it is God alone who performs all the man's works...
>
> The man who has God... grasps God divinely, and to him God shines in all things; for everything tastes to him of God, and God forms himself for the man out of all things. God always shines out in him.
>
> So a man must be penetrated with the divine presence, and be shaped through and through with the shape of the God he loves, and be present in him, so that God's presence may sing out to him without any effort."[11]

(JNH)

---

11. Griffin, Emilie, ed. *Meister Eckhart: Selections from His Essential Writings*. San Francisco: Harper Collins Publishers, 2005, 9, 11–12.

# Holy Week and Easter

*The Light Rises*

## IMITATIO CHRISTI

*(in memoriam—Thomas A Kempis May 1, 1471)*

The cruciform life to which we are called
In the crucible of life we give you our all
Shaped and sharpened
Enlightened and lead
In the footsteps of Him
Who rose from the dead.

By dying to sin and living anew
We boldly embody Immanuel who—
Through his grace has brought us,
With his word has taught us,
By his blood has bought us,

    —Lord Jesus Christ.

    May 1, 1990

## THEOLOGICAL MUSINGS

GOOD FRIDAY OF COURSE is only good, and God's Friday, because of Easter Sunday. Otherwise it would be the worst day in human history. But this day in the church calendar has special significance for the spiritual pilgrimage of Christians. I remember attending the Good Friday service in King's college in Cambridge when I was on sabbatical in the 90s. The music was somber, the procession of the choir boys was somber, the black crepe draped around the high altar suited the mood and the service concluded with the slamming shut of the triptych on the altar with its lovely pictures of Mary and Jesus. This seems to be the most final funeral one could imagine. Surely nothing good could come either from this or after this.

Fast forward to Easter day. The choir and a packed house in the same chapel are treated to Bach's St. Matthew Passion as well as a regular Easter service. The altar is now crowded with lilies and other aromatic flowers. The bells, instead of tolling a death are wildly jubilant as one peal after another rings forth well into the afternoon. What a difference a couple of days make. Ah, but it is not just the passing of time that makes a difference. Easter did not merely follow Good Friday automatically. It came as a miracle that eclipsed Good Friday. Thus, the trick in celebrating Good Friday when you know how the story turns out is not to jump the gun. To pilgrimage through Maundy Thursday, on through Good Friday and then stand with the church expectant on Easter Sunday morning awaiting the joyful climax of one church season and the beginning of another.

Thomas a Kempis was one of the great devotional writers of any era. He was perhaps John Wesley's favorite, along with Jeremy Taylor. A Kempis wrote a spiritual classic called *The Imitation of Christ* or sometimes dubbed *The Pattern of Christ*. Wesley adopted and adapted it and made it required reading for his itinerant ministers. Would that they would all read it today.

A Kempis talks about what it actually means to take up one's cross and follow Jesus. He reminds us that it is not Christ's cross we are bearing, indeed we could not carry that one, but rather our own. He reminds us that while we may have our thorns in the flesh that come unbidden, they have nothing to do with freely choosing to take up one's cross and follow Jesus. Rather this has to do with dying to sin and rising to walk in newness of life following the example of Christ. It has to do with some of the things Paul speaks about in Romans 6, where he likens the immersion rite of baptism to a burial service, and he reminds us that the old person that we once were has been crucified and should be left in the grave. Carrying one's cross daily (as Luke puts it) involves not only once having died with Christ, and no longer being that old person. It also involves the ongoing putting to death of sinful desires, longings, temptations and the like. It involves daily resisting the temptation to avoid the hard path of resisting temptation!

As Dietrich Bonhoeffer so often emphasized, when Christ calls us, he bids us to come and die. This involves not merely dying to self, and living for Him once or even repeatedly. It involves being prepared to die for one's faith commitment should you be called upon to do so. Bonhoeffer of course was one of the Christian martyrs to Hitler's madness. Taking up the cross involves being prepared to go down the road to Golgotha, not merely spiritually but physically if God should so will. Christ calls us to be cross bearers not merely cross wearers.

It is also not enough to flee temptation if one leaves a forwarding address. It is not enough to have been convicted, convinced, and converted once in the past. Taking up one's cross is a daily commitment, a daily exercise. Too many Christians today want a Gospel without the cross, without self-sacrifice, without self-discipline. Thomas a Kempis would never have understood such a thing. Like William Penn he would have said—no cross, no crown, no gall, no glory, no pain, no palm. Good Friday is the perfect day to think on these things.

## Spiritual Meditations

### "Imitatio Christi"

- Lectio Divina: Luke 9:22–27

- Thomas à Kempis believed that if we would simply spend time meditating on Christ's passion, we would find strength to stand in our own lives. Spend some time meditating on the crucifixion. Consider the anguish, suffering, and sorrow our Savior felt as he bore our sins. While we know the rest of the story to include the resurrection, it is important not to diminish the cost and sacrifice made on the cross.

- It is significant to note that the command that Jesus gives us is to carry our cross *daily* (Luke 9:23). Cross-bearing requires a daily dying to self. A key part of this is putting to death our sinful desires through the discipline of confession. Richard Foster reminds us that "confession brings an end to pretense." We live in a world that is hungry for a Church that knows its weaknesses and can admit its faults. This begins with a contrite heart and a humble spirit. "Honesty leads to confession," writes Foster, and confession leads to change."[1] Carve out some time to confess your sins to a trusted companion and to God this week.

## Thoughts for Further Reflection

*"Taking up one's cross is a daily commitment, a daily exercise. Too many Christians today want a Gospel without the cross, without self-sacrifice, without self-discipline."*

Ben Witherington III

*"If we are to follow Christ, it must be in our common way of spending everyday. If we are to live unto God at any time or in any place, we are to live unto him in all times and in all places."*

William Law

*"Set yourself, then, like a good and faithful servant of Christ, to bear bravely the cross of your Lord, Who out of love was crucified for you."*

Thomas à Kempis

*"There are no crown-wearers in heaven who were not cross-wearers here below."*

Charles Spurgeon

*"If we do not die to ourselves, we cannot live unto God, and he that does not live unto God is dead."*

George Macdonald

---

1. Foster, Richard. *Celebration of Discipline*. San Francisco: Harper and Row, 1988, 157.

# Holy Week and Easter

## Personal Ponderings on "Imitatio Christi"

"If anyone would come after me, he must deny himself and take up his cross daily and follow me" (Luke 9:23). We know these words of Jesus by heart. We repeat them to each other. Yet the daily application of them eludes us. We struggle to embody this in our lives. We are a stubborn, resistant people, frozen in fear and complacency.

In his classic work *The Imitation of Christ*, Thomas à Kempis addresses our resistance to living out this vital command of Jesus. He urges us to make ourselves "one with the Crucified" willingly in this life and experience salvation and life in the now. à Kempis knows well that there is no other way to experience the fullness of life and God's peace than to make the daily decision to carry one's cross. Why, then, do we resist it so? It is this very question that à Kempis reflects upon in the chapter "The Royal Road of the Holy Cross." Read and reflect upon these words and make them your prayer as you seek to carry the cross daily.

> "Why . . . do you fear to take up the cross when through it you can win a kingdom?
>
> In the cross is salvation, in the cross is life, in the cross is protection from enemies, in the cross is infusion of heavenly sweetness, in the cross is strength of mind, in the cross is joy of spirit, in the cross is highest virtue, in the cross is perfect holiness. There is no salvation of soul nor hope of everlasting life but in the cross.
>
> Take up your cross, therefore, and follow Jesus and you shall enter eternal life. He himself opened the way before you in carrying His cross, and upon it he died for you, that you, too, might take up your cross and long to die to upon it. If you die with Him, you shall also live with Him and if you share his suffering, you shall also share His glory."[2]

(JNH)

---

2. à Kempis, Thomas. *The Imitation of Christ*. Book Two, chapter 12.

## The Living Legacy
## AKEDAH

Did he ponder Isaac
Whilst hanging on the cross
A last second substitution
Just before all was lost?

Is this why he cried out
'My God, My God' so loud
Showing disappointment
Before a hostile crowd?

Where's God's intervention,
Offering a lamb
Or would He be passed over
A dangling great I AM?

Abandoned but begotten
Left to face his fate?
Would help arrive in 'nick of time'
Or would it come too late?

Where's the lamb, asked Isaac
And told 'God will provide'
But Jesus died in plain sight
No place for grace to hide.

Jesus, like old Isaac
An only begotten son,
Isaac was no substitute
But Jesus was the one.

We like sheep have gone astray
Unblemished lambs we're not
God led the One to slaughter
The Passover he'd begot.

Offering isn't 'finished'
Until the sacrifice
For any true atonement
Blood shed must suffice.

*Holy Week and Easter*

Behold the Lamb of God
Who takes away our sin
God accepts no substitutes
For Jesus, in the end.

## THEOLOGICAL MUSINGS

I HAVE ALWAYS BEEN fascinated by the story of the near sacrifice of Isaac in Gen. 22 which comes near the end of the Abraham cycle of stories in Genesis. In the Jewish discussion of this story, the tale came to be called 'the Akedah', which means 'the Binding.' One might think and expect that this story, because of various of its similarities to the story of Jesus' demise would have come in for some considerable theological reflection and typological comparison in the New Testament, but in fact it is hardly alluded to at all, and never discussed directly. I have always found this very strange indeed. But of course the two stories do have some notable differences which we should enumerate.

For one thing, the story of the death of Jesus is indeed about a human sacrifice, if one interprets the story theologically, whereas in Gen. 22 all we have is a near human sacrifice. In the Abraham story, while it appears to be God's will that Abraham offer his son as a sacrifice, in the end we discover otherwise. But in the story of Jesus there is the questioning of Jesus in the Garden about whether God's will might include letting the 'cup' pass from Jesus, but in fact that was not the way things were in Jesus' case. Jesus did indeed have to offer 'the last full measure' a person can give. In the story of Abraham of course Isaac comes along when Abraham and Sarah are incredibly old, but the child is conceived and born in the normal way. By contrast, Mary is a young teenage virgin when she conceives Jesus, and without the aid of a husband. These are two very different tales about how 'only begotten sons' come into the world. Obviously as well Isaac was no lamb of sacrifice, whereas Jesus came to be seen as the lamb of God who takes away the sins of the world. Yet in both stories, the element of 'substitution' is crucial and comes into play at the appropriate juncture. Jesus is the substitute for all of humanity, the one a ransom for the many. Isaac needed a last minute substitution or he too would be a sacrifice.

What I am especially pondering in this poem is whether the Isaac story in Gen. 22 might have been on Jesus' mind from Gethsemane all the way to Golgotha. Is this what prompted Jesus' request to let the cup of death pass from him—because there was precedent in the case of that other only begotten son, Isaac? Is this also what prompted the cry of dereliction from the cross? Was Jesus expecting a last minute substitution even on the cross? It is interesting that in the Islamic reflection on how Jesus' life ended, one scenario suggested is that Judas was substituted for Jesus at the last minute, as Moslems have difficulty imagining God would send the holy prophet to his death in that shameful fashion. Jesus was in a 'bind' alright, but God the Father refused to undo the bindings and let him go.

Though it is a great paradox, one way one can show that life is precious and indeed of sacred worth is by exacting the highest possible price for the taking of a life—in other words a life for a life. This is of course what the lex talionis suggests in the OT—the theology of commensurate price leads to—'an eye for an eye, a hand for a hand, a life for a life.' How much is a life worth? One life. But this is precisely where the mystery of Jesus' death deepens, because the expending of his life ransomed the many—that is many lives. The life of the only begotten Son of God was of such immeasurable sacred worth, that his life poured out in death was equal to and could be exchanged for the lives of all of the rest of humanity! If the wages of sin is death in each case, then the cost of redemption is also death, but only in one case. Herein lies a great mystery and its named shall be called atonement.

## Spiritual Meditations

### "Akedah"

- Lectio Divina: Colossians 2:9–15; 1 John 4:7–12
- Use your prayer time today to pray for the humility to accept the gift of the Atonement. Pray for the strength to receive God's grace freely and the fortitude to share that with others. Only when we come face-to-face with our own need for Him can we introduce others to His love and grace.
- Reflecting upon the mystery of the Atonement ought to call forth in us awe and wonder that cannot be contained. Worship God today through a medium that is comfortable to you. Write. Draw. Sing. Listen. Reflect. Whatever the medium, spend quality time in praise and worship to God.

*Holy Week and Easter*

## Thoughts for Further Reflection

*"The life of the only begotten Son of God was of such immeasurable sacred worth, that his life poured out in death was equal to and could be exchanged for the lives of all the rest of humanity."*

Ben Witherington III

*"There for me the Savior stands, shows his wounds and spreads his hands. God is love! I know, I feel; Jesus weeps and loves me still."*

Charles Wesley

*"To abandon all, to strip one's self of all, in order to seek and follow Jesus Christ naked to Bethlehem where He was born, naked to the hall where He was scourged, and naked to Calvary where He died on the cross, is so great a mystery that neither the thing nor the knowledge of it, is given to any but through faith in the Son of God."*

John Wesley

*"I cannot make myself right with God, I cannot make my life perfect; I can only be right with God if I accept the Atonement of the Lord as an absolute gift."*

Oswald Chambers

## Personal Ponderings on "Akedah"

We have all but eliminated the scandal of the cross in this modern age. It makes us uncomfortable to consider the agony and anguish Jesus experienced on the way to and on the cross. We will entertain the images of a suffering, sympathetic Savior, but ask us to remember the scandal of it all and we quickly retreat. Grace given to all through the disgrace of One. Salvation made possible through the shame of the Crucified . . . We scarce can take it in because we are unfamiliar with the most familiar scene.

Joel Green writes of the " scandal of the cross" in a number of his works. Through extensive personal study, he has determined that we must recover the scandal of cross. It is vital to our own understanding of the crucifixion that we grasp the shame and disgrace that happened on Calvary. Not only is it vital to us personally, it is a fundamental in our quest to take Christ into a world where shame and disgrace still reign.

Crucifixion was a "heinous mode of execution" even for the worst of criminals. For the Son of God to know this kind of death is difficult to swallow when we discover the ridicule, pain, and dishonor experienced there. "The victim of crucifixion," Green writes, "was displayed naked on the cross, ordinarily at a public crossroads, and was the object of public ridicule."[3] The suffering and shame of the cross was a central reality to the first Christians. They were forced to make sense of it, "interpreting it within the framework of God's redemptive purposes." It was of utmost importance that they understand for themselves as much as for others that "the expression 'Christ crucified' was not a contradiction in terms." [4]

In our own "unease with suffering,"[5] we have sought to minimize the shame of the crucifixion by looking past it to the resurrection. While the resurrection is a vital part of our story, it is not the whole story. We cannot "understand Jesus if we have not plumbed the depths of his passion," taking in the scandal of the cross. For only as we understand the scandal and the shame can we understand that the cross alone has crucified our own shame.[6]

(JNH)

---

3. Green, Joel B. *The Way of the Cross: Following Jesus in the Gospel of Mark*. Nashville: Discipleship Resources, 1991, 4.

4. Ibid., 6.

5. Ibid.

6. Ibid., 7–8.

*Holy Week and Easter*

### JOB DESCRIPTION

When comfort turns to torment
And solace leads to pain
Then Job will find his master and
Receive his life again.

When ashes without number
Burn on the funeral pyre
Then suffering is consumed
And an end is made through fire.

Yet through the fire a figure
Stands golden, purified
The one who once was taunted
Has now been justified.

Not through the will of mortals
Nor through the countless saints
Can come the vindication
Of Job's quite just complaints.

Let God be God, says Scripture
And all the world be wrong
For triumph comes through suffering
And life from life passed on.

The world has been left hanging
Upon a crooked tree
In Christ the microcosm
Life, through death, is set free.

At Easter dawn a trumpet
Blasts from an empty tomb
Announcing sin's destruction
And death's eternal doom.

" I Know my Redeemer lives
And will stand upon the earth,
And in my flesh I'll see him"
In resurrection's birth.

Darkness lasts a little while
But joy comes with the dawn,
Then Job will see his savior,
And lament will turn to song.

>October 21, 1992

## THEOLOGICAL MUSINGS

THE STORY OF JOB might seem an odd choice for a reflection on Easter day, but in fact no figure in the OT more bears the image of the man of sorrows, well acquainted with grief than Job, and he is also the only OT saint who speaks of seeing his Redeemer stand upon the earth at the resurrection. The parallels between his story and the Christ story are interesting and telling. Both cry out that they have been abandoned by God. Both are vindicated after great suffering, and both are unjustly suffering as righteous persons, though both Job's 'comforters' and Christ's tormentors assume otherwise. Vindication comes as a surprise ending in both cases.

One of my favorite recent stories is the story of the woman who could not understand why in the last book of the OT God is called a silversmith. Since she was leading a Bible study on Malachi she decided she needed to go and visit a silversmith and see what his job description looked like. She got there in time for the day's purification of the silver. The impure silver was poured into a heat resistant cup on the end of a very long pole and then inserted into the red hot kiln.

The woman noticed that once this happened the silversmith would no longer make eye contact with her, though they were still carrying on a conversation. Instead he concentrated on keeping the silver in the cup in the very hottest, the most blue part of the flame. He explained that this was necessary to purify the silver completely, and that if he took his eye off the silver even for a moment all could be spoiled for he needed to draw the silver out of the fire the very instant all the dross had been burned off. Suddenly, the light dawned in the woman's brain. God gives us trials by fire not merely to test our metal, but to purify us, but equally clearly God will not hand down more than we can handle by relying on his grace. Instantly, when the purification point has come, God will take us out of the fire. To be truly tested, and truly pure, one must go through the fire, not around it. Triumph comes through suffering, and through overcoming suffering, not by avoiding it.

Easter is of course about the triumph over the grave. But it only comes at a price—in this case not merely of suffering but of death. God's yes to life was proved to be louder than death's no, not merely by Jesus saying he was the Resurrection during his ministry, but by his being resurrected and becoming the living proof that this was so.

I was once preaching in the Durham and Darlington circuit in the late 70s in England. It was Easter Sunday morning and the little Methodist chapel was decked out for the occasion. The chapel steward raced out of the door when he saw me coming up the hill at a good pace and he stopped me. He looked flustered and like he was mustering up his courage. He asked me in his ever so polite British way: "I must ask you something sir, before we go in. You do believe in the resurrection don't you?" I reassured him I did and the relief was written all over his face. He then said "I'm ever so glad to hear it because last year we had a chap who didn't and he preached such utter rubbish about the blooming of the flowers and the coming of spring, as if the resurrection was an annual natural occurrence."

No indeed, resurrection is not a natural occurrence, and it requires death as its predecessor. It's something only God can bring about, the God who is the very definition of life, and who longs to give us all everlasting life. The story of Job in fact has a happy ending, but it comes at a great cost of suffering. The same can be said about the story of Christ. Real triumph comes after and sometimes through real tragedy in God's economy of things, it would seem. This is something to bear in mind throughout Eastertide.

## Spiritual Meditations

### "Job Description"

- Lectio Divina: Lamentations 3:1–33
- Silence is a centering discipline, one that has the capacity to undergird us with the strength we need to stand strong amidst hardship and difficulty. It is impossible to persevere long without the inner strength gained from participating in the discipline of silence. Spend whatever time you can afford in silent reflection this week. No matter if it is minutes or hours, take the time to be still and silent before the Lord. Refrain from speaking, only listen.
- The discipline of service must not be about the self. Service is other-focused and must be done with humility of spirit. However, oftentimes participating in service to others can help to take the focus off our own circumstances and onto what is eternal. This is why we all know stories of persons who, though in the midst of difficulty themselves, always seem to be helping others. Take some time to serve someone this week, in big or small ways. Be creative!

### Thoughts for Further Reflection

*"God gives us trials by fire not merely to test our metal, but to purify us, but equally clearly God will not hand down more than we can handle by relying on his grace."*

Ben Witherington III

*"Triumph comes through suffering, and through overcoming suffering, not by avoiding it."*

Ben Witherington III

*Holy Week and Easter*

*"God does not lead His children around hardship, but leads them straight through it. But He leads! And amidst the hardship, He is nearer to them than ever before."*

Otto Dibelius

*"It is well for those who find themselves in the dark night of the soul to persevere in patience . . . Let them trust in God, who does not abandon those who seek Him with a simple and right heart, and He will not fail to give them what is needful for the road, until He brings them into the clear and pure light of love."*

John of the Cross

*"The central reality for Christians is the personal, unalterable, persevering commitment God makes to us. Perseverance is not the result of our determination, it is the result of God's faithfulness. We will survive the way of faith not because we have extraordinary stamina but because God is righteous, because God sticks with us."*

Eugene Peterson

### Personal Ponderings on "Job Description"

The truest example of perseverance cannot be described in words, it must be evidenced in a life. The most resounding example of this can be found in the late, great missionary, E. Stanley Jones. The whole of his life is a testimony to the power of God, but especially his final years.

Late in his eighties, Jones suffered a massive and debilitating stroke that changed everything. Intelligence and mental acuity were not affected, but fine motor skills and speech—his livelihood as a missionary and preacher—were shattered. And yet somewhere in the midst of that, he found the strength to stand and say to himself:

> "Nothing has changed! I'm still the same person that I was. By prayer, I am still communicating with the same Person. I belong to the same unshakable Kingdom and the same unchanging Person. Nothing has really changed except my means of communication with the outside world."[7]

---

7. Jones, E. Stanley. *The Divine Yes*. Nashville: Abingdon Press, 1975, 30–31.

Herein lies the proof that faith, tried and tested, is not circumstantial. Real faith is lasting and enables us to make a pronouncement like this one. May we all find in ourselves such unwavering faith and steadfastness. Faith that asks, in the face of impossibility, "If it is now hard for me to preach a sermon; why not be one?"[8] May we ask ourselves that same question in the midst of our own difficulties and sufferings and answer it in the affirmative every time.

(JNH)

---

8. Ibid., 26.

# Eastertide

*The Light Rises*

## SCIENCE—FICTION

(This poem is meant to be read antiphonally by half line so that it has a call and response effect. Wherever one finds a dash line in the first and third lines of a stanza the first voice should say what comes before the dash, the second voice what comes after, and the first voice should say the whole of line two while the second voice says the whole of line four of each stanza).

Science—fiction
It happens every day
We're all—reduced
To things that pass away.

Mind/brain—soul/link
Material to the core.
When the flesh—desiccates
The person is no more.

Absent—from the body
Yet present with the Lord
Seems there's—something more
That we have ignored.

Immaterial—evidence
Empirical's dead end
If God—exists at all
Spirit's what transcends.

Reduced to—neurons
Synapses will misfire.
Behaviorism—sure leaves
Much to be desired.

In grief—in love
Where can these be found?
Non-material—realities
Larger and profound.

## The Living Legacy

Ashes—to ashes
Dusting off the flesh
Back to—the Life source
So we can refresh.

Saints cry—how long
Hiding near the throne
They're given—new robes
Told they're not alone.

Resurrection—new direction
Permanence resolved.
Spirit back—into flesh
Our conundrum solved.

January 3, 2005

## THEOLOGICAL MUSINGS

THE END OF THIS poem makes it quite appropriate to be included in an Eastertide collection. This poem was written after I was asked to be on a panel where the topics of discussion included: 1) Is there more to the mind than its hardware the brain?; 2) does the human spirit survive death, or are we monistic wholes?; 3) Is there such a thing as an non-material soul/spirit?; 4) if there is such a thing as a soul, why would we need resurrection after death? These questions of course are enough to keep us puzzling for a long time to come.

I entitled this poem Science—Fiction not because I think there is no value to science. Indeed, I have great admiration for much of what science has and can accomplish. I entitled it as I did because reductionism and hard core materialism is one form that the philosophy of science takes in our era, and it is indeed at odds with a Christian worldview in various ways. By this I mean there is often an assumption that the only reality is material reality, or put another way, the only things that are real and can be known are known through and by our five senses. This is but another way of saying the only real evidence is empirical evidence. This is sometimes coupled with an assumption that faith is something we have in things that are not subject to scientific scrutiny, where as science is based on the hard data of material reality.

*Eastertide*

A moments reflection however will show that it is a faith postulate to say "the only reality is material reality" or to say "we can only know something if it is known through our senses or produces some empirical evidence." These are hypotheses which are the basis of reductionist and purely materialist theories about reality, but I would stress they are just faith postulates or hypotheses. They are far from proven facts. This is what I would call science fiction as opposed to scientific fact. I would also be willing to say that some of the most profound realities of all, like love or God, cannot be studied under a microscope. The material universe as it turns out, is only part of reality, and in some ways not the most important part.

What is interesting however is that God who is spirit has chosen to manifest himself in material reality in various ways, including coming in person, and through resurrection God also demonstrates that there are greater forces at work even in the material universe than natural forces. The risen Jesus is a conundrum that scientific formula or measurement can never take the full measure of, even though he provided us with tangible proof he was back from the dead. One could say that as material creatures we needed some material evidence to bolster our faith, and the God who keeps intervening in human history is happy to oblige us and provide that evidence—one miracle at time.

## Spiritual Meditations

### "Science Fiction"

- Lectio Divina: Ephesians 1:3–14
- Spending time in quiet solitude re-orients us to the miracles that are present all around us. Extended times of solitude and silence refocus the eyes of the heart in a way that is not possible in the noise of our everyday. If you are able, spend a few hours this week or weekend in silence and solitude. A day apart can change a life, but a long walk or hike or just taking advantage of the little solitudes that fill our days can have the same effect.
- Grab some paper and go somewhere where you can reflect uninterrupted for an extended period of time. Using whatever medium you are comfortable with (journal, poetry, art, etc.) and reflect on the miracles that have filled your life up to this point. Allow yourself to reflect on each major period in your life (childhood, adolescence,

young adulthood, adulthood, etc.). It may take several periods of reflection, but resolve to reflect upon each major phase of your life and how God has met you along the way.

**Thoughts for Further Reflection**

*"The risen Jesus is a conundrum that scientific formula or measurement can never take full measure of, even though He provided us with tangible proof He was back from the dead."*

Ben Witherington III

*"One could say that as material creatures we need some material evidence to bolster our faith, and the God who keeps intervening in human history is happy to oblige us and provide that evidence—one miracle at a time."*

Ben Witherington III

*"Miracles, in the sense of phenomena we cannot explain, surround us on every hand: life itself is the miracle of miracles."*

George Bernard Shaw

*"In the long run God is no one but Himself and what He does is like nothing else."*

C. S. Lewis

*"The Voice has said: 'Because I live, ye shall live also.' Our hearts knew all along it must be so. It was what we wanted to hear, and now that we have heard it, we feel that we have solved the mystery of life."*

Peter Marshall

*Eastertide*

## Personal Ponderings on "Science Fiction"

The overwhelming reason that we do not see and experience miracles is not because they no longer happen in our day. No, the trouble is not the lack of miracles. The trouble is in our inability to listen to our lives and to our surroundings. This is where the discipline of silence can help us immensely.

Thomas à Kempis writes of the benefits of silence in his classic work *The Imitation of Christ*. He stresses the importance of the inner life and "leaving the crowd behind"[1] in order to truly walk with Jesus. He is careful to note that our time in silence need not exceed our time in public. Our time in stillness and solitude will only bless our time in community; the converse is also true.

"In quiet and silence," à Kempis writes, "the faithful soul makes progress." The Word is seen with greater clarity and the world as well. "Even as one learns to grow still," he writes, "he draws closer to the Creator."[2] What better way to have the eyes of our hearts opened and enlightened than through stillness and quiet? Only then will we be able to recognize the miracles already happening all around us. And what are miracles but evidences of the continuing power of the resurrection?

(JNH)

---

1. Foster, Richard J. and Emilie Griffin. *Spiritual Classics: Selected Readings for Individuals and Groups on the Twelve Spiritual Disciplines*. San Francisco: Harper Collins Publishers, 2000, 149.

2. Ibid., 150.

### OPUS MAGNUM

Weary, worn, welts on hand
Work has whittled down the man
To the bare necessities
Of what he is, and what he'll be
Was this then his destiny?

Defined, refined by what we do,
The toilsome tasks are never through
Thorn and thistle, dirt and dust
Sweeping clean, removing rust
All to earn his upper crust?

Sweat of brow, and carried weight
Rose too early, slept too late
Slaving, striving dawn to dusk
Til the shell is barely husk
Staunch the stench with smell of musk?

*Eastertide*

> But work is not the curse or cure
> By which we're healed, or will endure
> It will not save us in the end,
> It is no foe, but rather friend
> But while it molds us will we mend?
>
> Task Master making all things new
> Who makes the most of what we do,
> Let our work an offering be
> A timely gift from those set free
> From earning our eternity.
>
> When work is mission on the move
> By those whose efforts serve to prove
> That nothing's wasted in God's hands
> When we respond to his commands
> Then we shall hear him say "well done"
> To those who worked under the Son.
>
> October 4, 2005

## THEOLOGICAL MUSINGS

Work is something most of us share in common, and unfortunately too often even Christians succumb to the notion that work itself is a curse, even God's curse on fallen persons. This is a most unfortunate reading of Genesis. Work is something God assigned Adam to do before there ever was a Fall. He was to fill the earth and subdue it. He was to be fruitful and multiply. He was called upon to name the animals and to recognize none of them would be a suitable companion or life partner. Apparently there was much work to do before the Fall.

It is in fact the toilsome nature of work that is a result of the Fall. Work becomes hard work as a result of the Fall. The earth can be unresponsive and require much sweat of the brow to produce anything. And of course we have not made things easier on ourselves as we have fouled our own nests with pollution and garbage of numerous sorts. All kinds of work can be bone-wearying. Is there a way to look at work from a Christian perspective that neither writes it off as a curse and something to be merely endured, nor to see it as our salvation? Could it be our calling rather than a curse or a cure?

In this poem I am suggesting work can be a calling, a mission, a ministry, an offering to God, and in any case and at all costs it should never be seen as merely a way to 'make a living', which is an exceedingly odd phrase. We might do well to talk about making a Christian life before we talk about 'making a living', if what one means by that phrase is making money so one can survive. All too often 'making a living' really means 'making a comfortable living' or even 'making a killing' if we are a greedy sort of person.

From a Christian perspective all persons in Christ are called to both ministry and discipleship of various sorts. Labor is part of this calling some of which is remunerative, some of which will not be. Paul in 1 Corinthians is insistent that ministers of various sorts should be offered pay for their labors since Jesus says a workman is worthy of his hire, but of course they can refuse pay as well. If we see work as part of our life stewardship, just as play and worship and prayer and sleep and so many other things are part of our stewardship, we will begin to be on the right track.

Life is a gift from God, and work can be a blessing rather than a curse if it is done to God's glory and for Christ's kingdom. Work is part of what we offer to God on a daily basis as we respond to God's call to do various things that matter in life, even do things that change life for the better, or even save lives. There are several keys to a proper Christian attitude about work.

Firstly, work should be done in full remembrance that salvation is a gift of God's grace. Therefore we can neither work nor worm our way into God's graces, and we shouldn't ever see work as a means of doing so, or as a means of making amends, or as a means of atoning for things we've done wrong and the like. Work has no capacity to save us, nor can it compensate for our lack of salvation, nor can the doing of it make God an offer he can't refuse. Work done in service to God, as a grateful response to God's grace can however be a great good. It can even help feed, cloth, and even save the world.

Secondly, we should avoid the mistake of our culture by which I mean we should avoid defining ourselves by what we do. We are all creatures created in God's image (which is not an accomplishment but a gift) and if we are Christians we are creatures renewed in the image of Christ. This is who we are. What we do, whether we are doctors, lawyers, scientists, ministers, theologians is important but it does not define or eclipse who we are. We have all met doctors who had excellent skills but who were not very good persons. They were good at their tasks but bad at being a real human being, much less a Christian one. It is no accident that Paul in the Pastoral Epistles, when he is talking about ministers says precious little about what they ought to be doing, and quite a lot about what kind of persons they should be (cf. 1 Tim. 3 to Titus 1).

Thirdly, we should not evaluate the value of our work by how much we are paid to do it, nor by the amount of praise, fame, or kudos garnered for doing it. We should evaluate our work by whether we have done it well, done it to the best of our ability, done it honestly and in good time, done it to the glory of God, whatever the human response to the work may be. Unfortunately we live in a world where many people even Christians not merely define themselves by what they do, but define their true worth by their financial or net worth. This is both tragic and it gets in the way of finding out whom and whose we really are.

Lastly, it is right to take satisfaction from a job done well. This is in itself a reward, but since in the end we are playing to an audience of One, the evaluative voice that really matters when it comes to assessing our work is the one whom hopefully we will one day hear say "Well done good and faithful servant." It is no accident that there is a dialectic set up in Genesis between work and rest, between work and play, between work and worship. Work should never be a be-all and end-all experience, or else it will indeed be the end of us all, prematurely, as we work ourselves to death.

I was visiting the Billy Graham library in Charlotte and had finished the tour and was going to leave but there was one more outside spot to see—the memorial garden for Ruth Graham, Billy's wife. There was a very large tomb stone carved with her name and dates and the following words—"Construction Completed. Thanks for your Patience." It dawned on me that there is a whole different way of evaluating work and time. What if you evaluate life's work as something God has been doing in and to you? What if you conceive of it as a timed process that takes time? What if "work out your salvation with fear and trembling for it's God who works in you to will and to do" is viewed as the most important 'work' of all, a work dependent on God's doings in us which we cannot even work out unless God has first worked it in? What if this sort of working is the one that really matters and affects our eternal destiny? Think on these things.

## The Living Legacy

# Spiritual Meditations

### "Opus Magnum"

- Lectio Divina: 1 Corinthians 3:8–17; Colossians 3:23–24
- We are to do whatever we do as if we are working for the Lord (Colossians 3:23–24). Yet we are often guilty of compartmentalizing our lives, naming only certain acts of service as work for the Lord. True service is constant, not periodic. Find innovative ways to serve God throughout your days this week. Whether you are at work, home or somewhere in-between, find ways to give honor and glory to God in it all.
- Plan a small celebration for a family member or dear friend who works particularly hard at home, in the workplace, and/or elsewhere. Make dinner or dessert for that person and/or plan a small party where the attendees spend time praising and encouraging this friend or family member. Don't have time to plan a small get-together? Consider e-mailing or calling a few of that person's friends to commission them to write an encouraging note to him or her.

### Thoughts for Further Reflection

*"If we see work as part of our life stewardship, just as play and worship and prayer and sleep and so many other things are part of stewardship, we will begin to be on the right track."*

Ben Witherington III

*"Life is a gift from God, and work can be a blessing rather than a curse if it is done to God's glory and for Christ's kingdom. Work is part of what we offer to God on a daily basis as we respond to God's call to do various things that matter in life . . . "*

Ben Witherington III

*"Where our work is, there let our joy be."*

Tertullian

*Eastertide*

"*The responsible person seeks to make his or her whole life a response to the question and call of God.*"

Dietrich Bonhoeffer

"Seems to me then that the highest possible reward for man's labor is not what he gets for it, but what he becomes by it."

Brock Bell

"*Trying to do the Lord's work in your own strength is the most confusing, exhausting, and tedious of all work. But when you are filled with the Holy Spirit, then the ministry of Jesus just flows out of you.*"

Corrie ten Boom

### Personal Ponderings on "Opus Magnum"

As Christians we long to find meaning and purpose in our work. For many of us this is difficult, if not seemingly impossible. We find our work to be mundane, necessary at best. We struggle to see where our futile work is honoring God and contributing to his overall work in the world. We hold this view because we have a limited understanding, a skewed view of the value of any work to the kingdom of God.

In his book *A Long Obedience in the Same Direction*, Eugene Peterson reflects on the root and value of work. "Before anything else," he writes, "work is an activity of God." The sooner we realize this, the more we are able to see our work as done with and for God. Acknowledging that God himself works in and through us gives our work dignity, purpose, and meaning.[3]

As we understand all work as rooted in and established by God, we begin to be shaped "not by accomplishments or possessions" or lack thereof.[4] We are formed and informed by our overwhelming desire to allow God to work His plans through us vocationally and personally. We are no longer consumed with success in the worldly sense. Our work is motivated by the victory found in doing whatever we do with excellence,

---

3. Peterson, Eugene. *A Long Obedience in the Same Direction*. Downer's Grove, IL: InterVarsity Press, 2000, 108–9.

4. Ibid., 110.

to the glory of God, and through no power of our own. This approach to work blesses both God and others.

"Our work creates neither life nor righteousness," writes Peterson. In fact, our work is useless and futile if attempted apart from God. As we remind ourselves that it is first God who works in us, we are kept from making our work our lives. What we do is "not at the center; the Lord is at the center." Armed with this new perspective, our efforts at work are "at that periphery and God's work is at the center."[5]

(JNH)

---

5. Ibid., 111–12

*Eastertide*

## STREAM OF UNCONSCIOUSNESS

Stream of consciousness
Limits our flow
Sets boundaries on living,
On what we may know.

When floodwaters come
We can't take it in
We founder and sink
In the sea of our sin.

Shipwrecks on reefs
Of doubt and of fear
Islands of mind
Erode year to year.

## The Living Legacy

We yearn to dive in
To life's torrent and flow
But the soil of our minds
Will not let us go.

For we are not seamen
Just sailors of mind
On oceans of dreams
That leave us behind.

Our rivers of thought
Not catching the drift
We look for a seaman
To give us a lift.

Not knowing the purpose
Nor seeing the plan
Nor sensing direction
That life flows in man.

The mind's web is useless
And cast out like we
Apprentice fishermen
That must go to see.

Whence comes the Pilot
The captain that sails
Whence comes the rudder,
The wheel and the gale?

Whence comes the north star
The compass, the guide
Our own constellation
The ship on our side?

Look homeward angel
Turn facing the sun
Leave harbor of mind,
Your journey's begun.

        1972—Struggling toward faith

*Eastertide*

## THEOLOGICAL MUSINGS

THIS IS A POEM I wrote prior to really giving my life to Christ, or put another way prior to making my Christian heritage my own faith of choice. It reveals the hesitancy and yet also the longing I had to dive into a faith commitment, the longing to come home, but there was the soil of the mind which had not yet been washed clean, a soil I was clinging to in various ways. In my dreams I was brave and sailed forth into a new reality, but in reality I was still settled in the harbor of my mind, afraid to sail forth. What I intuited was that I should not sail off on my own, lest I drown. What I had an inkling of was that I needed a real captain of my soul to come and take me on the journey.

I include this poem in the collection not because it is a perfect poem, but because it reflects some of the mental struggles of life that even a person raised in a Christian home and presumed to be a Christian has. The struggle is not just on the conscious level it is also on the unconscious level, as one's dreams demonstrate. One of the real inhibitors to faith, at least in my case, was the recognition of how much I did not know, and of the limited capacity one human mind has for knowing. Was a God as enormous as the Bible suggests really knowable? Could I comprehend the evidence well enough to make a choice?

One of the things I did not fully grasp when I wrote this poem was that it was not just about knowing. It was the vision of the ancient Gnostics that salvation was about what you know, and in particular it was about having some kind of special, esoteric, inside knowledge of what makes the universe tick and what really solves the human dilemma. I remember vividly taking philosophy classes at Carolina that talked about the 'epistemic principles of the mind'—what we could know, and how we could know it. The implicit message was that we could redeem ourselves if we just found the right wisdom, the right knowledge.

What I did not know was that in the first place and primarily it was about Who you know, not what you know or how much you know. It is about having a relationship with God in Christ from whence comes some knowledge and insight, but is in the relationship, and the surrender to being changed by the love in that relationship that amounts to salvation. Salvation, as I was to learn later, is not a human self help program, no matter how many slick TV preachers tell you otherwise. I realized that doubt and fear were inhibitors to salvation, but what I did not fully grasp is that their opposite number is not knowledge and wisdom, but rather faith and trust in a Person who saves. Eastertide is a time to remember one's past and to take stock of how far one has come since Easter dawned in one's own life. In my case the mental journey was considerable, and it was not all about me setting sail on my own. It was about being rescued from a sea that threatened to overwhelm me, and trusting someone else enough to be taken on board His ship and going on the journey of a lifetime.

## Spiritual Meditations

### "Stream of Unconsciousness"

- Lectio Divina: Psalm 63:1–7
- Dietrich Bonhoeffer believed "The most promising method of prayer is to allow oneself to be guided by the Word of the Scriptures."[6] Take Psalm 63:1–7 or another passage of Scripture and use it as your prayer for the next several days. Cultivating the practice of praying through passages of Scripture is life-giving and life-changing. This vital practice provides us with encouragement as we commit passages to memory through repetition in prayer.
- The discipline of study affords us the opportunity to "see the Word of God at work in the lives of others,"[7] thus providing us with much needed encouragement on our own journey of faith. Study one of the pivotal players in the Old Testament (consider: Moses, Jacob, Isaiah, Job, etc.) or one of the communion of saints through the centuries (Athanasius, Chrysostom, Wesley, Bonhoeffer etc.). Learn from their lives and "make them your friends and associates in the way."[8]

### Thoughts for Further Reflection

*"Eastertide is a time to remember one's past and to take stock of how far one has come since Easter dawned in one's own life."*

Ben Witherington III

---

6. Bonhoeffer, Dietrich. *Life Together*. San Francisco: Harper Collins Publishers, 1954, 84.

7. Willard, Dallas. *The Spirit of the Disciplines*. San Francisco: Harper Collins Publishers, 1988, 177.

8. Ibid.

*Eastertide*

*"We are above all things loved—that is the good news of the Gospel—and loved not just the way we turn up on Sundays in our best clothes and on our best behavior and with our best feet forward, but loved as we alone know ourselves to be, the weakest and shabbiest of who we are along with the strongest and gladdest . . . "*

Frederick Buechner

*"It takes a profound conversion to accept the belief that God is tender and loves us just as we are, not in spite of our sins and faults, but with them. God does not condone or sanction evil, but he does not withhold his love because there is evil in us."*

Bernard Bush

### Personal Ponderings on "Stream of Unconsciousness"

In considering the cloud of witnesses—past and present—as our current companions on the way, one of the first names to come to mind is always Brother Lawrence of the Resurrection. There is not a book in print—short of the Bible itself—that offers more wisdom and insight into living abandoned to God than *The Practice of the Presence of God* by Brother Lawrence of the Resurrection. The title makes it sound like a daunting read. I myself avoided reading it for a long while, thinking it must be an impossibly large work and certainly difficult to embody. Imagine my surprise when I discovered it to be less than one hundred pages! I immersed myself in the book that very day and found it to be filled with practical, accessible insights into holy living. I have since returned to it countless times.

Hidden in this tiny volume of Brother Lawrence's letters and conversations are thoughts and ideas that have the power to help make walking with God in the details of life possible for anyone. Brother Lawrence considered union with God the supreme goal of every Christian. He found himself most united with God in the ordinary activities of the day rather than in the specifically religious. It was because he had made a "private chapel of [his] heart," a place to which he could return no matter what task he was performing at the time.[9]

---

9. Lawrence of the Resurrection, Brother. *The Practice of the Presence of God.* New York: Doubleday Publishing, 1977, 52.

Making friends with saints past and present serves to challenge and convict us to reach higher and dig deeper in our walk with the Lord. The beauty of Lawrence's work is that it does challenge, but is also encourages. In his conversations and letters he is always careful to balance his challenges with genuine encouragement. He understands from experience that the idea of practicing the presence of God at all times is a daunting task, but one we need not cower from the attempt of it in fear. Lawrence gently encourages the reader to come to God humbly and quietly, focusing the mind on God's presence and not on one's own limitations. When asked what to do when "troubled by wandering thoughts," Lawrence offered encouragement that the human mind is prone to wander and this is a practice difficult to overcome. Read the rest of his reply below and be encouraged in your own pursuit of practicing the presence of God.

> "I think one remedy for this is to confess our faults and humble ourselves before God; I do not advise much talking in prayer, long discourses often being the cause of wandering. Present yourself in prayer to God like a dumb and paralytic beggar at a rich man's door; concentrate on keeping your mind in the presence of the Lord; if it sometimes wanders and withdraws itself from Him, do not let it upset you; confusion serves rather to distract the mind than to recollect it; the will must bring it back calmly; if you persevere in this way, God will have pity on you."[10]

(JNH)

---

10. Ibid., 63–64.

*Eastertide*

## TIME

Time, unmoved but moving
Divider and dividend
Controlling not controlled—
And we often frustrated every minute of it,
Because of these things.

Time, in the final hours of analysis
We may take you—not always by surprise
And give you—the greatest and surest gift—

To take time to know many things/others
To take time to share many things/ourselves
And so to love each other
Not just the each other in ourselves.

And then to laugh—
When we see the time spent with/on
Others is never costly
When we understand that knowing
Sharing
Loving . . .

Though timed are timeless
And so we too are victors—
Jubilant children set free from father time
Set free by a sense of time
From further restraint—
For the time being—man.

    1970

# The Living Legacy

## THEOLOGICAL MUSINGS

The issue of the relationship of time to eternity, like the issue of this world and the heavenly realm have always been major theological issues in the Christian tradition. There has been for instance the debate as to whether eternity is just time infinitely extended. There has been the debate about whether there is time in heaven. Some of this debate has focused on the remarkable statement in 2 Pet. 3.8 "With the Lord one day is as a thousand years, and a thousand years as one day." What actually should we make of this remark? It surely cannot mean that time doesn't matter to God, or else we would not hear about God's remarkable sense of timing, of the appropriate time for something (see Gal. 4.4). And we might be able to understand how God might be able to slow all things down and remarkably extend the length of a day. After all, science and space travel have already let us know that if we could only reach something approximating the speed of light time would indeed slow down or bend. Einstein was on to something with his theory of relativity which affects the issue of time. But what would it mean to say that 'with the Lord' a thousand years is as one day'? Perhaps the key phrase here is 'with the Lord.' God is an eternal being, a timeless, not a timed being. God can operate either in or out of time, either with or without time, either within the time-space continuum or beyond it. We on the other hand, while we are on earth, are on the clock. We are the time beings par excellence.

Let us consider the human relationship to time. For one thing, consider the fact that while there are natural rhythms in nature, rhythms observed by other creatures, only humans seem to be concerned about 'telling time' 'making time' for something, finding 'the appropriate time', and the like. Only humans wear watches. Is it just that we are more aware of time and its passing? Or is it that time is simply a mental construct that helps us organize life? Aging is one thing—it is a physical process. Time and timing is another and it seems in the main to be an arbitrary mental construct. By this I mean, why should someone in Greenwich England have decided how we should all tell time? Why should we have time zones around the world? These are obviously of human creation and origin. And yet, and yet, God also seems to be concerned from time to time about the timing of things, and even about time running out.

In this poem I have tried to stress that human beings have some control over what they do with their time on earth. They can choose to use their time wisely and for the benefit of others, or not. They can choose to spend time loving, caring, helping, serving, or not. My theory is that if we choose to do things of eternal importance, doing the Lord's work, there is a timeless quality to that. Sometimes you even read about epitaphs that say "if I'd only had a little more time." But maybe when one truly knows they have everlasting life, they can be set free, at least to some degree, from the tyranny of the urgent. Maybe at least they can get a sense of perspective on what's really worth doing and what is not, what is really worth our time, and what is not. My theory is if we get lost in loving others, we will not be losing time or wasting time, but acting in time as if we are everlasting creatures. Isn't this how we are supposed to act as Christians?

It has been said that God has placed eternity in our minds so that we will long for it. Perhaps most of us have had the odd experience of seeing someone who is an old friend after a long interval of time. We anticipate the meeting and in our minds we have this mental image of what they look like. Then when we see them we are surprised, and remark on how much they have aged, or at least make a mental note of the fact. Why are we surprised, since 'time and tide wait for no man'? My suspicion is that it is because God has indeed put eternity in our hearts, the longing for it, and when we see the ravages of time we are shocked, even offended by it. There is a still small voice within that says— "It is not supposed to be like this. Charlie should look just like he did when I last saw him face to face." Whatever we make of such experiences it is clear that it is both the timely and the timeless that should most matter to us since they most matter to God. Otherwise, we are just marking time.

## Spiritual Meditations

### "Time"

- Lectio Divina: 1 Timothy 6:11–16
- We are a scheduled people. Many of us have our hours and days scheduled down to the second. The irony of this is that in our efforts to control time, we are losing it. Carve out some extravagant time to sit and meditate. Find a comfortable place outside in nature or another place that is a sort of sanctuary for you. Take whatever time you have to contemplate time as it relates to your life in the now and the not yet.

## The Living Legacy

- The pressures of the everyday will pull our focus away from God if we do not constantly take time to reorient ourselves to our Center. The discipline of worship helps us to concentrate our thoughts on God, even in the midst of the chaos that is life. Work on finding time(s) each day to worship God. Whether it be five or fifteen minutes or more, give that time to God. As you create specific times and spaces to worship God, you will find it easier to return to your Center throughout each day.

### Thoughts for Further Reflection

*"God is an eternal being, a timeless, not a timed being. God can operate either in or out of time, either with or without time, either within the time-space continuum or beyond it."*

Ben Witherington III

*"[I]f we get lost in loving others, we will not be losing time or wasting time, but acting in time as if we are everlasting creatures."*

Ben Witherington III

*"The life with God is the center of life, and all else is remodeled and integrated by it. It gives the singleness of eye."*

Thomas R. Kelly

*"Think of Him often, adore Him continually, live and die with Him; that is the glorious business of a Christian; in a word, it is our calling; if we do not know that calling we must learn it."*

Brother Lawrence

*"Listen to your life. See it for the fathomless mystery that it is. Touch, taste, smell your way to the holy and hidden heart of it because in the last analysis all moments are sacred moments and life itself is grace."*

Frederick Buechner

*Eastertide*

## Personal Ponderings on "Time"

There is within us this sense that eternal life is something that has not yet begun. "We think of eternal life," Frederick Buechner writes, "if we think of it at all, as what happens when life ends. We would do better to think of it as what happens when life begins."[11] In the gospel of John, Jesus reminds us that he has come that we might have life, and abundant life at that (10:10)! The Greek word in this passage implies a life far more blessed than anything we could imagine. A life meant to be experienced both now and forevermore. This theme resurfaces again and again throughout the New Testament and the whole of the Bible.

In the Word, eternal life is discussed as both "the end goal and process of salvation" and our current position as people in Christ. We are called to fullness and completeness of life in Christ in the now and the not yet. Put another way, we are only able to experience the fullness of eternal life in the hereafter as we allow ourselves to live in the fullness of it now. To live the eternal life now and forever is "to be with God as Christ is with him, and with each other as Christ is with us."[12] We all want, or ought to want, this very thing as Christians. May we begin to experience eternity not just as something to be experienced at the end of time, but from this time forth and forevermore.

(JNH)

---

11. Buechner, Frederick. *Wishful Thinking: A Theological ABC*, 22.
12. Ibid., 22–23.

# The Living Legacy

## FIRE ON ICE

Fire on ice
Ice on fire
Unbridled ambition
Unending desire,
Golden hair
Midas touch
'I am Alexander.'

Ice on fire
Fire on ice
Gory glory
Beyond advice
One world vision
Flickering flame
'I am Alexander.'

Macedonian monarch
Aristotle's ward
The great commander

*Eastertide*

> Without reward,
> Without peers
> Without an heir
> 'I am Alexander.'
>
> All the world's glory
> All the acclaim
> The Greek colossus
> The mythical name
> Builder of empire
> Finder of fame
> 'I am Alexander.'
>
> Child of the gods
> Destined from birth
> Harvest of Hellas
> Spread through the earth
> Conqueror conquered
> Food for the worms,
> 'I was Alexander.'
>
> November 1972 and 2004

## THEOLOGICAL MUSINGS

I MUST ADMIT I have always had a fascination with Alexander the Great. I went to see the recent movie on this great historical figure, and was deeply disappointed. Not only did it fail to do justice to the man, it made small things great by exaggeration, and it made his greatness seem small. The figure of Alexander is important for Christians not least because the NT would not likely have been written in Greek had it not been for the Hellenizing of the entire Mediterranean world through the conquests of Alexander. Even Jews, even in the Holy Land did not escape the legacy and harvest of Hellenism.

Alexander is much like some of the larger than life figures in the Bible, particularly like David, the great warrior king of Israel. Only David's exploits on the battlefield pale in comparison with Alexander's. David did on a small scale and in a small geographical region what Alexander did on a much grander scale. This is one reason movies have been made about Alexander, but David has been largely ignored. What the story of

Alexander tells us however is not merely the lesson we learn from the Goliath tale that 'the bigger they are the harder they fall.' We learn from Alexander that unbridled human ambition, while it can seem to accomplish much, in the end leads to the same outcome—the hero dies. In this case the hero dies prematurely, while he is still young. In fact, he dies at about the same age that that other towering figured died who has continued to have ongoing influence. I mean Jesus of course.

Let us consider for a moment a comparison and contrast between Alexander and Jesus. Alexander had the very best education money could buy, from no less a figure than Aristotle himself. He gained a vision of there being one world, with one civilized culture, one language. In a sense he set out to reverse the effects of the Tower of Babel episode recorded in Genesis, and indeed he even conquered Babylon in the process. He traveled widely, married a woman from another race and another culture in the East, conquered all the way to India, and in his wake Greek culture and Greek language became like the influence of Midas—changing everything it touched, even the Hebrew people of God, even their Scriptures which were translated into Greek. Peter Green's wonderful biography of Alexander the Great should be read by everyone interested in the period that led up to the New Testament era. It would be hard to imagine a person who had more impact on more people and cultures than Alexander, judging by human standards. Hard to imagine that is, unless one ignored Jesus.

Jesus trod a very different path to glory. He hardly ever left his own country, and so far as we can tell had only occasional communication with or dealings with foreigners. Unlike Alexander he led no armies, fought no battles (in the normal sense), conquered no lands, and spread no cultures or languages across the globe. Or did he? It is hard to dispute that this one single life of Jesus, which never involved war or political triumph or vast wealth, or wide travel and influence in his own day, not only eventually eclipsed the influence of Alexander, but spawned a new world religion which is still very much alive and vital today. You will find no temples where Alexander is worshipped today. The story about Jesus is different. If a person should be judged by the impact crater they have left, then Alexander made a dent, but Jesus has left a crater even larger than the one in Arizona or any of the ones on the moon. Considering the seeming lack of immediate impact of Jesus' life this is remarkable. Indeed one can even say that it appears that one of these two persons definitely must have had God on his side, or else he would have disappeared into the sands of time. I mean Jesus of course. Had there been no resurrection of Jesus and no ongoing Jesus movement, he surely would have been relegated to an interesting chapter in early Jewish history at most.

It has been said that we become what we admire. It seems clear to me that most major world leaders have been admiring and following the blueprint of Alexander not Jesus. There are of course exceptions to this rule. Ghandi comes to mind, or Martin Luther King, but both of them clearly patterned themselves on Jesus. But of course the big difference between Alexander and Jesus, is that Alexander was, while Jesus still *is*. He is still calling disciples, still inspiring sermons, still guiding churches and the like. It raises the question—which of the two greatest leaders of antiquity are we patterning ourselves after?

## SPIRITUAL MEDITATIONS

### "FIRE ON ICE"

- Lectio Divina: Psalm 145
- Celebration is simply coming together to remind each other that the God who spoke in Jesus still speaks in our lives. Get together with friends in Christ this week to celebrate and enjoy fellowship. Intentionally share stories of God's presence in your life and in the people around you.
- Dallas Willard once remarked that fasting is really feasting on God. Through fasting we are reminded that God is the source of all things, that he alone is the giver of life.[13] Fast from food today (for one or all meals) and drink only water or juice throughout the day. Pray that God will use your time of fasting to open your eyes to His constant activity in your life.

### THOUGHTS FOR FURTHER REFLECTION

*"Jesus still is. He is still calling disciples, still inspiring sermons, still guiding churches and the like."*

Ben Witherington III

---

13. Willard, Dallas. *The Spirit of the Disciplines*. San Francisco: Harper Collins Publishers, 1988, 166.

## The Living Legacy

*"The Jesus who walked the roads of Judea and Galilee is the one who stands beside us. The Christ of history is the Christ of faith."*

Brennan Manning

*"Christ is an ever-flowing fountain; He is continually supplying His people and the fountain is not spent. They who live upon Christ may have fresh supplies from Him to all eternity; they may have an increase of blessedness that is new, and new still, and which never will come to an end."*

Jonathan Edwards

### Personal Ponderings on "Fire on Ice"

Witherington's words in the theological reflections stir something deep within me. I am a lover of history both sacred and secular. Character studies of significant figures in history, living and dead, fascinate me. The statement Witherington makes just fascinates me. Jesus not only was, "Jesus still is." Jesus stands not just as a part of history, but as the God of history. His was an actual life in the flesh spent calling disciples, preaching sermons, and pointing others on the way. He has continued to do the same throughout the centuries since his earthly life, informing our past, present, and future.

Harry Emerson Fosdick explores the person of Jesus in his book *The Man from Nazareth*. He looks at Jesus from a variety of viewpoints. Each of these perspectives points to the conclusion that "whatever else his contemporaries saw in Jesus, they saw *him*; he was a real man."[14] This man walked and is walking among us even now.

Jesus' teaching alone has a timelessness about it that cannot be duplicated. His words had immediate appeal in their original surroundings and "continuing pertinence to all men, always, and everywhere," making "all men everywhere his contemporaries."[15]

---

14. Fosdick, Harry Emerson. *The Man from Nazareth*. New York: Harper and Brothers, 1949, 42.

15. Ibid., 243.

## Eastertide

In the epilogue, Fosdick concludes the following about the ever-presence of Jesus,

> "He was to them that most powerful force in human experience, an incarnation, embodying and revealing in his own person the truths he represented. When they thought of God, it was more and more in terms of Jesus; when they thought of goodness, it meant likeness to him. So he became to them not only Teacher, but Lord and Savior, revealer of the divine, ideal of the human, who having died for their sakes still lived, and to whom, in God's good time, the future belonged.
>
> "For the deep and abiding needs of man, [now] as in the first, call for a living, personal revelation and symbol of God, for pardon, power, faith in divine purpose and courage in serving it, for inward peace, a cause worth ultimate self-sacrifice, and for hope here and hereafter. The process which started in the experience of the first disciples has proved to be endless: man's profoundest spiritual wants finding their satisfaction in this Eternal Contemporary..."[16]

(JNH)

---

16. Ibid., 248.

# Pentecost

*The Light Bursts into Flame*

## A BARRISTER'S BRIEF BRIEF ON PENTECOST

The filigree flame of fire fell on the fellowship
Pursuant to the prayer and praise and paeans of the plaintiffs
Such that there was no room in the upper room,
And they fled like men fleeing a burning building.
But even the Temple courts could not contain the ebullience and effervescence
And so they were deemed drunk, tipplers before their time.
Yet all that they had imbibed was Spirit,
Which was so like fire in their bones that their wayward words
Leaked out in languages unknown to the speakers,
As if the babble of Babel had been set in reverse,
To unite a divided Empire that pretended Pax Romana.

Who knew the cost of Pentecost then or there,
Or the momentousness of the movement set in motion?
Who could have guessed the Guest who had inhabited them that day?
If possession is nine tenths of the law, then this magnificent possession
Became a magnificent obsession to lay down the Law and take up the Gospel,
And so tip the world upside down such that peace came from grace and truth,
Not law and order,
And testimony was borne not to a crime but to a crisis
Not to progress but to rescue,
Not to an Emperor, but to a Savior,
Not merely to the end of the old age,
But to the dawn of the new one.

As for me it appeared that at Golgotha,
Court was adjourned once and for all,
For the sentence had been executed,
The price paid,
And no appeals, summons, pleadings, stays or briefs

## The Living Legacy

Could now change that outcome.
No de facto or de jure actions could in anyway retrieve the prior state of affairs.
But oddly with this outcome it is now the Law,
And all those under it have ever since been on trial.
As if it were not enough that a 'criminal' had become King of Kings
Now on top of all else, all those who live in the Domain he has laid claim to
Are told that new occasions call for new duties,
For there is a new pact called new covenant governing the way the wheels of justice turn.
They grind slowly no longer, for they have ground to a halt until he returns.

And what interim rules he left!!—'no oaths' 'no violence' 'no depositions' 'no suits'
Only testimonies on His behalf, only confessions of his lordship, only mandates to love One and all, as if it were 'all for one' instead of free-for-all.
Thank goodness he did not demand we like our enemies!

Yes, of course I have perused the Deposit, the nomina sacra, the ancient words,
Full of odd stories, ad hoc letters, rhetorical discourses, even apocalypse of sorts
I must say—it hardly reads much like lex nova, more like sage sayings, and prescient promises.
So what's left for a lawyer to do?

Consider this my last will and testament—
I have laid down the law, and determining I have a stake in this matter, I have taken up a cross. While dying daily is painful, it beats facing the music and the musings of the messiah, when he sits on the bema seat on judgment day. I trust my day in court then will go better than his did in A.D. 30 although as it turned out, he was vindicated by a surprising reversal, ex post facto, for it appears that the Spirit was as good at revivifying bodies as inspiring proclamations at Pentecost.

    March 5, 2005

*Pentecost*

## THEOLOGICAL MUSINGS

THIS POEM IS WHAT is called a literary conceit. It is spoken in the voice of a lawyer who has given up his profession, in order to make a profession of faith in Jesus. I have tried to use as much legal language as possible to give the sense of this being a legal brief of sorts written about what happened on Pentecost. I have written it for a friend who is a J. D. though not a practicing lawyer, and his initials are J. D. as well.

Pentecost is interesting from many different angles. It was of course a Jewish festival long before it ever was a Christian one, and as the name implied it was a festival that took place some 50 days after Passover. The Jewish liturgical calendar is of course partly responsible for the Christian one. What is of importance for us is that Pentecost is portrayed in Acts 2 as the fulfillment of Joel 2, in which the gift of the Spirit which had in the past fallen on select prophetic individuals now was falling on the entire body of believers in the upper room, empowering them to bear witness. Thus a new evangelistic movement is born.

Luke's portrayal of Pentecost makes it appear that we should see this event as the reverse of what happened at the tower of Babel, where the language (singular) of human beings became the languages of human beings, hence confusion and division. Notice that what happened at Pentecost is not a Pentecostal experience, if by that one means the giving of the gift of glossolalia, speaking in angelic tongues. No, what happened at Pentecost A.D. 30 was that the miraculous gift of instantly speaking in human foreign languages was bequeathed, a gift my seminary students studying Greek and Hebrew pray for regularly! The Greek text is quite clear—the audience heard the disciples of Jesus each 'speaking in our own languages.' The miracle happened only to those speaking, not those hearing. We would need to go elsewhere in Acts, for instance Acts 10, to find a story about glossolalia. But tellingly, this doesn't lead to a one world language story. Rather the language differences are transcended but not eliminated by means of the Holy Spirit.

The prophetic gift is given to both men and women on Pentecost which of course is important for it means that both men and women will be expected to proclaim the prophetic Word of God as part of this evangelistic movement. Then too Jer. 31.31–33 lies in the background here which speaks of a new covenant written by God's Spirit on the human heart. This Pentecost event then signals both the fulfillment of old prophecies and promises and the beginning of a whole new relationship, a new covenant relationship between God and God's people.

One more thing should be noted. You don't accuse people of being drunk first thing in the morning unless you have noticed something about their behavior. In this case it must surely be that people saw the incredible enthusiasm and great desire to share some very important news with those worshippers in the Temple precincts. The proclaimers must surely have been both effervescent and ebullient. And why not? The eschatological age had begun with a bang. First Jesus had risen from the dead and appeared to his disciples, then they had received empowerment from on High to accomplish what Jesus had commissioned them to do. If you can't get excited about these sorts of things you are a Christian without a pulse.

## Spiritual Meditations

### "A Barrister's Brief Brief on Pentecost"

- Lectio Divina: Jeremiah 31:31–33
- Pentecost serves as a reminder to us of the power of the Holy Spirit in the life of a Christian. Pray for the humility and grace to surrender to the stirrings and gifts of the Spirit in your own life. We will not all have the same gifts (i.e.—prophecy, speaking in tongues, teaching, etc.), but we do all have gifts given and are empowered by the Spirit. Pray for a revelation of those gifts in your own life and for the ability to employ them with confidence.
- Spend some time studying the Pentecost event in Acts 2. Grab a pen and paper and write down your own observations and reflections. Consider how the ripples of this event are still being felt today. Reflect upon your own part in the continuing Pentecost.

### Thoughts for Further Reflection

*"[The] Pentecost event . . . signals both the fulfillment of old prophecies and promises and the beginning of a whole new relationship, a new covenant relationship between God and God's people."*

Ben Witherington III

*Pentecost*

"Holy Spirit, descend plentifully into my heart. Enlighten the dark corners of this neglected dwelling and scatter there Thy cheerful beams"

Saint Augustine

"O consuming fire, Spirit of love, descend within us and reproduce in us, as it were, an incarnation of the Word, that each of us might be another humanity wherein he renews his mystery."

Elizabeth of the Trinity

"The trace of the Trinity appears in creatures."

Saint Augustine

### Personal Ponderings on "A Barrister's Brief Brief on Pentecost"

Pentecost is a vital, important season in the church year. It commemorates the descent of the Holy Spirit on a gathering of Christ's disciples (Acts 2:1–4). This pivotal event in the first days of the church was a fulfillment of prophecies and a sign of things to come. Such an event demanded a response from those that saw and experienced it. The ripples of the event and the responses of those present are still being felt today.

One of the more beautiful aspects of the descent of the Holy Spirit on the people is often overlooked. The power and energy experienced are significant, but the wonder of this passage is the humility with which Peter approaches the event and the response to it. We often think only of the sensational power of the Holy Spirit when we consider the Pentecost event in Acts, but there is so much more that the passage has to tell us. When asked what the response should be to the Holy Spirit, Peter's reply was simple: humility. Reception of the Holy Spirit and the gifts therein requires humility and grace only found through a bending of the knee in repentance and baptism. Only with such a spirit can the Holy Spirit be received and exercised rightly.

François Fénelon writes of this need for humility in his work *Let Go*. He writes of the paradox that the Holy Spirit works best in us when we recognize our own powerlessness. "Humility," he writes "is good in every situation because it produces that teachable spirit which makes everything easy."[1] When we walk in humlity we are more receptive to the Spirit's leadings. As we allow God through the Holy Spirit to do His work in us, we are more able to "concentrate on living a selfless life in each and every moment, as though each moment was the whole of eternity."[2] It is to this we are called and this we can only achieve through humble submission to God.

(JNH)

---

1. Fénelon, François. *Let Go*. Springdale, PA: Whitaker House, 1973, 1.
2. Ibid., 75.

## THE MIRAGE

Shimmering, glimmering
Enticing to a fault
Always in the distance
Beckoning to be caught.

The illusion, projection
Of what we hope and dream
Always better imagined
Not being what it seems.

Leading the thirsty one
Down a dusty track
Through a blistering desert
Never turning back.

Oasis, respite
Mirror or mirage
Foretaste of glory
Or desert camouflaged?

## The Living Legacy

Fantasies, fairy tales
Broken, borrowed schemes
Dead end ideas
Ephemeral moonbeams.

Prosperity, wealth
Beyond one's wildest dreams
Pleasure though fleeting
Glistens and it gleams.

Longing, lusting
For things beyond our reach
Driving our behavior
Not practicing what we preach.

Consumer, consumed
By the inner fire
Not the Holy Spirit's,
Insatiable desire.

Transitory, temporary
Shelter from the storm
Something to nurse a life along
Someone to keep you warm.

Like David, wizened
And his Shunammite
A beautiful young virgin
To get him through the night.

Settling's unsettling
To the heart and soul
Made for everlasting love
Not fleeting human dole.

Look in the mirror
Remember what you saw
The person you've just glimpsed
Is you in the raw.

## Pentecost

Stop praying for mirages
To suddenly be real
Stop measuring yourself
By how it makes you feel.

Stop measuring your worth,
By how much you've achieved
How much you have bought or won
Or suffered or have grieved.

The image has been broken
But Christ's image can emerge
Not its ghost or fleeting token,
You are living on the verge.

August 9, 2006

## THEOLOGICAL MUSINGS

I REMEMBER WELL THE five hour long trips to the N.C. beach in the back of an un-air conditioned 1955 Chervrolet. It was hot as a fire cracker and the windows were rolled down so there would be a breeze. My sister and I, when we were not busy antagonizing and playing with each other enjoyed looking at the flat ribbon of road through the front windshield. We could always tell when we were getting closer to the coast because there would magically appear a mirage of water on the road ahead, always fading into nothing by the time we reached the spot where we had just glimpsed it. It was shining, gleaming in the summer sun, but actually it was all an optical illusion, all a mirage. Its brightness and beauty attracted immediate attention, but alas it was all form and no substance, all flash and no cash, all appearance and no reality.

This particular poem deals with how many things are mirages in our lives, that cannot deliver the things for which our heart most deeply longs. Even when they have some reality or substance to them, like a good meal, they come and they go quickly, leaving us still longing for more. What happens when all too soon a person realizes that we should all be singing Mick Jagger's classic song—"I Can't Get No Satisfaction?"

Do we simply settle for second, third, or fifth best in life? Is life all about 'settling' because life can't deliver all it seems to promise? Or do we embrace the illusions and live out of touch with reality, living in a fantasy world? Or alternatively do we embrace the reality of both the goodness and temporal and temporary quality of so many things in this fleeting existence and realize they were only meant to point us to a greater good, to a God who is good, and who along can fill the God-shaped vacuum in our souls?

Do we also recognize that we are on a journey towards the really REAL, towards being all we can be, as the image of Christ is formed within us over time? Do we realize that it's a process of growth into the full measure of the stature of Christ? Do we realize that that incomplete and in-process reality in Christ has an everlasting quality, whereas many things which seem more fully formed and immediate attractive and satisfying, in fact are not 'as advertised'?

In the deserts of Nevada in a town called Las Vegas (or as it is sometimes euphemistically dubbed 'Lost Wages') stands a huge casino of a hotel aptly named the Mirage. When you see this place up close it is a glimmering palace, promising instant gratification of many sorts, including instant wealth without work, free meals without pay, cheap rooms without effort, and best of all we are promised that no one needs to know since "what happens in Vegas stays in Vegas."

If you go down the strip beyond the Mirage a ways, and past the faux Wedding Chapel, you will find a much less impressive structure—a small church on the outskirts of the 'Strip.' Stripped of all glamour and glitz, and gala buffets, you will find in there food for the poor and hungry, clothes for the naked, counseling for the abused and troubled, vibrant worship for one and all, good fellowship and friendship with no one trying to pry your money out of your hands, and of course you'll find the living Word of God and even salvation. You must decide however which of these two places offer a mirage in the desert, and which manna from heaven in the desert. One is real, the other only surreal. But one thing is certain—what happens in that little building doesn't 'stay in Vegas', it echoes in eternity.

*Pentecost*

## Spiritual Meditations

### "The Mirage"

- Lectio Divina: 1 John 5:1–5
- A poem like this one exposes in each of us a proneness to wander toward the mirages of success, wealth, and temporary pleasures. These mirages in our life, as Witherington noted, "cannot deliver what our heart most deeply longs for." Even those mirages which are not inherently evil in and of themselves cannot satisfy us for long. And yet we are so often guilty of focusing not on the eternal, but the temporal. Spend some time confessing where you have wandered recently. Ask God to give you a new awareness of those areas where you have a tendency to seek after that which is not of Him.
- Conversation with a trusted friend about your own weaknesses can be liberating and freeing. Find a friend with whom you can confide your struggles in fully surrendering to God and accepting His blessings and not the fleeting pleasures of the world.

### Thoughts for Further Reflection

*"[W]e embrace the reality of both the goodness and temporal and temporary quality of so many things in this fleeting existence and realize they were only meant to point us to a greater good, to a God who is good, and who alone can fill the God-shaped vacuum in our souls."*

Ben Witherington III

*"When we meet God and live with him, we discover who we are in the light of who God is. God is the one who gives a realistic picture of human life."*

Dennis Kinlaw

*"It is no good trying to 'be myself' without Him."*

C. S. Lewis

# The Living Legacy

*"Teach us, O Lord, to use this transitory life as pilgrims returning to their beloved home; that we may take what our journey requires and not think of settling in a foreign country."*

John Wesley

## Personal Ponderings on "The Mirage"

The surest way to loose ourselves from the chains of the world is to surrender. There can be no real freedom without a real letting go. The paradox of this is that we are made "captive" to Christ instead, as the old hymn suggests.[3] There is freedom to be found in this sort of captivity.

C. S. Lewis writes of this surrender of self in his classic work *Mere Christianity*. He proposes that until we give up our self to God, we will not have a real self. Our search for an identity in the world is futile apart from our connection to God. Our personality is God's gift to us as we identify ourselves with Him and "there are no real personalities anywhere else."[4]

Lewis writes, "Your real, new self will not come as long as you are looking for it. It will come when you are looking for Him."[5] In coming to know Jesus Christ deeply and personally, we find our own personality hidden in His.

> "The principle runs through all life from top to bottom. Give up your self and you will find your real self. Lose your life and you will save it. Submit to death, death of your ambitions and favorite wishes every day and death of your whole body in the end: submit with every fiber of your being, and you will find eternal life. Keep back nothing. Nothing that you have not given away will ever be really yours. Nothing in you that has not died will ever be raised from the dead. Look for yourself, and you will find in the long run only hatred, loneliness, despair, rage, ruin, and decay. But look for Christ and you will find Him, and with Him everything else thrown in."[6]

(JNH)

---

3. See *Make Me a Captive, Lord* by George Matheson, c. 1890.
4. Lewis. C. S. *Mere Christianity*. New York: Touchstone, 1996, 190.
5. Ibid., 191.
6. Ibid.

*Pentecost*

### THE ORACLE

Call them forth,
Call them forth,
From the passive past.
The soothsayers and truth sayers
The yea sayers and nay sayers
The foretellers and forthtellers,
Scanning the skies,
Hoping for the horizon,
Acting out the plan
Signing forth the ban
Boon or bane
Commendation or condemnation

Blessing or curse,
Let them wrap their mantles
'Round their hoary heads
And cry: 'Thus sayeth the Lord'
Once more.

September 13, 1997

## THEOLOGICAL MUSINGS

THIS POEM IS WRITTEN for the Pentecost season, reflecting on what Peter says in Acts 2 when he quotes the prophecy from Joel 2. We tend to forget that Peter lived in an oral culture and that the literacy rate was 10% or thereabouts. In such a culture, the phrase 'Word of God' normally referred not to a text, but to an oral proclamation. In particular it referred to a word of prophecy, where the prophet or oracle became a mouthpiece for the Almighty. The oracle would use the formula "thus says Yahweh" and whatever followed that formula was considered the words of the Deity, not merely the words of the prophet.

We tend to stereotype the Biblical prophets as if they were simply foretellers, predictors of the future. Of course it is true that they were foretellers at times, but they were as often forth-tellers as they were foretellers, truth tellers, so to speak. But there was another dimension to their work as well, namely prophetic sign acts. Sometimes prophets would dramatize or act out what they saw coming, like when Hosea married a prostitute on divine order (Hos. 1) or when Ezekiel was forbidden to mourn his wife's passing in a normal way (cf. Ezek. 24) or when Jesus cleanses the Temple (see John 2). It has been a custom in OT scholarship to call Israel's prophets 'prosecutors of the covenant lawsuit.' By this is meant that their job is to call Israel to account, and reveal to them the judgment or salvation that is coming from God because they either have, or have not, kept the covenant.

Perhaps it will be useful to say a word about how ancient covenants or treaties worked. If we are talking about a suzerain-vassal treaty, a treaty between a superior power and some subordinate person or state that is under the rule of this particular monarch, then the terms of the covenants made are dictated by the dominant power, by the ruler in question. This does not mean that the covenant is unilateral in the sense that the monarch has to do nothing, and the vassal has to do everything. With any such treaty the sovereign makes promises and also makes stipulations. There are both blessing and curse sanctions in such treaties. The prophets then are sent to warn Israel that the curse sanctions are about to be applied to God's people unless they repent. Of course if they do repent and turn back to God, such sanctions do not apply.

In the case of the Pentecost event, we see Peter playing the prophetic role and calling Israel to repent and believe in their own messiah, Jesus. We should not overlook the fact that Peter's Pentecost speech is not just a celebratory one over the fact that God has poured out his Spirit. He has done so in order that there might be many prophets who can call many persons to repent and believe the Good News about Jesus. The assumption is that God's people are in a spiritually precarious condition. But the warning given on that occasion to Jews, could just as well be given today to Christians who take their 'chosenness' for granted or assume God will not judge their sin. In the midst of the celebrating of receiving the prophetic gift, we need also to count the cost of Pentecost. The gift has been given so God's prophetic word about both redemption and judgment may be spoken. Peter, to his credit, even on a day when he is tremendously excited, does not skimp on offering the whole Gospel.

## Spiritual Meditations

### "The Oracle"

- Lectio Divina: Joel 2:28–32
- In Joel 2:12–13, the Lord pleas with the people, "Return to me with all your heart, with fasting . . . rend your heart and not your clothing" and the Lord will be "gracious and compassionate, slow to anger and abounding in love." Fasting has great power in our lives, revealing to us what is binding us and keeping us from giving God our whole heart. Fast this week from food or something else. Come with a readiness to be exposed and learn what binds you. Leave with that knowledge and the confidence that "the Lord your God . . . is gracious and compassionate" and will not leave you there.
- Journal through the Lectio Divina passage for this particular poem (Joel 2:28–32). Reflect upon this passage through free-writing, creative writing, poetry, prose, art, or another avenue of expression.

## The Living Legacy

### Thoughts for Further Reflection

*"In the midst of the celebrating of receiving the prophetic gift, we need also to count the cost of Pentecost. The gift has been given so God's prophetic word about both redemption and judgment may be spoken."*

Ben Witherington III

*"The New Testament proclaims that at some unforeseeable time in the future God will ring down the final curtain on history, and there will come a Day on which all our days and all the judgments upon us and all our judgments upon each other will themselves be judge. The judge will be Christ. In other words, the one who judges us most finally will be the one who loves us most fully."*

Frederick Buechner

*"We must choose for God if we want to be with God."*

Henri Nouwen

*"[T]he greater any man's mind is, the more he knows of God and himself, the more will he be disposed to prostrate himself before God in all the humblest acts and expressions of repentance."*

William Law

### Personal Ponderings on "The oracle"

The task of sharing the whole Gospel with the whole world is a daunting one when we seek to do it on our own. Attempted apart from God, evangelism is nothing more than empty words about a God we claim to know but do not. We can only communicate the power of the Gospel as we allow that power to infuse our own lives.

In his book *Tell It Well*, the great missionary J. T. Seamands speaks of the importance of telling God's story well. He writes, "The uniqueness of the gospel lies in the person of Jesus Christ and His transforming power. We are effective communicators only when we center our message around Him."[7] Seamands understands evangelism to be "a divine-human cooperation or

---

7. Seamands, J. T. *Tell It Well*. Kansas City: Beacon Hill Press, 108.

partnership. God is at work; He calls us to work; we now work together."[8] Seamands' thoughts on the power and necessity of Pentecost in taking the Gospel to the world bears repeating and reflecting upon today.

> "[H]ow we need the fullness and power of the Holy Spirit in our lives! Pentecost is not a spiritual luxury; it is an utter necessity for Christian service. It is not an adornment, but essential equipment; not something we can take or leave as we like, but a must. We are shut up to the alternative: Pentecost or failure. For the human spirit fails unless the Holy Spirit fills."[9]

(JNH)

---

8. Ibid., 116.
9. Ibid., 120.

# The Living Legacy

## ESSE QUAM VIDERE—TO BE, RATHER THAN TO SEEM

Take me to the just side of justice
And the right side of righteousness,
Not the vindictive side of vindication,
for otherwise—I do not wish to go.

Lead me to the passionate side of compassion,
And the gracious side of grace,
Not the condescending side of mercy
for otherwise I remain remote—for pity's sake.

Push me past the truant side of trouble
And the pleasant side of pain
Not allowing me to wallow in it—
Lest I marvel at my martyrdom

Carry me to the service side of serving
And the sacrificial side of sacrifice
Not the calculating side of caring
for otherwise, my generosity remains too frugal.

Put me outside my selfish Eden
And beyond my creature comforts
Without raising Cain in my life
for I desire to be a remarkable, not a marked man.

*Pentecost*

Fill me with an inextinguishable blaze
A peerless and fearless love,
Not a faltering flame or a fumbling forgiveness
for I desire to be christened with real Christ-likeness.

May the Spirit make me spiritual
And the Son shine in my life
And the Father find me faithful,
Lest I miss the Kingdom's goal.

July 4, 2005

## THEOLOGICAL MUSINGS

THIS POEM IS IN essence a plea to God to help me manifest the proper Christian virtues in ways that are not sanctimonious nor self-righteous nor unhelpful. There is a kind of Christian piety that can be very self-absorbed and self-focused. I have even known persons who were proud that they were so humble! Pride is not a sin we talk much about in Christian circles these days, but we ought to, as it is one of the most deadly sin, as it stifles true holiness.

There is indeed a right side of righteousness which is not self-righteous, and there is also a compassion that is selfless and does not draw attention to the giver and is in no way condescending. It lifts up the wounded or needy without singling them out. There are as well some Christians that have something of a martyr complex, and they use their suffering to get attention, to spark sympathy or pity. This is not what Jesus had in mind when he told us to take up our crosses and follow him. We should not be seeking suffering, but when it finds us, we should try and react in a Christ-like manner.

This poem is intended to make clear the total dependency of the believer on God for all good things, and indeed even for one's own virtues. God is called upon to take, lead, push, carry, put, fill and even prod the prayer into the right place, the right actions, the right temperament. It is not assumed that God has left us with a bunch of commandments that we must fulfill without divine help. It is fair to say that Christians cannot be Christians without a lot of help, a lot of grace, a lot of divine intervention, for what we are called to is not natural—it is supernatural.

What I mean by this last remark is that self-sacrificial behavior is not natural for a fallen self-centered person. Righteous behavior is not natural for one who has been wronged. Forgiveness is not natural for one who has been wounded. Compassion for the less fortunate is especially not natural in a culture that assumes that everyone makes their own bed, makes their own fortune and therefore should live with it.

This radically individualistic assumption goes beyond the normal expectation of individual responsibility for one's own actions to the point of assuming that the poor are always or at least normally victims of their own mismanaged lives. There is no concept or taking into account of the effect of circumstances, upbringing, social networks, ethnic prejudice and a host of other factors. God however has other views of why some people are poor and others are wealthy, and it doesn't just have to do with intelligence, being in the right place at the right time, good hard work and honest labor. It also has to do with oppression, dishonest dealing, cheating and a host of other sins. God alone is impartial, and it is our task to try and view the world in the way that He sees it, not according to 'conventional wisdom.'

The poem ends with a doxology of sorts, really more of a plea that God will inspire, empower and motivate the petitioner so that he will be found faithful when Christ returns. Faithfulness is a very different concept from success, and indeed it may often come at the expense of success, as defined by the world. This poem is a prod for all Christians to be real Christians, rather than just seeming to be Christians, and this means being real Christians in their business ethics, in the way they treat their families and neighbors and even enemies, and realizing that this is far more important than some forms of ephemeral worldly success. As John Wesley suggested in his famous sermon "On the Use of Money" it is possible to be a living person and be a dead Christian if you do not practice the Christian virtues without compromise. When one sees erosion on the horizon, erosion of character, then turning to the Lord with the sort of concepts we find in this poem is in order. It assumes that we need to be prodded, directed, enabled, led from time to time. It assumes that we regularly need outside help to be a Christ-like person.

*Pentecost*

## Spiritual Meditations

### "Esse quam Videre"

- Lectio Divina: Romans 12:1–8
- Witherington has remarked that "self-sacrificial behavior is not natural for a fallen, self-centered person." Service may not be our natural inclination as fallen creatures, but participating in it recalls who we were created to be before the fall. Find ways to be in service to others this week. Consider contacting a local shelter, food pantry, or hospital to volunteer your time. Explore a variety of options before finding your fit and making it a regular part of your schedule
- Pray for a spirit to receive God's help, grace, and intervention in your life to be more Christ-like. In order to be righteous, not self-righteous and pious, not prideful, we must fully rely on God for strength. Write out a brief prayer to memorize and repeat throughout the week. As you allow yourself to receive God's help and grace, you will be better able to give the same to others in His name.

### Thoughts for Further Reflection

*"It is fair to say that Christians cannot be Christians without a lot of help, a lot of grace, a lot of divine intervention, for what we are called to is not natural—it is supernatural."*

Ben Witherington III

*"God alone is impartial and it is our task to try and view the world in the way that He sees it, not according to 'conventional wisdom.'"*

Ben Witherington

*"To love is to think, speak, and act according to the spiritual knowledge that we are infinitely loved by God and called to make that love visible in this world."*

Henri Nouwen

## The Living Legacy

*"The mystery of the Spirit is the mystery of selfless love. We receive Him in the 'inspiration' of secret love, and we give Him to others in the outgoing of our own charity. Our life in Christ is then a life of both receiving and of giving. We receive from God, in the spirit, and in the same Spirit we return our love to God through our brothers."*

Thomas Merton

### Personal Ponderings on "Esse Quam Verde"

God alone is purely impartial, yet we are called to solidarity and intimacy with our brothers and sisters without prejudice. A true encounter with God is the only way to fulfill this mandate. Those who have encountered Jesus cannot escape the "discovery that solidarity is the other side of intimacy." A right understanding of forgiveness and grace grows us in the knowledge that "the intimacy of God's house excludes no one and includes everyone."[10] Nouwen further charges, "We cannot live in intimate communion with Jesus without being sent to our brothers and sisters . . . intimacy manifests itself as solidarity and solidarity as intimacy."[11]

We are called as Christians to share with others the mercy and grace we have received. Reciprocity. Solidarity. Unity. You may call it what you want, but the more important work is to embody it. We cannot do this apart without a new set of eyes and ears—God's. Nouwen calls this "divine perception" and puts it thus,

> "We need new eyes to see and new ears to hear the truth of our unity, a unity which cannot be perceived by our broken, sinful, anxious hearts. Only a heart filled with perfect love can perceive the unity of humanity. This requires divine perception. God sees his people as one, as belonging to the same family and living in the same house. God wants to share this divine perception with us. By sending the only beloved Son to live and die for us all, God wants to open our eyes so that we can see that we belong together in the embrace of God's perfect love."[12]

(JNH)

---

10. Nowen, Henri J. M. *Lifesigns: Intimacy, Fecundity, and Ecstasy in Christian Perspective.* New York: Doubleday, 1986, 30–31.

11. Ibid., 32.

12. Ibid., 33.

### ODE FOR A SUMMER'S DAY

The spray, the foam, the salty air
The sound, the roar, the silent prayer
The way the waves roll cares away
The way the sun beats down all day.

The sound of gulls, the sound of wind
The simple, silent peace that mends.
The tide, the crabs, the sand fiddlers too,
The pools of warm water caressing you.
Your hair bleached out, your skin quite red
The feeling of languor in your head.
The children making sand castles near,
The fishermen casting lines from the pier.

All this and more awaits your eyes
In summertime, a wonderful surprise
Your heart will mend, your will will bend,
Your mind stops racing, your feet stops pacing.

> And stillness and awe, and wonder come,
> The sense of God that strikes you dumb.
> So hush and ponder on this dark night
> Why God made it all, and made it just right.
>
> February 8, 2002

## THEOLOGICAL MUSINGS

THIS POEM IS WHAT is called a revery, in which one reflects on something beautiful or wonderful and has something of a day dream about it. Normally such a poem involves remembering something that was a blessing, which one is not now or not yet experiencing. From a theological point of view this poem is an exercise in creation theology, in this case reflecting on what one sees and hears and feels at the beach.

In the creation story in Genesis 1, the story is brought to a climax in vs. 31 where it says "And God saw all that he had made and it was very good." No created thing is evil in itself. The material realm is seen as a good thing in toto, at least as it was originally made. Air is good, water is good, land is good, animals are good, people are good, warmth is good, cold is good, and we could go on. There is no moral dualism of spirit and matter in this theology as if only spiritual things were good. This poem then revels in the sheer goodness of ordinary and mundane experience of God's beautiful creation.

Creation theology does not reflect on God's special providences, his intervention in human lives, his role in historical processes and the like. It reflects on what God made and the goodness of that. Of course we ourselves are a part of what God made. We are placed into an ecosystem on which we depend, and the interesting thing is that it was all made for our good. As long as we don't destroy our environment it is there to sustain us, to maintain us, to provide for us.

Creation theology involves the recognition that God indeed did make a human centered world, which was nonetheless meant to be God focused. What I mean by this is that God made creation for the benefit of the crown of creation—human beings. We see a measure of this in the declaration that all the lower life forms (e.g. the plants, the fruit trees, the grains) are given to humans and animals for food. And then of course there is the further declaration that the animals are to be ruled by the humans (Gen. 1.28–30).

*Pentecost*

One clearly gets a sense of the divine satisfaction of having created all things good, and indeed for our good, and occasionally we get glimpses of this, such as is expressed in this poem. The poem not only reflects on the beauty of the experience but also on the harmony between the creation and the creature in such a setting. This produces a profound sense of joy. There is a sense in which one is in a safe haven, a wild life sanctuary, and one needs to take care of such a precious place.

Of course the creation story reflects not only on the privilege and position of humankind as rulers over the creation, it also reflects on our responsibility. Consider just for a moment the process of naming the animals. What was the point of this exercise? Surely part of what is going on in that story is that animals are to be treated with kindness, with respect, as beings worthy of being named. Names in the Biblical world were not just ciphers or mere labels. They were meant to say something about the nature of the person or animal named. Just as the privilege of doing the naming is given to the superior being, so also the responsibility is give to treat the lesser creatures with respect, as having their own dignity.

I have always enjoyed watching the pelicans as they fly low over the sea looking for fish. They do not go fishing just for the fun of it. They fish to survive, as do all animals. There is no wasted motion, no wasted effort. There are things humans could learn from the way some animals relate to other animals. As one poet put it "life and death upon one tether, and running beautiful together." But there is a wisdom not just in learning from creation, there is wisdom in just appreciating it and thanking God for making it all as he did. This poem is mainly about the latter.

## Spiritual Meditations

### "Ode for a Summer's Day"

- Lectio Divina: Genesis 1
- Reflecting on creation and the goodness of it does nothing if not call us to worship. We ought to stand (or kneel!) in wonder and amazement at what we see each day. More often than not, this is not the case. We take the goodness of creation for granted, especially when it comes to ourselves. We must remember that everything around us, *including* us, is a part of what God made and called *good*. Ponder

this today and spend some time in worship, giving thanks to the creativity and generosity of our God.

- Another equally worshipful response to creation is to sit in silence in it. Schedule a day this week to spend an extended period of time just sitting in and observing nature. Whether it is simply sitting for a while on your porch in a rocking chair or relaxing at the lake or a beach somewhere, enjoy all the sights and sounds of creation and soak it all in as best you can. This practice will bless and humble you in such a way that just the remembrance of it will become a sanctuary in your heart.

### Thoughts for Further Reflection

*"[T]here is wisdom not in just learning from creation, there is wisdom in just appreciating it and thanking God for making it all as he did."*
Ben Witherington III

*"We cannot assume that [God] feels about us the way we feel about ourselves, unless we love ourselves intensely and freely."*
Bernard Bush

*"[T]he heavens rejoice when God's creatures honor their Creator with the gifts and abilities he has given them. Why? Because that was His original plan. And it is still God's plan for us—today and in the world to come."*
Stan Gaede

*"We cannot love ourselves unless we love others, and we cannot love others unless we love ourselves."*
Thomas Merton

### Personal Ponderings on "Ode for a Summer's Day"

Not many of us look at creation—trees, flowers, birds, animals and the like—and scoff. We appreciate what we see around us and revel in the opportunity to enjoy it. We love a long walk on the beach, beautiful mountains, and a colorful sunset. Where we often fail in our appreciation of creation is in recognizing the beauty within ourselves. We love creation itself, but not what God has created in us. This causes all sorts of problems with our fulfilling the mandate to love our neighbors because we have so miserably failed at the "as ourselves" part of that command.

Brennan Manning's book *A Glimpse of Jesus: The Stranger to Self-Hatred* explores this human bent toward self-loathing. With remarkable tenderness and transparency, Manning offers personal insight and practical help in recovering the image of God within and learning to love ourselves as God already does.

Recalling the countless stories of the Old and New Testaments that tell of God's unwavering mercy and love for imperfect people, Manning reminds us that God loves us fully and completely the way we are right now. He is our "deliverer from self-hatred through love." His love for us is not conditional on our having it all together, it is available to us as we are in the now.[13]

> "The unflinching, unwavering love and compassion of Jesus Christ, the stranger to self-hatred," writes Manning, "is the ultimate source of our healing wholeness." If we wish to know Jesus as God and love ourselves and others, "we must let him be who he wants to be for us."

And who is it Jesus desires to be for us but the lover of our souls? May we learn to let Him love us so that we might turn and love the world through Him.[14]

(JNH)

---

13. Manning, Brennan. *A Glimpse of Jesus: The Stranger to Self Hatred.* San Francisco: Harper Collins Publishers, 2003, 36.

14. Ibid., 39.

# The Living Legacy

## WAR'S WISDOM

They say there is no wisdom
They say it isn't so,
They stir up rainy weather
But then it starts to snow.

Poor prognosticators
Pungent pundits too
They trust their own predictions
But don't know what to do.

The politics of fear,
And self protection reign
As if killing all our foes
Was possible and sane.

We alienate our allies
We say we'll go alone
We ignore prevailing wisdom
And enter a war zone.

*Pentecost*

And no one's even asking
What would the Master say
We sing our patriotic songs
When things go wrong we pray.

It's right to ask for sacrifice
Whene'er the cause is just
Whenever truth is being served
When God's the one we trust.

Vengeance is no solution.
Observe the Holy Land
Sick cycles of destruction
Bad blood flows in the sand.

There surely is a wisdom
It's spoken in God's Word
It speaks of holy sacrifice
Not one that is absurd.

It calls for love of enemy
And giving lives for friends
It calls for taking up the cross
Through suffering, violence ends.

Lamech called for vengeance
Seventy-seven fold,
Jesus said forgive that much
Before the night grows cold.

"Vengeance is surely mine"
Thus speaks a sovereign Lord,
And when we try to play God's role
We violate his Word.

An 'eye for an eye's myopic
Or else it leaves both blind.
Endless reciprocity
Leaves humanity behind.

# The Living Legacy

Someday the lion will lie down
Next to the harmless lamb.
Someday the swords will be retooled
For plowing up the land.

Someday we'll see that 'just wars'
Are never just enough
Someday we'll realize the kingdom's for
The meek, not for the tough.

Until that day we all must pray
For forgiveness for what we've done
For those who live just by the sword
Lose, even when they've won.

Somewhere there is an endgame
Without the sound of taps
A plan to play a different role
Blessed peacemakers perhaps.

## THEOLOGICAL MUSINGS

This is a poem that some Americans will have a hard time stomaching. I understand this, but I am a pacifist because I believe that is exactly what Christ demands of me in the Sermon on the Mount and what Paul says as well in Rom. 12–14. Of course I do not think that Christ was trying to make public policy when he taught his disciples to turn the other cheek and love one's enemies, but I do think he was offering an ethic that he expected his own followers to embrace. Jesus believed in suffering for, and even at the hands of his enemies. He did not believe in killing them. Jesus it will be remembered even stopped to heal the ear of the high priest's slave as he was being carted off to trial, and told his disciple to stop the violence. Jesus it will be remembered even forgave his executioners who had wrongly nailed him to the cross saying with his dying breath "Father forgive them . . . "

What this all means for me is that while I certainly pray for our troops safety and that they may come home unharmed, I find that I have a Christian duty to oppose war which overrides any patriotic duty to support it. I am well aware that other equally sincere Christians think differently about this matter, though for the life of me I don't see how they get around the obligation for Christians to follow the example of Christ when it comes to the matter of non-violence, the obligation to embrace personally the ethic of the Sermon on the Mount.

Yes, I am well aware of Romans 13, which suggests that governments have the right to bear some kinds of arms for some sorts of defensive purposes. I do not dispute this, but what I do dispute is that Christians have any obligation to serve their country in capacities that involve violence. This means for me, that I could never be any kind of soldier, except of course the Christian sort spoken of in the familiar hymn or in Ephesians 5. I suppose it also means I could never be some kinds of law enforcement officers either. I believe there is a place for this opinion not merely in a democracy like America, but especially in the body of Christ, though it surely is a minority opinion, I realize.

Sometimes people point to the OT for justification for fighting wars. Sometimes they even talk about wars sponsored or endorsed by God. I understand this, but I think it involves a misreading of several things. In the first place, those texts are about God's chosen people and their taking of the Holy Land. Americans, though they may like to think otherwise, are not God's chosen people anymore than any other modern nation state is. According to the NT God's people at this juncture are "Jew and Gentile united in Christ" (Gal. 3.28), an ethnically and racially and nationally diverse group that comprises a world-wide fellowship of Christ. In other words, those texts provide no justification for secular governments of any sort going to war. Modern wars are not holy wars, no matter who's fighting them.

Secondly, Christians are under the new covenant, not any forms of the old covenant, and there are decided differences between the new covenant Jesus inaugurated and the old covenants. One of the most obvious differences has to do precisely with this matter of non-violence. Jesus believed he was bringing in the Dominion of God upon the earth, the eschatological state of affairs. He believed he was bringing in the state which Isaiah spoke of when he talking about the lion lying down with the lamb. This among other things is why we have a blessing on peacemakers as one of the inaugural beatitudes.

The already-not yet nature of the coming of this kingdom of course makes our ethical situation not always clear, but what is clear to me is that if I am going to err, I should err on the side of love not hate, peace not war, forgiveness not vengeance, because at the end of the day it is those qualities which will endure and prevail one day when the kingdom has fully come on earth. I think it is high time for Christians to have a more adequate theology of peacemaking, rather than seeking justification for participating in more wars. I may be wrong about this, but if so, I want to err on the side that I see the Savior took for he is the one who believed that there were many things worth dying for, but nothing worth killing for. Indeed, he believed that killing violated the values that were worth dying for.

## Spiritual Meditations
### "War's Wisdom"

- Lectio Divina: Matthew 5:1–11

- Intercessory prayer paves the straightest path to loving others. William Law once said, "There is nothing that makes us love a man so much as praying for him; and when you can once do this sincerely for any man, you have fitted your soul for the performance of everything that is kind and civil toward him."[15] We cannot love others—especially our enemies—if we do not enter into prayer on their behalf. Call to mind a specific person or place you have trouble thinking of with love. Commit to pray for this person or place from this day forward and see how God changes your anger into compassion, your rage into tenderness.

- Meditate on the mandates that Jesus gives to us in Matthew 5:1–11. Let your meditations lead you into a time of concentrated prayer that God would do the work of this Word in your life.

### Thoughts for Further Reflection

*"[I]f I am going to err, I should err on the side of love not hate, peace not war, forgiveness not vengeance, because at the end of the day it is those qualities which will endure and prevail one day when the kingdom has fully come on earth."*

Ben Witherington III

*"Intercessory prayer might be defined as loving our neighbor on our knees."*

Charles Brent

---

15. Law, William. *Selections from a Serious Call to a Devout and Holy Life*. San Francisco: Harper Collins Publishers, 2005, 92.

*Pentecost*

*"Compassion is the sometimes fatal capacity for feeling what it is like to live inside somebody else's skin. It is the knowledge that there can never really be any peace and joy for me until there is peace and joy finally for you, too."*

Frederick Buechner

*"The most eloquent prayer is the prayer through hands that heal and bless. The highest form of worship is the worship of unselfish Christian service. The greatest form of praise is the sound of consecrated feet seeking out the lost and helpless."*

Billy Graham

### Personal Ponderings on "War's Wisdom"

The late Trappist monk Thomas Merton was passionate about peace and unity. Much of his thoughts centered around an overwhelming conviction that we, as humans, are interconnected. He understood deeply that brokenness anywhere must mean brokenness within ourselves. We must become one with our brothers and sisters in their woundedness and brokenness. If we really believe we are one body, we cannot afford to be divided against each other or the world itself. Merton's words capture this far better than mine ever could. I leave you with his thoughts:

> "Compassion teaches me that my brother and I are one. That if I love my brother, then my love benefits my own life as well, and if I hate my brother and seek to destroy him, I seek to destroy myself also . . . Hate itself is the seed of death in my own heart, while it seeks the death of the other. Love is the seed of life in my own heart when it seeks the good of the other . . .
> 
> Violence rests on the assumption that the enemy and I are entirely different: the enemy is evil and I am good . . . But love sees things differently. It sees that even the enemy suffers from the same sorrows and limitations that I do. That we both have the same hopes, the same needs, the same aspiration for a peaceful and harmless human life. And that death is the same for both of us. Then love may perhaps show me that my brother is not really my enemy and that war is both his enemy and mine. War is *our* enemy. Then peace becomes possible."[16]

(JNH)

16. Merton, Thomas. *Essential Writings.* Maryknoll, NY: Orbis Books, 2003, 114.

# The Living Legacy

## THE MAZE

*Voice One—The Conscience*

You don't get there sooner
Running faster in that direction,
It only ruins your temper
Your color and complexion.

*Voice Two—The Emotions*

If you can't remember
Whether you've been here before
I fear you'll never find
The exit or the door.

*Pentecost*

*Voice Three—The Will*

You grow weary of the game
You grow wary of the claim
Cause all paths look the same,
And no one is to blame.

*Voice Four—The Mind*

Did you take the trouble
To think the path through,
Before you even started,
Before you turned blue?

*Voice One*

Are you going round in circles,
Retracing your selections,
Has it occurred to you,
To ask for directions?

*Voice Two*

Every turn you take,
Every move you make,
Every path you forsake,
Could be a mistake.

*Voice Three*

Some are not phased
By a complex maze,
It doesn't take days,
Or leave you amazed.

# The Living Legacy

*Voice Four*

Seeing the end from the beginning,
Shows you which way to go,
If only you'd had the foresight,
To start off quite slow.

*Voice Two*

And now it's getting dark,
And all the noises gone,
Should I just stop and rest,
Or should I be moving on?

*Voice Five*

'My Word is a lamp unto your feet,
And a light unto your path'

BW3
July 17, 2007

## THEOLOGICAL MUSINGS

We've all seen the commercials where a person is in a store and there are two voices in competition in the man's poor head—one telling him to buy, the other to abstain, or one telling him to be good, the other to indulge. Sometimes voice one is depicted as a little devil, the other as a little angel. This poem attempts to portray the paralyzing nature of being deeply conflicted and having multiple voices enticing one to do this, that or the other. What I have tried to show is that the mind and the feelings aren't the only voices in the house. There is also the will and the conscience as well.

It is interesting that the New Testament concept of conscience doesn't just involve a sort of policeman of the brain always alerting you to when you are about to do something wrong. No the Greek word often translated 'conscience' could just as well be translated 'consciousness' and at its most basic level refers to awareness of moral realities, both good and evil. In the New Testament the conscience is said to be a faculty that approves as well as disapproves, confirms as well as denies, permits, and well as prohibits. It is clear however that the New Testament writers could never have offered up the advice "let your conscience be your guide" for there is a deep conviction on the part of the New Testament writers that even the human conscience is fallen and tends to be self-serving. There is need for an outside voice, that can speak clearly and shed light on the situation.

C. S Lewis once bemoaned that he was unable to crawl one inch outside his mortal skin, by which he meant he couldn't escape his own solipsism the fact that everything he thought and felt was filtered through his own limited point of view. This is why at the end of the poem I have brought in the concept of revelation which can break through our cloud of unknowing and reveal not only what is true about ourselves, however painful that revelation may be, but also give us light for the path so we can see which way we ought to travel.

The ancient Jews used the verb 'to walk' to refer to the moral life of a believer—they are to walk not in the ways of the flesh, but according the fruit of the Spirit and the guidance of the Word. What penetrates the maze of voices in the head, and makes sense of life is God's Word, both as external guide, but also as implanted Word nurtured by the Spirit. Instead of being a maze, one is amazed how clear one's thoughts can become and how obvious it can be which path to follow when one listens to 'the still small voice' of God speaking order out of chaos, direction out of wandering, a plan instead of frantic running about, looking for the way out. The question is, which voice will we listen to when we are lost in the maze of life, and will we make the mistake of only listening to an external voice as a last resort, when we are exhausted, and have exhausted other options?

## Spiritual Meditations

### "The Maze"

- Lectio Divina: Psalm 119:105–112; Isaiah 26:3–8
- The discipline of study helps to renew our mind and refocus our energy on the abundant life in Christ and off of the exhausting life the world says we need. Spend some time renewing your mind by studying God's Word this week. Choose a book of the Bible (consider Esther, Hosea, or one of the Epistles) to study. Take notes and reflect upon how these stories/letters might inform your own journey.

- Fast from worry this week. This may seem a strange suggestion at first, but when we consider the power that worry has in our lives to keep us from truly walking with God, we will recognize the need for such. Commit a passage of Scripture to memory that deals directly with worry or stillness of soul (Psalm 46:10a, Philippians 4:6–7, etc.) and call it to mind each time your mind is given to worry. Your mind will be transformed and renewed through this exercise.

## Thoughts for Further Reflection

*"The Ancient Jews used the verb 'to walk' to refer to the moral life of a believer—they are to walk not in the ways of the flesh, but according to the fruit of the Spirit and the guidance of the Word."*

Ben Witherington III

*"Going home is a lifelong journey . . . As we walk home we often realize how long the way is. But let us not be discouraged. Jesus walks with us and speaks to us on the road. When we listen carefully we discover that we are already home while on the way."*

Henri Nouwen

*"He . . . is the devout man who lives no longer to his own will, or to the way and spirit of the world, but to the sole will of God, who considers God in everything, who serves God in everything, who makes all parts of his common life parts of piety by doing everything in the name of God and under such rules as are conformable to His glory."*

William Law

## Personal Ponderings on "The Maze"

Witherington speaks a word of peace into the chaos that is our life in this poem and theological musings. "What penetrates the maze of voices," he writes, "and makes sense of life is God's Word." God can change our wandering to wonder and bring order where once there was chaos. This does not mean that we are headed for a life of ease and bliss, but one of abundance and joy in all circumstances.

*Pentecost*

We do not experience inner peace and abundant life because of our unwillingness to truly follow Jesus. We want a life of ease and self-satisfaction. We seek after pleasure and get lost because we crave a life of personal fulfillment and worldly success. This is why life becomes for us an unending, frustrating maze. Stan Gaede challenges this in his book *An Incomplete Guide to the Rest of Your Life*. Read and reflect upon his ruminations and consider where you might fall in his words. May his words convict and challenge you as they have me.

> "You know, we say we are followers of Jesus Christ, and yet I fear that we crave a life almost in opposition to the one he lived. We want what's easy; he chose what's hard. We want life for ourselves; he chose to give his life for others. We want approval for our own deeds; he chose to do the deeds of his father in heaven.
>
> Jesus says to take up our cross and follow him and he will give us life. Not easy life . . . but abundant life. Not painless life . . . but life worth living. Not joy just for today . . . but forever. With him."[17]

(JNH)

---

17. Gaede, Stan. *An Incomplete Guide to the Rest of Your Life*. Downer's Grove, IL: InterVarsity Press, 2002, 124–25.

# Kingdomtide

*The Dimming of the Light*

### THE WORD'S WORTH

Spoken into being
The world from the word
Silence starts nothing
The void absurd.

His word was action
Not null or annulled
The darkness divided
His light not dulled.

The word became story
Symbol and sign

## The Living Legacy

Metaphor and meaning,
Salvific design.

But the story was tragic
The plot past belief
The Creator rejected
His word came to grief.

The word seemed to falter
Its laws disobeyed
Its prophecy left dangling
Its promises mislaid.

But the word became flesh
His word was his bond
He fulfilled it himself
He came and was gone.

He disciplined disciples
He crucified sin
He passed on the story
The word born again.

Alpha, Omega
From first word to last
The living word creates
Future from past.

Light from darkness
Life from the grave
The New Testament story
Continues to save.

## THEOLOGICAL MUSINGS

Kingdomtide is perhaps the least familiar of the church seasons. It is a time to contemplate some of the major features of the sacred story and particularly the nature of God's divine saving reign on earth—God's Dominion or Kingdom. One place to start such discussions is by focusing on God's Word.

Sometimes less is more. Ben Jonson the great English writer once said 'perspicuity is the chiefest virtue of a style.' Clarity and brevity are important when one is conveying the truth, especially when one is in an emergency situation and one needs to be brief. In a modern world full of words, there has been a devaluation of the precious nature of the word. Sometimes we say "his word is his bond" and this is often said as if we are surprised when someone keeps their word. But when we are dealing with the Word, and it is God's, we need to have a clear sense that God means what God says and vice versa. Furthermore, God's word is an action. When God speaks, things happen, like for instance the coming into being of the whole of creation.

But this poem is not just about the power of God's Word, it is trying to explore the nature of the relationship between Word and sacred story, a complex matter indeed. Salvation is not just about God's pronouncements or God's actions but both, which make up the theological substance of sacred story. Stories have plots, characters, developments, climaxes, denouements, endings. And God's Word is not merely the catalyst or commentator on the story, it is in fact, in the person of Jesus, an actor in the story. In fact the Word who became flesh is the most important actor in the story. He's the one who dramatically turns the story in a new and proper direction so there will be a satisfactory ending. This Word not merely acts in the story, he is the major determiner of its outcome. As it turns out, God not merely gets the first word, God gets the last word as well. It is much like the sign I saw on the highway the other day. It said at the top in bold letters- "God is Dead"—Nietzsche. Directly under this it said "Nietzsche is dead."—God.

Yet it would be true to say that when Jesus came into the world, he was not merely acting out a pre-ordained script. Yes, there is a sense in which at various junctures he sought to fulfill Scripture, even fulfill all righteousness, but no his every move was not scripted. There were things that happened to Jesus that he surely did not expect. For instance, when the woman with the long term flow of blood touched the hem of his garment, Jesus asked "Who touched me?" Since Jesus' life was not a charade, what he meant by this was "Who touched me?" He had neither expected, nor did he know who had suddenly touched the tassels on his garment. He asked for information. The Incarnation among other things means that Jesus assumed human limitations of time, space, knowledge and power. He asked honest questions. He swam through the same sea of possibilities and temptations we all face. His interactions with other human beings were genuine and much hung in the balance not only for the others whose lives he touched, but also for his own life. The story of his life developed on the fly, it was not all pre-scripted or prescribed.

And we need to bear in mind that sin always is against God's word and will, it's a violation of how God wants the story to go. Jesus asks his disciples to pray for the coming of the kingdom on earth and for God's will to be done on earth for the very good reason that it often is not done on earth. Jesus operated in a world full of contingencies, and yet also a world in which God has plans and acts. Both things are true. Jesus was both an actor in the drama and an enactor of the intended drama as well such that the intended future is created out of the past and present. God indeed works all things together for good for those who love God, but sometimes this involves weaving together the good and the less good for not all things are good in themselves.

God, as it turns out, is a performance artist who enters into his own work and steers it in certain directions. He is not really a maker of pre-fab paint by numbers kits which we get to fill in on the basis of the instructions given and the paint provided. If our painting of our scenes was really pre-determined, then it is hard to explain why we have so many instructions in the training manual (called the Bible) that remind us over and over again to paint inside the lines! Robots on the assemble line neither need nor can respond to such instructions. But we do need them if responding to the Word, and recognizing its worth is something we must do freely and personally.

## Spiritual Meditations

### "The Word's Worth"

- Lectio Divina: Psalm 33
- In his theological reflections on this poem, Witherington writes that in our "modern world full or words, there has been a devaluation of the precious nature of the Word." This could not be truer. Our lives are saturated with words and noise, so much so that words are losing their value. Spend some time in silence this week in your home and/or your workplace. Speak when necessary, but allow yourself to listen more than speak when you can. Journal about this experience

- or share with someone else at the week's end about the joys and difficulties you encountered along the way.
- Commit to pray that God would show you the power of His Word and your own words this week. Ask God to reveal to you in new ways the power of His Word in your life and the lives of the people around you. Spend part of your prayer time asking God also to show you—good and bad—the power of words in your own life.

### Thoughts for Further Reflection

*"God's word is an action. When God's speaks, things happen . . . "*
Ben Witherington III

*"Whatever we do and wherever we go, let us stay close to the words of Jesus. They are words of eternal life."*
Henri Nouwen

*"Anything that forces you into the presence of Christ and into an openness to His Word will make a dramatic difference in your Christian life. He positions Himself right in the middle of our lives so we can look at Him and talk to Him everyday. He wants to tabernacle in us."*
Dennis Kinlaw

### Personal Ponderings on "The Word's Worth"

In order to be people through whom God can speak, we must first allow ourselves to be spoken to by God. If we want to be living illustrations of His Word, we must first be informed by it. Henri Nouwen speaks of this very thing in his book *The Living Reminder*. Nouwen writes of the necessity of being a people of "living faith," a faith that recalls what God has done in the past, what He is doing in our present and what He will do in the future. The key to this is to "become good storytellers again."[1] This is something we can do only when we immerse ourselves in God's Word and become a part of the greater Story.

---

1. Nouwen, Henri J. M. *The Living Reminder*. New York: The Seabury Press, 1981, 65.

> "How then can we be spiritual people through whom God's divine counselor and guide can become manifest? If we really want to be living memories, offering guidance to a new land, the word of God must be engraved in our hearts, it must become our flesh and blood. That means much more than intellectual reflection. It means meditating and ruminating on God's Word—chewing it... day and night. In this way the Word of God can slowly descend from our mind into our heart and so fill us with the life-giving Spirit."[2]

As Christians we are a people who are called to take the message of the Word into the world. This is an impossible task if we have not first been transformed by the Word ourselves. Nouwen writes that "meditation on God's Word is indispensable if we want to be reminders of God and not of ourselves, if we want to radiate hope and not despair, joy and not sadness, life and not death. Since the greatest news is that the Word has become flesh, it is indeed our greatest vocation and obligation to continue this divine incarnation through daily mediation on the Word."[3]

(JNH)

---

2. Ibid., 68.
3. Ibid., 69.

*Kingdomtide*

## THE TEST

The dust of the earth,
The sand by the shore,
The stars in the heavens
Descendants galore.

'Abraham, Abraham
Where are you?'

'At your service,
What may I do?'

'Take your son
Beloved Isaac,

And then, in sacrifice
Offer him back'

The knife in his hand
The fire by his side,
The brush on the back
A son set to die.

The promise hanging
By a mere thread,
Sacrifice the son,
The promise is dead.

'Father, Father
Where's the lamb?'

'The Lord will provide
The Great I am'

Tied him to the altar
Reached out his hand
The knife blade glistened
God shouted —'ABRAHAM'!

'Here am I'
He replied.

'Withdraw your hand,
God's satisfied'

The fear of the Lord
The font of insight,
On the mountain of God
You'll see respite.

The stars in the heavens
The sands by the shore
God keeps promises,
Who asks for more?

> For Bill
> December 16, 2007

## THEOLOGICAL MUSINGS

THIS IS THE SECOND poem in this collection that deals with Gen. 22 and the near sacrifice of Isaac but this poem is dealing with a very different issue indeed. Instead of a comparison between Isaac' and Jesus' story, here I am dealing with the tension between promise and test. On the one hand God had promised Abraham descendants as numerous as the grains of sand on the seashore and God had thwarted Abraham's attempts to enact a self-fulfilling (or do it yourself) promise by having a child with someone other than Sarah. Abraham failed that test, but in Gen. 22 he passed the test in question.

This story reminds me so very much of the story Corrie ten Boom told frequently of her conversation with her father about what to do if the Nazis came to the door asking if any Jews were present in the house. In fact the answer to the question was yes, but to reply in the affirmation would cost Jews their freedom, and indeed potentially their lives. Corrie's father responded to her question by asking Corrie—"When do I give you the ticket for the train? Weeks in advance, or right before you get on the train?" Corrie replied that it was the latter. "Exactly," said her father "so you will use it for what it was intended for and not lose it." Similarly, God provided the lamb at the crucial juncture when Abraham was raising the knife to take Isaac's life. Corrie's father was suggesting that God would provide her the proper words when the time arrived. As it happened, the time did come, but before then Corrie's father had asked the Jews hiding in his basement if they would be willing to become honorary Christians for a time, or 'friends of Jesus.' They gladly said yes. So when the Nazis came calling Corrie was able to respond "there are only friends and servants of Jesus in this house" when asked. In the hour of need, the Lord will provide.

But it may well be asked about either of these stories, why does God deliberately put us to the test? So that we will have to prove our faith is genuine? So we will be forced to trust God's word of promise? So that we will learn the lesson Paul spoke of in 1 Cor. 10 when he assured "God will not allow you to be tested past your power to endure?" The truth is, any and all of these questions could be answered yes, but a more important clue to what is going on in such testing and trying episodes in life is shown by Rom. 5.3—"we know that suffering produces perseverance, perseverance, character, and character, hope."

Would Abraham abandon the promise and his hope of having a legitimate son and heir by Sarah? Would the test reveal his failings, or show that his character had been and was being strengthened by the whole ordeal? Gen. 22 comes at almost the end of the cycle of Abraham stories and it serves as something of a climax, for here, unlike various occasions in the past Abraham obeyed, and passed the test, though it was a severe one. This story gives us hope because despite his previous failings, God still kept testing and strengthening Abraham and he finally was refined so that it could be said of him not only in Gen. 12, but also in Gen 22—"Abraham trusted God, and it was reckoned to him as righteousness."

## Spiritual Meditations

### "The Test"

- Lectio Divina: Romans 5:1–5
- M. Robert Mulholland reminds us in his book *Invitation to a Journey* that the "essence of fasting is the separation of ourselves from something in order to offer ourselves in greater measure to God."[4] God

---

4. Mulholland, M. Robert. *Invitation to a Journey: A Road Map for Spiritual Formation.* Downer's Grove, IL: InterVarsity Press, 1993, 118.

calls us to fast to shift us from "dependence upon God's gifts and enable us to become dependent upon God alone."[5] Consider in prayer what God might be calling you to lay down for a season (this may be for days, weeks, months, etc.) and begin your fast.

- The story of Abraham and Isaac is a story of surrender and sacrifice. It is also a story of God's blessing of Abraham's trust, faith, and righteousness. In prayer we simply offer ourselves to God in a like way. In our prayers we surrender our own will and lay down our plans on the altar. Use all or part of your prayer time this week talking to God about the areas in your life where you need to more fully surrender and lay things down at His altar. Be careful to listen to what God might be saying to you and commit to act on what you hear.

### Thoughts for Further Reflection

*"In the hour of need, the Lord will provide."*

Ben Witherington III

*"The life of faith is not a life of mounting up with wings, but a life of walking and not fainting. It is not a question of sanctification; but of something infinitely further on than sanctification, of faith that has been tried and proved and has stood the test."*

Oswald Chambers

*"My Lord and my God, take from me everything that keeps me from reaching You. My Lord and my God, give me everything that will bring me close to You. My Lord and my God, take me away from myself and give me to You."*

Nikolaus von der Flue

*"Faith never knows where it is being led,
but it loves and knows the One Who is leading."*

Oswald Chambers

---

5. Ibid., 119.

*Kingdomtide*

## Personal Ponderings on "The Test"

The scene from Genesis 22 that this poem and theological musings recalls is a difficult one to grasp. We are fixed upon the part of the story where Isaac is bound to the altar, the "tension between promise and test." Why would God ask this of Abraham? What must Abraham and Isaac have been thinking in the midst of it all? We do not know the answer to the latter question, but the Word itself provides us the answer to the former.

A close reading of Genesis 22 and other passages that speak of this scene reveal to us a God who will ask us to lay anything down which hinders us from walking in step with Him. At first glance, we look at this story and are filled with fear. We see a God who just wants us to give up things for no apparent reason and we wonder what He will ask of us. Oswald Chambers speaks of this in his classic work *My Utmost for His Highest*. He writes, "God nowhere tells us to give up things for the sake of giving them up. He tells us to give them up for the sake of the only thing worth having . . . life with Himself."[6]

Chambers writes of the journey of Abraham and Isaac in Genesis 22 as the "supreme climb," one which demanded deep conviction and confidence from a man who had shown himself to be lacking both previously (see Genesis 16). This time Abraham's faith proved much more steadfast and sure, and God took him "through an ordeal which [brought him] out into a better knowledge of Himself." [7] In faith, Abraham showed his preparedness to do whatever God asked of Him. If we "will remain true to God, God will lead [us] straight through every barrier into the inner chamber of the knowledge of Himself," our task is to trust.[8]

(JNH)

---

6. Chambers, Oswald. *My Utmost for His Highest*. Uhrichsville, OH: Barbour & Company, Inc., 1963, 8.

7. Ibid., 84.

8. Ibid.

The Living Legacy

## THE GREAT PHYSICIAN

They call him 'great physician'
And surely it is so
He always had that healing touch
Was always in the know.

Thru countless hours and countless trials
He came and prayed and touched
He left them in a better place
He loved them all so much.

God only knows the sacrifice
The healer must endure.
To help a suffering world survive
To find the sick a cure.

Thru fevers, aches, and pains so deep
The end seems close at hand
The healer never gives up hope
He knows the son of man.

The human doctor knows as well
All lives are in God's hands
It takes great love from God above
To make the cripple stand.

Somewhere up there in heaven's realm
The singing starts to swell
They're praising all the doctor's deeds
They're singing 'all is well.'

They're saying how he pays the price
So others could live on
His 'mark' is always on their lives
And never will be gone.

    March 21, 2006

*Kingdomtide*

## THEOLOGICAL MUSINGS

ONE OF THE PERSONS I have most admired for most of my life was our family pediatrician from my home town, Dr. Marcus Aderholdt. He was indefatigable and seemed to always be there when we had a health crisis of one sort or another. Yes, he made house calls as well. He was one of my father's very best friends over a long lifetime. Even when I was away at college, and long since out of the realm of a children's doctor Dr. Mark would always take my health questions and take an active interest in me and my well being. He would spend many long hours researching a medicine that might help me, or whether this sort of surgery was advisable for me. He would consult with other doctors in a B.C. age (by which I mean Before Computers). It was not hard for me to believe there was a Great Physician when I had always been treated by a scale model who was himself a great physician. But there is something different about The Great Physician.

The Great Physician was not merely a healer who brought the cure, he was the cure. Remember when he told Martha not merely "I give the resurrection" but rather "I am the resurrection and the life"? An ordinary doctor can give treatment, and hope the medicine or surgery works. Mostly he is counting on the body's own healing powers and ability to respond to stimulants that aide healing. Jesus however didn't need medicines or magic, he could simply heal. And it was not just merely spiritual healing or just merely physical healing he offered, but the whole package. When Shakespeare's Macbeth lamented "who can minister to a mind diseased" it was clear he had never met the Great Physician who even forgave sins and healed guilty consciences. And it is important to stress that Jesus did not do healings as a public relations stunt or to increase his following. He did them as acts of compassion.

Reg Mallett is a British Methodist lay person who has been a doctor and he tells the following story. It seems that an amazing cure for a major malady hit the front page of the Times and was credited to a well known medical figure who had a laboratory where many researchers were looking for cures. Dr. Mallett says that when the news came out, the 'great man' was interviewed about the matter and he was surprisingly vague as to how he had found the cure. This aroused suspicions and so one reporter went to the lab himself and began to ask a bunch questions. He was pointed to a researcher off in one corner of the lab staring into a microscope. The reporter asked the man—"Was it actually you who discovered this amazing wonder drug?" "Yes," said the man, "C'est moi." The reporter scratched his head and said 'Well, doesn't it bother you that your boss is taking the credit and may well get all sorts of awards for this discovery?" " No," said the man, "It doesn't matter who gets the credit, what matters is who gets the cure."

This story reminded my of the story in John 9 about the man born blind whom Jesus healed. Jesus did not wait around for the man to discover who Jesus was, he simply healed the man and went on to the next thing he needed to do. It was often thus in Jesus' ministry. He wasn't interested in taking credit, he was interesting in handing out cures. How rare it is in our age to see this approach, an age where most people are so litigious when someone steals another's supposed original idea about this or that. And yet the story Reg Mallett told reminds us that there are still people more concerned for the right things than for their own career enhancement. The question is, are we such persons? The Great Physician wants to know.

## Spiritual Meditations

### "The Great Physician"

- Lectio Divina: John 9:1–12
- Confession can be one of the most freeing disciplines for us. As we confess our sins to God we are freed to be the people that God desires for us to be. Our lives are opened up through confession in a way not possible otherwise. Use your time of confession and prayer this week to admit to God where you have sought your own gain over the advance of the kingdom. Ask God to give you humility and strength to be wholly and completely available to His will and not just your own.
- Consider the healing that Jesus and the disciples did during their day and all the many miracles across the centuries since. Spend some time worshipping God with a grateful heart. Recall those miracles and healings that have touched your own life in some way and simply thank the Lord for His continued presence in your life.

*Kingdomtide*

## Thoughts for Further Reflection

*"The Great Physician was not merely a healer who brought the cure, He was the cure."*

Ben Witherington III

*"Jesus did not do healings as a public relations stunt or to increase His following. He did them as acts of compassion."*

Ben Witherington III

*"You may call God love, you may call God goodness, but the best name for God is Compassion."*

Meister Eckhart

*"He became what we are that He might make us what He is."*

Saint Athansius

## Personal Ponderings on "The Great Physician"

We are unwilling to admit it, but we are a self-important people. We want credit for what we have done for others, even if only unconsciously. Jesus was not like this. He brought healing wherever He went, whether physical, emotional or spiritual. Yet he rarely stayed around long after any healing or miracles took place. He did so because He knew He was not here for Himself. He came as the Compassionate One to show the depths of God's love and power in our lives.

In the devotional book *Bread for the Journey*, Henri Nouwen speaks beautifully of Jesus compassion. He writes, "The great paradox of Jesus' life is that He, whose words and actions are in no way influenced by human blame or praise but are completely dependent on God's will, is more 'with' us than any other human being."[9] Jesus shows He is with us in the personal way he approaches each individual and crowd to which he brings healing and wholeness. We read that he is moved with compassion and

---

9. Nouwen, Henri J. M. *Bread for the Journey*. San Francisco: HarperCollins Publishers, 1997, May 21.

that he even weeps with us. We learn in Luke that everyone who touched him was healed and empowered (Luke 6:19).

Jesus' deep and abiding connection with the Father and His will enabled the same sort of connectedness with us. Such an intimate connection with the Father of Compassion could only call forth a compassionate life. I leave you with these final thoughts from Nouwen on Jesus' compassion. May we seek to abide in Christ the way He abides in God the Father, knowing that such a connection can bring healing and wholeness to a hurting people.

> "Jesus' compassion, his deep feeling-with-us, is possible because his life is guided not by human respect but only by the love of his heavenly Father. Indeed, Jesus is free to love us because He is not dependent on our love."[10]

(JNH)

---

10. Ibid.

### SETTLED

Clodhoppers and sodbusters
Creeping across the plains,
Finding their own domain,
Praying each week for rain,
Settled.

Thrill seekers and risk takers
Pushing the envelope
Racing up the slope
Until they no longer coped
Settled.

Mate seekers and date seekers
Combing the internet
Deciding to hedge their bets
Tired of not finding yet
Settled.

## The Living Legacy

Politicos and Pac Men
Always testing the wind
Always prepared to bend
Whatever it takes to win
Settled.

Lawyers and Litigants
Suing to get their way
Heedless of what they pay
Until the judgment day
Settled.

Sports stars and movie stars
Shining in media's light
Getting their image right
Stylin' both day and night
Settled.

Teachers and preachers
Thinking they know it all
Ignoring verity's call
Pushed up against the wall
Settled.

Pastors and ministers
Envisioning great success
Placing themselves under stress
Never confront or confess
Settled.

'Enter through the narrow gate; for the gate is wide and the way is broad that leads to destruction, and there are many who enter through it.'

>BW3
>December 4, 2007

*Kingdomtide*

## THEOLOGICAL MUSINGS

ONE OF THE THINGS I have found most 'unsettling' in spending a lot of time with ministers is their propensity to 'settle.' I don't mean 'settle' as in 'settle a law suit', or 'settle' in a particular town. I mean 'settling' for taking the path of least resistance in church crises, and 'settling' for doing less than what they vowed at their ordination, and 'settling' for re-treading various of their own sermons, not to mention using the sermons of others. And then there is the 'settling' involved in no longer attending to their own spiritual growth and maturation.

There are a lot of contributing causes for this problem, and in fact as the poem suggests, ministers are hardly alone as examples of those who have settled for less than God's highest and best for their lives. It happens in all walks of life. But why? Do people just give up the dream? Do they simply despair? Do they just get tired? Do they simply grow weary of not getting the outcome for which they were striving? I suspect that part of this is a result of the fact that our culture conditions us to want and expect everything 'immediately' or at least quickly. We have fast food, fast cars, fast tax refunds, quicky divorces, instant coffee—you get the picture. And so when we do not get the results we want rapidly, we just assume it's not going to happen, or we simply haven't been taught and conditioned to have the intestinal fortitude and character to persevere until we get the preferable outcome. In other words, all those teachings in the NT about perseverance being necessary in prayer, in faith, in suffering, in work and so on are too seldom trusted, or even tried in some quarters. But there are other cultural obstacles we have to overcome to avoid being a 'settler.'

Our culture is one preoccupied with appearance, and form over substance. We have commercials that keep stressing "image is everything." In such a culture people do not even realize that they are settling for less than their best when they settle for 'fame and fortune', for 'publicity and notoriety' and the like. You can tell a lot about a culture's values by what it is willing to pay the most for—entertainment, for example.

And then there is another factor. Life is seen as a negotiation in which one needs to make some compromises, some concessions, to get ahead in life, to get what one wants. Consider the whole legal system which is more about 'negotiating settlements' than finding the truth, or the peace process where compromise is assumed to be the essence of good diplomacy.

My point is that this whole approach in various spheres of life leads to a climate which assumes that nothing is sacred or absolute, it can all be bought or finessed, or at least a price can be put on it, and then it can be bargained for. We even have a term for what happens when ethics is approached in this way—'situation ethics' where the situation dictates the ethics, and not the other way around.

Then too the win at all costs attitude pervades such a culture and leads to cheating in numerous forms, including performance enhancing drugs. It was refreshing of late to see a Christian person named Andy Pettite, a baseball pitcher, not only admit he took steroids, but say in public that he needed to come clean and stop compromising his integrity, because someday he was going to have to answer for his behavior to the Judge. Indeed, so shall we all. And what all the examples in the poem have in common is they fail to see that there is an absolute standard by which they are being measured and they will one day be responsible for their life choices and behavior.

Settling for second best, or even a personal best, fortunately was not how Jesus lived his life. Imagine where we would be if Jesus had decided in the Garden of Gethsemane to 'settle' for the easy way out, and not take up the cup that his Father wanted him to drink. And it does not sound like 'settling' to me when Jesus suggests, "if any one would come after me, they must take up their crosses daily, and follow me." In fact nothing in the NT calls us to 'settle for 'whatever works for you.'

It is no accident that Peter in his wonderful letter we know as 1 Peter keeps reminding his Christian audience that they are not 'settlers' on this earth, they are rather resident aliens. And resident aliens cannot afford to settle, indeed they have no legal right to do so. They need to keep their eyes on the heavenly city to which they are journeying, all the while focusing on the task at hand. Settling for less than one's highest and best is settling for less than entering or inheriting the Kingdom, which is in the end, exchanging one's 'new' birth rite for a bowl of lentil soup. The one thing God doesn't want when we arrive at the door of the Kingdom for our character examination is to find a label on our chest that reads—"Warning: Contents may have settled during shipping."

*Kingdomtide*

## Spiritual Meditations

### "Settled"

- Lectio Divina: 1 Peter 1:13–25
- It has been said in countless ways by many different saints through the ages that we will not truly be content unless we are walking in God's will. Contentedness is much different than settling. Contentedness is simply acknowledging, as Saint Augustine once said, "Thou has made us for thyself and our hearts are restless until they find their rest in Thee." We are often unaware of our own settledness and complacency because habits are formed gradually over time. In order to know our own complacency, we must spend time in quiet contemplation and prayer. Carve out some time to be still before the Lord and consider where you might be settling instead of growing. Close your time(s) of contemplation with prayers for strength to press forward.
- We live in a world that longs for authentic, consistent, compassionate people. As Christians we are called to fill that role. We cannot hope to do this if we are content simply existing and standing still. It is easy for us to fall into such a pattern, but we mustn't! We must seek always to be who God has called us to be in a world that is hungry for Him. We need the help of others to accomplish this and to resist the urge to settle in our spiritual lives. Grab a friend (or a few) and spend some time in conversation about your own complacency. Be sure to encourage each other and find ways to "spur one another toward love and good deeds" (Hebrews 10:24) and resist the temptation to settle.

### Thoughts for Further Reflection

*"Resident aliens cannot afford to settle, indeed they have no legal right to do so. They need to keep their eyes on the heavenly city to which they are journeying, all the while focusing on the task at hand."*

Ben Witherington III

*"Settling for less than one's highest and best is settling for less than entering or inheriting the Kingdom . . . "*

Ben Witherington III

## The Living Legacy

*"A Christian who stays put is no better than a statue."*

Eugene Peterson

*"You cannot stay where you are and go with God."*

Henry T. Blackaby

### Personal Ponderings on "Settled"

This poem warns against our propensity to settle as Christians. It is so easy for us to get so involved in our lives or even in doing the work of the Lord that we fail to move forward in any way. This is so true and should not be so. And yet as I read this poem and the theological musings that followed, I found myself thinking of the paradox of our faith. We are called to go, to press on, to follow, and to dare mighty things for God. We are also called to abide, to stand firm, and be still. There is immeasurable tension in this.

Eugene Peterson offers helpful thoughts on this paradoxical part of our journey as Christians in his book *A Long Obedience in the Same Direction*. In his chapter on obedience, he talks of the need and desire of Christians to have a "sense of stability and the spirit of adventure." He begs the question, "How do we get the adult maturity to keep our feet on the ground and retain the childlike innocence to make a leap of faith?" Peterson asserts that we can and should have both a rooted and responsive faith. If we are to truly and actively live in the present and vision for the future, we must have "roots in the past to give obedience ballast and breadth."[11] We must connect ourselves to the past, live in the present, and press on toward the future.

A living faith is one that "develops a strong sense of continuity with the past and a surging sense of exploration into the future." Such faith is vibrant and alive. It is this kind of faith that the world needs to see, the kind that has "the strength to stand and the willingness to leap, and the sense to know when to do which."[12]

(JNH)

---

11. Peterson, Eugene. *A Long Obedience in the Same Direction*. Downer's Grove, IL: InterVarsity Press, 200, 163.

12. Ibid., 171.

*Kingdomtide*

## SEER'S TOWER

*(the other one in Chicago)*

From here I can see tomorrow,
From here I can see the shore,
From here I can see the future,
But I ask myself, what for?

Somewhere between curse and blessing
Between help and hindrance
Is knowing exactly what's coming
Preparing for the dance.

Would you want to know the outcome,
If it turned out you would lose?
Would you want to know the verdict,
If it's not what you would choose?

Would you want to know the future,
If it crushes those you love?
Would you want to know the future
If it's a vulture, not a dove?

But what if the future's not quite fixed
And there's still time for a change?
What if it's not all written in stone,
And hope's not out of range?

What if God only gives us glimpses
Of what will someday be,
But he let's us fill in the blanks
Between here and eternity?

What if we have a role to play
In the grander scheme of things,
What if we have at least some say,
In who will wear the rings?

What if God only reveals
Enough of the future today
To give us hope and encouragement

## The Living Legacy

Not removing the need to pray?

What if we see through a glass darkly,
And most of the objects aren't clear,
Things look closer in the mirror,
Than they actually are from here?

Pundits and prognosticators
The weather men of time,
Are often over-confident
Ridiculous, not sublime.

Take predicting the return of Jesus,
Many have boldly bet,
They all have one thing in common,
They've never been right—yet.

When you have that sort of failure rate
Reticence is required
Lest you be dubbed false prophet,
Your predictor's license expired.

The prophecies raise expectations
That God will see all things through
They don't encourage calculations,
Which tell God when's he's due.

Prophecy is not about calculation
Nor prognostication at all
Those are human preoccupations
Not part of the Almighty's call

Prophecy is about God's promise
That all will be well one day,
It does not tell us when or where
It's not for us to say.

Prophecy paints the big picture,
Of justice and mercy at last,
It does not give us the co-ordinates
It does not say how fast.

## Kingdomtide

There's a reason for this reticence
God's in control of time
He has not handed us the helm,
Only He knows the reason and rhyme.

Only he knows what is best for us,
Only he brings it all to pass
Only he knows where it's all going,
And how long it ought to last.

God will never make our lives
So we don't need to trust
He will never make his creatures
So that prayer is not a must.

We will always be his creatures
Who must rely on his loving care
I am sure he is tired of our asking
"Aren't we already almost there?"

When faith finally becomes sight,
And hopes are realized,
When the eschatological dust clears
And we see with new creation eyes

There will be one thing left standing
That we've been trusting all along,
A loving God's desire and ability
To finish his own love song.

The reason love is yet greater
Than faith or even hope,
Is because it endures forever
And enables us to cope.

Climb down from your own seer's tower
Place your life in the Father's hands,
For he always knows what's best for us,
And he gives what he commands.

## The Living Legacy

Stop writing fear-based fiction
It needs to be 'left behind'
It dishonors our loving Maker
Abandon's the faith-based design.

Someday we will see our Savior
Someday we will know, as we're known,
In the meantime stop playing God,
And leave the future alone.

When Christ returns let him find you,
Doing what he made us for,
Loving people into the kingdom,
Feeding and clothing the poor.

Inasmuch as you've done it unto the least of these,
You've done it unto the Lord,
Let him find you imitating his actions,
Not frightening the faithful, but bored.

Let him who runs read the writing
That's written on the wall,
'Take up your cross and follow me,
Sacrifice and serve them all.'

'Parting is all we know of heaven,
And all we need of hell'*,
Those who simply trust the Lord,
Will find that they've done quite well.

    July 20, 2007
    BW3
    * from E Dickinson
        —Poem 96, 'My Life Closed Twice . .

## Kingdomtide

### THEOLOGICAL MUSINGS

I MUST CONFESS AN irritation, a bee in my bonnet, so to speak. As a NT scholar I have enormous problems with the popular forms of Dispensationalism, and even the more scholarly approaches ('progressive Dispensationalism') leave me scratching my head. So yes, this poem is a critique of the LaHaye and Jenkins phenomenon called the 'Left Behind' series. In my judgment it is such a poor reading of Biblical prophecy and theology that it is very aptly titled— those books should be entirely 'left behind' if you really want to understand the nature of Biblical prophecy.

Of course a good deal of Biblical prophecy did not involve prediction or foretelling. Rather it involved forth telling, telling the truth about something in the present. Thus when the prophet Nathan confronted David about his sins involving Uriah and Bathsheba, he was revealing the truth about a past and present situation, not a future one. Then too, much of Old and New Testament prophecy when it is predictive deals with the near horizon, offering a message of relevance for the prophet's own immediate audience. It is really not until one gets into exilic and post-exilic prophecy, and it begins to morph into apocalyptic forms, that we begin to get more clear interest in the distant horizon, and what God ultimately has in view. And this is where the matter gets really interesting, because what happens is that prophecy about the distant horizon tends to be highly imagaic and metaphorical and poetic and even multivalent, especially in its apocalyptic forms.

If one compares for example the throne chariot vision in Ezekiel 1 and the similar one in Revelation 4 it immediately becomes apparent that the seer is not describing a reality literally. He keeps saying 'it was like . . . it was like . . . it was like' and he uses as big a metaphors and impressive language as he can find to describe what he saw. The very differences between Ezekiel 1 and Revelation 4 show the plastic and malleable nature of the images. Notice for example the difference in where the eyes appear in relationship to the wheels in each vision. The visions are similar, but not identical. This is of course because what is being described is a vision of God and his heavenly throne, and God is quite frankly grander than even our most creative efforts to describe the divine nature.

What is the function really of predictive prophecy about the more distant future, if it is not meant to reveal in detail exactly what will transpire down the road in literal terms? Firstly, it functions to reassure the audience that God is in control, and that in the end God's will, will be done on earth as it is in heaven. In particular, it reassures God's people that God will vindicate them and that justice and redemption will be accomplished in due course. Secondly, when such prophecy is referential, what it is meant to accomplish is to give the audience a big picture glimpse, from God's perspective of the future. Not the minute details, timing, and the like, but the character of the future. I like to put it this way—God reveals enough of the future to give us hope, but not so much that we do not have to live by faith, day by day.

And this brings me to my next point about the problems with prognostication. It involves a failure to live by faith. It involves an attempt to nail God and his plans down to a specific timetable and often even specific actions involving specific countries and persons, and quite frankly this reflects a failure to leave matters in God's hands. But alas for such attempts at specificity, they have all been wrong throughout church history. As it turns out Mr. 666 is not Stalin or Hitler or Saddam Hussein, or for that matter some future ruler of a supposedly united Europe. The anti-Christ image tells us what kind of person will vaunt himself against all things godly, but not who precisely that person will be. We must be content to know that the battle between good and evil will go on until the Lord returns and brings the matter to closure. To say more than this is to pretend to know more than the prophets were willing to reveal or than God intended his people to know. We walk by faith, not by sight.

Finally what most disturbs me about this whole approach to Biblical prophecy is that when it continually fails to tell the truth about the future, it calls into question the veracity of the church. It makes us all look like the gang who couldn't shoot straight, or get it straight. Why should the world believe us if our message no more corresponds with reality than the tabloid papers at the grocery counter checkout line? Perhaps it is time for us to realize that it is not the timing and details about Christ's second coming, but rather the unalterable fact of his return which should shape our view of the future. We must live in such a fashion that when he returns we will hear the words "well done good and faithful servant, inherit the Kingdom." The warriors that Gideon picked were not those who laid down their weapons and gulped the water from the stream, nor those who simply stared off into the distance, but rather those who got on with the task at hand, while still keeping one eye on the horizon. This also should be the posture of Christian saints awaiting the second advent of their King.

*Kingdomtide*

## Spiritual Meditations

### "Seer's Tower"

- Lectio Divina: 1 Corinthians 13
- Find a place where you can go and meditate on the poem "Seer's Tower." There is much to ponder and consider in this poem that demands more than just a quick reading. Read through the poem several times (aloud if you can) and allow yourself to gravitate toward words or phrases that stand out to you. Pray through those words and ask God what He might be trying to say to you through this poem and the specific words or phrases that grab your attention. Spend some time writing down your thoughts and prayers so that you can return to them.
- Study one of the passages in the New Testament where Jesus speaks of the second coming. You might consider a parable (Matthew 25:1–13, Luke 12:35–40, Luke 14:15–24, etc.) or another passage (Mark 13:32–37, 1 Thessalonians 5:1–11, etc.). Utilize whatever resources are available to you in your study, being careful only to consult commentaries after personal study and meditation.

### Thoughts for Further Reflection

*"God is, quite frankly, grander than even our most creative efforts to describe the divine nature."*

Ben Witherington III

*"God reveals enough of the future to give us hope, but not so much that we do not have to live by faith, day by day."*

Ben Witherington III

*"If we are going to be ready for Jesus Christ, we have to stop being religious and be spiritually real."*

Oswald Chambers

*"Rejoice in hope. He is our future."*

Dennis Kinlaw

# The Living Legacy

## Personal Ponderings on "Seer's Tower"

I once heard Dr. Witherington say something in a sermon that has been burned on my heart and in my mind ever since. He was speaking of that first Advent and the one to come and he said, "It is not the timing of the event that matters, but that God has a track record, and what Christ has promised, He will indeed one day perform . . . ." These words brought immeasurable encouragement to the heart of one who has fought a life-long battle with worry. The important thing we must rehearse and remember is that God has a history. That same God "has both the love and power to accomplish his aims" in our present and our future. This should give us an immeasurable hope and a confident faith.[13]

Witherington reminds us in this poem that our task in getting ready for the Advent yet to come is simply to be ready. Our attempts to definitively determine what it will all look like and when it will happen are futile at best. At worst, they are nothing more than adventures in missing the point. Eschatological study is fine and should be done, but our studies must not divorce us from the truth of all prophecy. As Witherington reminds us in his poem, "prophecy is not about calculation," it is concerned with "God's promise that all will be well one day."

As Christians we often get bogged down in what we do not know when we should be rehearsing what we do know. We know that God has a history of helping his people and that His promises are sure. We know that what he asks of us in preparation for what is to come is simply to be ready. To be ready and alert is simply to walk by faith and live by love, following the example of Christ in our everyday.

(JNH)

---

13. Witherington III, Ben. *Incandescence: Light Shed through the Word*. Grand Rapids: William B. Eerdmans Publishing Company, 2006, 27.

*Kingdomtide*

## THE TRUTHFUL PAIN—THE PAINFUL TRUTH

Pain
Like gravity,
Like love
Like all the prime movers
Of human behavior,
Cannot be found
Through surgical operation
Or empirical investigation,
And yet it is profoundly real.

To be sure, pain can be physically induced
And physically manifested.
But why do we say "my arm is in pain"
Rather than just there is a pain in my arm?
Could it be that pain is a larger category
And we know it?

And of course physical pain is on occasion
The least of our pains
Heartache may involve no physical pain.
Grief may have few physical manifestations
Love may produce an exquisite agony
When one is separated from the beloved,
But no doctor could find a physical source
Of this pain.

C. S. Lewis said that pain was God's megaphone
By which he shouts to get our attention.
It's a shame he must use such blunt instruments with us,
Yet it shows the length to which God will go
So we will focus on God.

And what can we say to the anesthesia culture
Which thinks no pain is all gain,
And the goal in life is to avoid it
At all costs. To insure against it,
Protect against it,
Prevent it, even at the cost of failing to do many
  important things.

## The Living Legacy

Had God wanted us to avoid all pain,
He would not have made us mortal in the first place,
Or given us nerve endings in places like fingers
So that even a small child knows
That pain means NO, "don't go there."
Or is a reminder— "you went there,
Though you were warned not to."

Pain reminds us
We live in a moral universe,
Where there are consequences for actions.
Pain reminds us,
We are not immortal just yet.
And yet, pain reminds us we are still alive.

Pain reminds us, that there is a state of normalcy
Which does not involve pain,
For pain itself is not inherently good.
To mask the pain,
Is to mask the truth
About some aspect of life.

Pain is not a disease which can be cured,
It is not merely a feeling,
Though it certainly involves feelings.
It is not something we should hope for,
Or desire, but it is also often something
We ought not to avoid.
Pain, like suffering has no inherent value
Or worth, save when worked together for good
By God.

The ultimate irony is—
We would be in an even bigger world of hurt,
(In view of our self-destructive tendencies),
Were it not for pain.
Pain can break the cycle of violence,
If its message is heard and heeded.

The cross is not merely
The example of God in pain,
Or God taking our pain,
But of God absorbing pain
Within the divine being
And transforming it into something redemptive.

For if redemption only comes through a death,
It only comes through pain,
A lot of pain,
Pain where God's Son cried out
About his own God forsakenness.

Thank God, pain was transcended
Not by a sedative,
Nor a masking agent,
But by a transformation of mortality
By means of resurrection of a body,
No longer subject to disease, decay, death.
Take pains to think about this truth.

BW3
November 17, 2005

## THEOLOGICAL MUSINGS

WHAT A BLESSING IT is to live in the age of modern medicine, most persons would say. And yet, and yet, modern medicine does as much to prolong the dying as it does to prolong the living. We are all mortal, and a part of mortal existence is pain, suffering, and eventually dying. This particular poem tries to present a balanced reflection on the issue of pain. There are some forms of religion which are almost entirely focused on the issue of the problem of pain and why a good God would allow it. Take for example Christian science, which is a 'mind over matter' religion, or put another way, suggests that pain and suffering are merely or at least mostly forms of cognitive dissonance which can be overcome by the right mental frame of mind and reference. The irony of course of this whole approach is that Mary Baker Eddy herself suffered horribly in a physical way.

So let us ask the question, why would a God of love allow there to be such pain, and consequent suffering in the world? Well let us consider for a moment what would happen to a small child that had mortal flesh, but no nerve endings in her finger tips? What would happen if there was no pain response when she placed her fingers on the hot burner on the stove? Would she not simply destroy her fingers altogether? Indeed she would. It seems then that pain provides a sort of early warning system that something is badly wrong.

I remember vividly when I began to have sharp pains in my gall bladder region many years ago. When I went to see my doctor, he said—"apparently you have not been listening to what your body has been telling you by that pain." He was right. I tried to ignore it, or mask the pain, or simply avoid ice cream and the like, but it was all to no avail. I was still hurting and something needed to be done. Should we see pain as a good thing? Well in one sense yes, if we want to avoid even greater suffering and premature mortality. Pain is not an inherent good, but it's a boundary defining thing, which helps us know when we have crossed some line. Like one of those electronic dog collars, pain gives us a freedom within certain limits, but lets us know when we have gone too far or are crossing a limit or a boundary that ought not to be crossed.

What happens when you mask pain, rather than make sure you check out its source? Well often enough this can lead to a person's entire demise. Of course when a person is already terminal, masking the pain is a good thing as it gives a person a little quality of life in their final days. And the same can be said about sedatives and pain pills to help one get over a temporary condition, such as a normal headache or when one is healing from surgery. It is interesting that healing hurts in ever so many cases, but healing is a good thing. Instead of leading to death it leads to a better quality of life. Perhaps the same can be said about the healing of the human heart and emotions. The process can be anguishing but helpful.

J. R. R. Tolkien used to talk about the difference between what he called a eu-catastrophe and simply a disaster. The former does indeed involve struggle and suffering and pain, but the purpose and the outcome are good. It is then a complex matter to be able to distinguish between pointless pain and suffering, and a pain through which comes gain, of various sorts. But the death of Jesus on the cross reminds us repeatedly that not all pain and suffering can be seen as a surd, or absurd, or without a reason or point. This then implies as well, that not all pain should be masked or avoided if we want to live well, and wisely, and even for a good length of years as well. As Lewis says, pain is indeed God's megaphone, and while this may be a sad truth, at the very least it ought to drive us into the arms of our Maker, rather than leading us to lament in Job like fashion.

## Spiritual Meditations

### "The Truthful Pain—The Painful Truth"

- Lectio Divina: 2 Corinthians 4:7–18
- Henri Nouwen writes that the heart of solitude is spending time "in the presence of our Lord with empty hands" on a regular basis.[14] It is far better for us to spend short, regular times in stillness and solitude than extended periods only every once in a while. "Simplicity and regularity are the best guides in finding our way," Nouwen writes. Examine your schedule and determine where you can spend ten minutes in solitude each day. Regular time spent in solitude will help you whether you are experiencing the pain and suffering spoken of in this poem or your heart and life are filled with joy. As you become faithful in the discipline of solitude in a specific time and space, your heart will become a place where God's peace and comfort reign wherever you are.[15]
- Intercessory prayer is an indispensable part of our lives as Christians. Bonhoeffer once wrote, "Intercession means no more than to bring [another] into the presence of God."[16] Call to mind people in your life who are presently experiencing great difficulty and suffering. Create some sort of daily reminder to intercede on their behalf, asking God for his peace, protection, and provision in their lives.

### Thoughts for Further Reflection

*"The death of Jesus on the cross reminds us repeatedly that not all pain and suffering can be seen as a surd, or absurd, or without reason or point."*

---

14. Nouwen, Henri. *Making All Things New*. San Francisco: Harper Collins Publishers, 1981, 76.

15. Ibid., 79.

16. Bonhoeffer, Dietrich. *Life Together*. San Francisco: Harper Collins Publishers, 1954, 86.

# The Living Legacy

## Ben Witherington III

*"Happiness and sadness may play havoc with our emotions, but once we learn that God dwells in darkness beneath the shifting surfaces of our souls, we know that that is where we must go to find him. There we will pray in peace and silence, attentive to the God who never changes."*

Brennan Manning

*"Christ invites us to remain in touch with the many sufferings of every day and to taste the beginning of hope and new life right there, where we live amid our hearts and pains and brokenness."*

Henri Nouwen

*"The heart is stretched through suffering, and enlarged. But O the agony of this enlarging of the heart, that one may be prepared to enter into the anguish of others! Yet the way of holy obedience leads out from the heart of God and extends through the Valley of the Shadow."*

Thomas Kelly

*"Are you asking God to give you life and liberty and joy? He cannot, unless you will accept the strain. Immediately you face the strain, you will get the strength."*

Oswald Chambers

## Personal Ponderings on "The Truthful Pain—The Painful Truth"

When we are walking through personal pain and suffering, our spiritual vision often fails. We find it difficult, if not impossible, to see God with us in this and all things. We fix our eyes on our circumstances instead of our God. We lose faith and we forget that God has promised to provide comfort and peace even in this.

Henri Nouwen explores the journey through suffering in his book *Turn My Mourning into Dancing*. He writes with the conviction that we cannot only survive, but thrive in the midst of sufferings. The journey begins with a recovery of faith. "Faith," writes Nouwen, "is the deep confidence that God is good and that God's goodness somehow triumphs."[17] This faith gives way to hope and hope to joy.

> "Hope does not mean that we will avoid or be able to ignore suffering, of course. Indeed, hope born of faith becomes matured and purified through difficulty. The surprise we experience in hope, then, is not that, unexpectedly, things turn out better than expected. For even when they do not we can still live with a keen hope. The basis of our hope has to do with the One who is stronger than life and suffering."[18]

Our vision will be restored as we walk in faith, trusting in the One who suffered all that we might live. "Faith opens us up to God's sustaining, healing presence. A person in difficulty can trust because of a belief that something else is possible. To trust is to allow for hope."[19] And our hope is not hollow and will not disappoint, for it is rooted in the God of Hope who is our Peace.

(JNH)

---

17. Nouwen, Henri J. M. *Turn My Mourning into Dancing*. Nashville: W. Publishing Group, 2001, 51.

18. Ibid., 53.

19. Ibid.

## The Living Legacy
## DISRUPTIVE GRACE

Shattering the smattering
Of calm I had created
Grace, a gratuity
Disrupted my day

Interrupting the ennui
I kept on feeling
An alien intruder
Stepped in my way.

Pacifying the pestering
Voice that kept nagging
I sought out a sanctuary
Any port in a storm.

Reluctantly resigned
To divine solicitation
The carols and bells
Beguiled me again.

Unbidden, unwanted
Joy overcame me
In spite of reluctance
Immersed once more.

Profoundly pregnant
Stuffed with the sacred
I wondered as I wandered
Out the back door.

Who sent out the signal
That lured and allured me
Called me and caught me
On that cold day?

A Father frantically calling?
A Son prodigally prodding?
A Spirited homing device?
GPS grace?

*Kingdomtide*

Or was it the familiar
Plaintive lament
Of a newborn child
Who was Heaven sent?

Some calls must be answered
Some cries must be heard
Some voices are insistent,
Especially the Word's.

BW3
December 12, 2006

## THEOLOGICAL MUSINGS

THIS IS A POEM of course which could be placed in the Advent section of our book, but it also suits a late fall placement as well, as we begin to prepare for the Advent season. There is something wrong with considering God and his grace an intrusion into the human sphere and our individual lives, and yet that is often how it seems to us. Sometimes we say things like 'life is what happens when we are making other plans', but sometimes it is not merely life, but God who intervenes. And of course the Bible is replete with stories of divine intervention over and over again, so why exactly is it that it catches us by surprise?

Well there are a lot of possible reasons, not the least of which is that our day to day focus is mostly on mundane things, not on God. Like a child playing with toys on the floor and ignoring all the adults standing around talking in the room, we seem to have a good capacity for ignoring the biggest things in our area when we want to concentrate on other things. If we are honest, sometimes we get so wrapped up in our own plans, and what we want to do, that the clarion call of God comes as not merely jarring, but as something of an annoyance. Remember the story of Moses and the burning bush? He did everything he could to bow out of being tapped as the person to go down to Egypt and confront Pharaoh. He definitely was saying "here I am Lord, take my brother"!

The feasting season, beginning with Thanksgiving and carrying on into Christmas reveals to us our level of tolerance for surprising interruptions, unwanted solicitations, annoying and intrusive relatives, and the like. And even though we know what's coming, we still find ourselves ill prepared to deal with it, and often not exhibiting the patience and focus needed to address what has come our way on such occasions.

One of the big problems with the feasting season is that not only does familiarity breed contempt, or at least mere tolerance of what is coming, but it breeds a numbness to the real encounters possible during such times. Sometimes I find that how I react to the coming of Christmas tells me a lot about where I am spiritually. If I am just going through the motions, or merely lamenting all the commercialism, how open am I really to receiving the Lord once more into my consciousness, my context, my inner sanctum? It is easy to understand how for some people the feasting season is the season they most dread and find depressing. It is the season that most indicates whether we are outsiders looking into the windows of God's world, or like mere shepherds we are occasional visitors to Bethlehem's manger, or whether we actually 'belong' in the house of the Lord at such times.

One thing that is clear to me—the Hound of Heaven is insistent. He keeps calling, keeps knocking, keeps intruding. But then wait a minute. Whose world is it anyway? And to whom do I belong? Am I not living on borrowed time, more specifically on God's time? So why should I ever think that my life is my own and that I should be able to deal with God on my own terms and time? That whole egocentric approach to God's overtures is precisely what this poem is suggesting we need to consistently program out of our thinking. Hopefully this Advent, we will make a better effort in that direction.

## Spiritual Meditations

### "Disruptive Grace"

- Lectio Divina: Jeremiah 29:10–14
- Confess to God where you have become so wrapped up in your own plans that you have abandoned His for you. Ask God for forgiveness for trusting in your own strength instead of His and for wisdom to see such patterns in your life. Continue your time of confession by praying for an open heart and mind to see and experience His overtures of grace along the path He has cleared for us.

*Kingdomtide*

- Gratitude and praise can work wonders in our spirit and our willingness to seek and follow the will of God. "Worship," writes Eugene Peterson, "is the primary and most accessible means we are given for orienting ourselves in the invisibilities, in God."[20] Begin this day by praying for an overwhelming attitude of worship and praise to color your day that the Invisible might be made visible around you. Go about your usual tasks, asking God to give you a clear view of His sacred presence in the mundane activities of your day.

### THOUGHTS FOR FURTHER REFLECTION

*"Sometimes it is not merely life, but God who intervenes."*
Ben Witherington III

*"[T]he Hound of Heaven is insistent.
He keeps calling, keeps knocking, keeps intruding."*
Ben Witherington III

*"The call of God is like the call of the sea.
No one hears it but the one who has the nature of the sea in him."*
Oswald Chambers

*"[O]pen up your heart to the riches of God's grace . . .
Simply trust everything into the hands of God,
be humble, and open up to His grace."*
Fénelon

*"The most important thing going on right now is what God is doing. The most important thing being said right now is something God is saying, marvelous things are being done and said right now. Look. Listen."*
Eugene Peterson

---

20. Peterson, Eugene H. *Subversive Spirituality*. Grand Rapids: William B. Eerdmans Publishing Company, 1997, 90.

## Personal Ponderings on "Disruptive Grace"

Opening our hearts to the riches of God's grace is a daily task. We must choose each morning to live for God and not for self, to bask in God's riches instead of seeking our own. It is this that Eugene Peterson writes about in his book *Subversive Spirituality*.

In the chapter entitled "Back to Square One: God Said," Peterson speaks of our need to "return to Square One for a fresh start as often as every morning, noon, and night."[21] We are human and, as such, prone to wander.

> "We are always beginners. We begin again. We hear Jesus say, 'Unless you turn and become like children, you will never enter the kingdom of heaven' (Matthew 18:3). And so we become as little children. We return to the condition in which we acquired subject permanence, God said. We go back to Square One. We adore and we listen."[22]

The reason for spiritual staleness and personal preoccupation in our lives is our unwillingness to begin again. The Christian life is about returning each day to "the place of wonder, the realization of infinity, and the worship of God."[23] To return to God each day is to listen and to respond. As Peterson put it, it is reminding ourselves that God speaks and tuning our ears to listen and obey anew each day.[24]

(JNH)

---

21. Ibid., 31.
22. Ibid., 30.
23. Ibid., 22.
24. Ibid., 23.

## CRAVEN IMAGE

When icon becomes idol
The image turns grave
With darkest deception
Convex turns concave.

Windows on heaven
The icon's true aim
If means becomes end
It's not quite the same.

But breaking the making
Iconoclasm's wrath
Is equally misguided
A mis-chosen path.

See through the icon
The larger design
Wineskins best function
To convey wine.

Sacred cows gilded
Become golden calves
We worship the image
Of things that we have.

Beauty without truth
The glass becomes stained
Discoloration
Verity strained.

Like art that is tainted
Like thoughts quite insane
Showers of blessings
Become Noah's rain

July 31, 2006

## THEOLOGICAL MUSINGS

I MUST CONFESS A love for icons. No I am not talking about sports heroes, or even persons of note. I am referring to the Christian art known as iconography. I have on my wall in my study two icons—a large one of the OT Trinity by Rubliev (the scene of the three angels dining with Abraham), and a smaller icon of Peter and Paul reconciled and embracing. The second of these especially is moving when one knows their stormy history and relationship.

Despite low-church Protestant protests, icons are not idols. Idolatry is the mistake of worshipping something less than God as God, whatever it may be. No Orthodox Christian who knows their theology of icons would ever make such a mistake. Icons are intended to be windows into heaven, not heaven itself, much less God. They are meant to help the worshipper's imagination be stimulated by the beauty and truth and love of God and look upward in their worship.

But sometimes of course, sadly even Christian worshippers mistake the means for the ends itself. And then unfortunately icons can be transformed in the imagination of the worshipper into some sort of magical talisman or supposed source of spiritual protection, power, healing and the like. But of course this does not happen just with icons. If one reads the Bible closely enough you discover that images of anything can become 'graven' ones, whether images of animals, birds, human beings, saints (including Mary), angels, if they are used and approached in the wrong manner. Golden calves are by no means the only form that idols can take. And what is at issue here is a violation of the creation order. Some 'thing', or some creature is worshipped or approached as if they were the Creator and could give or dispense things only the creator could dispense.

Notice at the very close of the book of Revelation the reaction of the angel when John of Patmos decides to venerate him and do obeisance for what he has revealed—"I fell down to worship at the feet of the angel who had been showing them to me. But he said to me 'Do not do it! I am a fellow servant with you and with your fellow prophets and of all who keep the words of this book. Worship God!!! [alone]" (Rev. 22.8–9). This is the persistent and insistent cry of the entire Bible—there is only one God, and that One alone is worthy of worship in all the universe and beyond. If even angels are not worthy of human worship, then certainly no human being is either, even exalted saints.

At the heart of Orthodox worship however is a belief in the communion of saints, by which I mean a belief that worship on earth is connected to worship in heaven. That is, we are all worshipping God together, whether above or below. Not only does God come down and inhabit our praise, the Orthodox theology suggests that the church militant and triumphant are one entity, and in worship our unity is most evident, resulting in both worship and communion, not only with God, but with the whole company of heaven.

Unfortunately, it is possible for any good and true and beautiful thing to be turned to a bad end, not merely mistaking the means for the ends, but even deliberately using the means for one's own anthropocentric ends, and this poem addresses this very point towards its conclusion. A good example of this would be the selling of faux holy relics, as some sort of source of blessing or protection. Is there anything wrong with revering what Christ did on the cross?—Of course not. Is there problem with wearing a cross as a sign of allegiance to the Lord?— Of course not. But when one uses the holy to manipulate people for one's own ends, it is the worst sort of sacrilege.

A good example of this phenomenon is depicted in the movie "There Will be Blood." There is a scene in this movie where the hard-bitten and truly self-centered oil man Mr. Plainview is coerced into a false confession (and a sizable donation to the Pentecostal church in the little Texas town where he is drilling for oil), by a scheming teenage evangelist who himself is a charismatic charlatan preying on people's spiritual weaknesses and vulnerabilities. Sacrament can so quickly turn into sacrilege in the wrong hands, with the wrong intent. Paul warns in 1 Cor. 11 that some have become sick and died because they partook of the Lord's Supper in an unworthy manner.

The encounter with the holy can be a sanctifying and purifying one, one that conveys grace. But in the wrong hands, and with the wrong hearts, it can have just the opposite effect or result. Think on these things.

## Spiritual Meditations

### "Craven Image"

- Lectio Divina: Psalm 95:1–6
- Using a Psalm as your guide, spend some time in worship.[25] You might rewrite and recite a Psalm as an act of worship. Consider using another medium (song-writing, art, poetry, etc.) to express your gratitude and turn your heart to God in worship and away from those things that divert your attention from Him.
- The discipline of simplicity is one that brings freedom from bondage. Richard Foster notes that it is this discipline that "brings joy and balance" to our lives.[26] It begins with an inward inventory of the heart. The experience of simplicity is only possible through examination and prayer. Spend some time in concentrated prayer, asking God to reveal to you the things you crave that are keeping you from Him. Ask God to awaken you to the idols in your life and help you to set "possessions in proper perspective."[27] The goal of simplicity is not simply the renunciation of otherwise good things, but "to seek the kingdom of God and the righteousness of his kingdom *first*."[28] Make this your prayer today.[29]

---

25. Psalm 29, 96, 100, etc.
26. Foster, Richard. *Celebration of Discipline*. 79.
27. Ibid., 84.
28. Ibid., 86.

29. Richard Foster closes his chapter on simplicity with this prayer: "May God give you—and me—the courage, the wisdom, the strength always to hold the kingdom of God as the number-one priority of our lives. To do so is to live in simplicity." May this be your prayer and mine.

## Kingdomtide

### Thoughts for Further Reflection

"[T]here is only one God, and that One alone is worthy of worship in all the universe and beyond."

Ben Witherington III

"[E]ncounter with the holy can be a sanctifying and purifying one, one that conveys grace."

Ben Witherington III

"God is to be loved, of course, most of all: heavenly things too are to be much loved; but little love, or at least no more than is necessary, may be given to earthly things. This surely is the way we turn to Christ to desire nothing but Him."

Richard Rolle

"To worship is to see God as worthy, to ascribe great worth to Him."

Dallas Willard

"God is most glorified in us when we are most satisfied in Him."

John Piper

### Personal Ponderings on "Craven Image"

We do not understand the need and necessity of worship. We speak of and even sing of returning to the heart of worship, but we fail with almost every attempt. The reason for this is preoccupation with self. Our self-centeredness touches every aspect of our lives, not the least our time in worship. Perhaps this is why we have turned our attention away from the Object of our worship and onto the order of worship.

Twentieth century mystic Evelyn Underhill explored the call to worship in her work *Worship*. She writes, "Worship . . . is an avenue which leads the creature out from his inveterate self-occupation to a knowledge of God" and a union with God that frees us to truly live. To worship God "in spirit and in truth" is to set aside self and praise and proclaim God's glory instead. Such a practice frees us to "enter that great life of the spiritual universe which consists in the ceaseless proclamation of the Glory of God."[30] This cannot help but prevent us from preoccupation with self and possessions.

Underhill writes that true worship has the power to purify, enlighten, and transform us into people concerned only with God's glory and not their own. And in this is true life. "Worship," writes Underhill, "is therefore in the deepest sense creative and redemptive. Keeping us in constant remembrance of the Unchanging and the Holy, it cleanses us of subjectivism, releases us from 'use and wont' and makes us realists." It is this that moves us toward "our true destiny" as creatures made in the image of the Creator.[31]

(JNH)

---

30. Foster, Richard and Emilie Griffin, ed. *Spiritual Classics*. San Francisco: Harper Collins Publishers, 2000, 254.

31. Ibid.

*Kingdomtide*

## WATER RITES

Can sin be drowned in water,
E'en with a flood of tears?
Or is it rather Spirit
That grafts the sinner in?

Does parting of the waters
Make exodus come true?
Or is it rather death to sin
That makes the sinner new?

Between the two creations
Two baptisms confess
The one depicts the story
The other makes one blessed.

Immersion in Christ's story
Death, burial, new birth
Begins the tale of Christians
New creatures on old earth.

## THEOLOGICAL MUSINGS

THE DEBATES ABOUT THE nature of Christian baptism have been ongoing since the dawn of the Christian movement. Paul, in a moment of frustration because his Corinthian converts were making too much of baptism says that he thanks God he has not baptized more of them (see 1 Cor. 1). We can understand this lament when we come to the end of his discourse and he lets slip that some Corinthians are practicing proxy baptism on behalf of the dead. Apparently they think it is such a magical ritual even the dead can benefit from it.

Whichever side of the baptismal waters one stands on in the infant vs. adult baptism controversy, one thing is sure. Baptism is the sign of the new covenant and we really ought to be practicing it. Indeed Jesus commanded that we do so in Mt. 28. If only he had told us how to do it, how much water to use, and who the recipients ought to be!

By definition a sacrament is an outward and visible sign of an inward and spiritual reality. It can also be seen as a means of grace. It is this last idea that becomes a sticking point for some. Yet it is interesting that most of both the Paedo-Baptists and the Baptists want to insist that this rite is not just a matter of symbol and sign that points outside of itself to a spiritual reality. Most do want to say that something happens in baptism. It is interesting to me however that what we usually say happens is not in fact what Paul in Romans says happens.

In Romans 6.3 Paul asks his audience whether they know that those who have been baptized into Christ were baptized into his death. This is interesting language in many respects. What does it mean to be baptized into Christ? Is this just exalted language for being baptized into the body of Christ or into his church? The problem with this conclusion is that in 1 Cor. 12.13 Paul probably tells us that it is the Holy Spirit, not a human being who baptized us into the body of Christ. This was a spiritual transaction and it happened even for those in Corinth who truly became Christians but had not received water baptism. Whatever else Rom. 6.3 means it is clear at least that Paul identifies water baptism with death, Christ's death, rather than with the Spirit or the new life. He goes on to say "we are therefore buried with him through baptism into death in order that, just as Christ was raised from the dead . . . we too may walk in newness of life" (6.4). Baptism is likened to death and burial. Presumably Paul envisions immersion as being like going into the ground and being covered with dirt, though he mixes the metaphors here. Baptism then seems to be a symbol of the death of the old self, rather than a simple cleansing from sin.

Indeed it seems to be about the old self which has been crucified, dead, and buried, which is why Paul calls it being baptized into Christ's death, Christ's story. His story is recapitulated in the believer's story when they are converted. Only those who have died can rise to newness of life and walk that way, and so baptism is seen as depicting the end of the old person, to be followed by the arising to newness of life, just as Jesus received the Spirit, not with the water or in the water but as he was leaving the water (see Mk. 1:10). To put it in a contemporary fashion, it is the baptism by the Spirit rather than the baptism by the water that gives the believer the new life, and the ability to live a new life. Water baptism symbolizes the end of the old self, baptism by the Spirit not only grafts the believer into the body of Christ, but enables that person to live a new life. If this is correct then we need to not only know about two baptisms, both of which matter, but the one by the Spirit is more crucial than the one that involves water.[32]

## Spiritual Meditations

### "Water Rites"

- Lectio Divina: Romans 6:1–14
- To live in the "newness of life" that comes with death to self, we must daily immerse ourselves in prayer. In prayer we present ourselves to God and submit to His will. It involves both asking and action. In prayer we present not only our requests but our wills to God, ready to do what He asks of us. Focus your prayers this week on asking God where He might be calling you into action. Ask for wisdom and discernment, spending more time listening than speaking.
- Spiritual journaling can be a great way to regularly take an inventory of our walk with God. Grab a pen and paper and spend some time journaling through your thoughts on baptism—by water and Spirit—and what this symbolizes for you. If you prefer another medium (art, poetry, prose, song-writing, etc.), use it to express your own musings on this the two types of baptism spoken of in this selection.

### Thoughts for Further Reflection

*"Only those who have died can rise to newness of life and walk that way . . . "*

Ben Witherington III

*"[I]t is baptism by the Spirit rather than baptism by the water that gives the believer the new life, and the ability to live a new life."*

Ben Witherington III

*"The Christian lives in Christ and Christ lives in the Christian through the Holy Spirit. He is empowered to lead a new life where sin has no place."*

Brennan Manning

---

32. See Witherington, *Troubled Waters. Rethinking the Theology of Baptism*, (Waco: Baylor Univ. Press, 2007).

# The Living Legacy

*"A fire comes to a person's soul when that believer is filled with the Spirit, and there comes a passionate burning to know Christ and share His gospel. An ignited person with an ignited heart is the one baptized by the Spirit's fire."*

Dennis Kinlaw

## Personal Ponderings on "Water Rites"

Water baptism symbolizes the death to self and baptism by the Spirit an enabling to experience and live a new life in Christ. We understand this on paper, but are often left without the daily assurance that either has occurred in our lives. Many of us do not remember our water baptism and cannot pinpoint when we received the baptism of the Spirit. We must ask ourselves the question Dennis Kinlaw asks in his daily devotional *This Day with the Master*. "What are the evidences of the Spirit in the life of the believer?"

To be filled with the Holy Spirit is to desire spiritual things. The Spirit "brings alive within us a hunger for God's Word. The Scripture becomes a staple without which we cannot live."[33] The Spirit-filled believer has an appetite for God's word and study that are constant. God's Word and witness through the saints of the ages "becomes the food of our soul."[34]

Another evidence of the Spirit is the desire to pray. Kinlaw writes that those who walk in the Spirit, "long for the Spirit's company." Time spent in prayer is "not a burden, but a delight" because it affords us the opportunity to be with our Companion.[35]

The final two characteristics of the Spirit-filled Christian are a love for other believers and a desire to share "knowledge of the Spirit with others." We long for deep fellowship with others in the Spirit because such relationships allow us to experience a renewal and refreshment of the Spirit in our own lives. Those who walk in the Spirit are always ready to share that with others because they are filled with the love of God which is "an other-oriented love." If God's Spirit and love is within us, we will long to share that love others.[36]

(JNH)

---

33. Kinlaw, Dennis. *This Day with the Master*. Grand Rapids: Zondervan, 2002, April 14: *Touches of the Spirit*.

34. Ibid.

35. Ibid.

36. Ibid.

*Kingdomtide*

## BOUND TO BE FREE

In freedom there's a bondage
Which leads to endless choice.
In bondage there's a freedom
Excusing loss of voice.

What frees a person shows us
What bound them long before.
What binds a person demonstrates
The thing she loves the more.

Commitment and concession
Contrast in this respect
One's accepted freely
The other with regret.

Freedom is hardly freeing
If only freedom from.
What good is escaping evil
And missing Kingdom come?

Freedom from's inadequate
Unless there's freedom for.
What good is no encumbrances
Without an open door?

Redemption's more than freedom
From chains that bind the heart.
It's also a fresh purpose,
A goal, a brand new start.

The yokes we cast off tell us
The things that held us down.
The yokes we take up freely
Remind us where we're bound.

No matter our opinions
The truth will set us free.
For freedom I have been released
To bind my heart to Thee.

# The Living Legacy

## THEOLOGICAL MUSINGS

Americans are a tough audience to speak to about freedom. Most of them think they have a PhD in understanding freedom. After all we have been letting it 'ring' all over the land ever since the American Revolution. But what really is the nature of freedom? What freedoms do we really have?

Sometimes we talk about being free to do whatever we want. This of course is not true. We are not free to slander another human being. We are not free to murder someone. We are not free to steal someone else's property. We are not free to do ever so many things because of course there are laws against them. If all you mean by freedom is "no one is stopping me from doing this at the moment" this is really not saying much because though you can do some things that are illegal or immoral, they almost always have consequences which result in a loss of freedom. And furthermore, sometimes even God's messengers intervene and limit our freedoms (see Num. 22.21–33). It's not just the Law that limits our freedoms.

And then there is this further problem with raw voluntarism whose mantra is "I'm free to do as I please." In fact it is not true, because fallen human beings are all caught in the web of sin, are all in bondage to sin. Apart from the grace of God, sinning is inevitable which is another way of saying we are not free from sin unless God's grace frees us.

We do not talk enough about what we are freed for, once Christ sets us free. We are freed to bind ourselves to Christ and to his commandments. We are freed to serve, minister, pursue our calling. We have not been freed to do whatever we please but rather to do what pleases God. That's a very different matter than the sort of freedom we usually discuss in America.

Janis Joplin famously used to sing "freedom's just another word for nothing left to lose." St. Francis could have understood this definition of freedom. At the juncture at which he became a monk he divested himself of all his worldly goods, even the shirt off his back. He definitely had 'no thing' left to lose, except his life. There is a kind of freedom which comes when we divest ourselves of our possessions and discover that in one sense they had been possessing us rather than the converse. But divesting one's self of sin or property is certainly not all there is to Christian freedom.

Paul in Galatians 4–5 has a good deal to say about freedom and slavery. He tells us that a person who has been freed by Christ is free indeed. But that does not answer the question of what they are free to do with their freedom, or why they have been freed. He goes on in Gal. 5–6 to talk about walking according to the Spirit, manifesting the fruit of the Spirit, and obeying the Law of Christ. This is not usually what Americans mean when they talk about what they are free to say or do.

Perhaps then what we need to do is take back the concept of freedom from its secular definitions. Perhaps we need a new thesaurus. Perhaps we need to talk about sacred freedom, freedom in Christ and what it does and does not mean. Perhaps we need to de-enculturate ourselves from the propaganda of the Founding Fathers and stick with the vision of the Church Fathers. Freedom is a heady drink for anyone to imbibe. My suggestion then to fallen people would be when it comes to this drink—"drink responsibly" and from the right source.

## Spiritual Meditations

### "Bound to be Free"

- Lectio Divina: Galatians 5:1–15
- True fasting is a giving of the whole self to God that He might reveal himself in a new way. While the discipline of fasting seems a time of poverty, it is really a time of gain and feasting. However, for it to be thus it must be an act of the heart. In fasting, we are giving God our heart and our desires. Fast from food or something else today. You will find your participation in this discipline to be liberating in more than one way.
- Witherington's words and Paul's in Galatians encourage us to live free, but not in an indulgent kind of freedom. We are freed to live no longer for self, but for God and for others. The discipline of service frees us to do this. Find a way to serve others this week in some way and discover the freedom that comes from thinking of and caring for others.

### Thoughts for Further Reflection

*"We are freed to bind ourselves to Christ and to his commandments. We are freed to serve, minister, pursue our calling. We have not been freed to do whatever we please but rather to do what pleases God."*

Ben Witherington III

## The Living Legacy

*"Make me a captive, Lord, and then I shall be free!"*

George Matheson

*"God delivers us from sin: we . . . have to present our natural life to God and sacrifice it until it is transformed into a spiritual life by obedience."*

Oswald Chambers

*"The wholly obedient life is mastered and unified and simplified and gathered up into the love of God and it lives and walks among men in the perpetual flame of that radiant love. For the simplified man loves God with all his heart and mind and soul and strength and abides trustingly in that love."*

Thomas R. Kelly

### Personal Ponderings on "Bound to be Free"

Paradox is a fascinating concept, especially when it applies to our spiritual life. There is no greater and more blessed paradox than that we are freed to be bound in Christ. Each time this particular paradox surfaces in my life, I return again to that old George Matheson hymn entitled "Make Me a Captive, Lord." The whole of the song and our life in Christ is summed up in the first few words, "Make me a Captive, Lord, and then I shall be free."[37] Such freedom cannot be explained; it must be experienced.

Freedom in Christ allows us to be taken captive in the things of God instead of the things of the world. As Henri Nouwen says in the devotional *Bread for the Journey*, captivity in Christ frees and empowers us to be. "[T]he Spirit of Jesus given to us reveals our true identities," writes Nouwen. This frees us from pursuing our identity in the world and in others and instead in God. "The world enslaves us in fear; the Spirit frees us from that slavery and restores us to the true relationship." No longer are we unsure of who we are or concerned about what others say about us. We know who we are. "We are God's beloved sons and daughters." That is the most liberating truth there is![38]

(JNH)

---

37. See *Make Me a Captive, Lord*, by George Matheson, c. 1890.

38. Nouwen, Henri J. M. *Bread for the Journey*. San Francisco: Harper Collins Publishers, 1997. June 10: *Empowered to Be*.

### THE SHEPHERD

The shepherd tends his precious flock
One eye upon the sky.
His staff and crook are both in hand,
The Adversary's sly.

The sheep are quite oblivious
They sense no danger there
They graze on what they find to hand
They seem without a care.

# The Living Legacy

Bur danger lurks without, within
The shepherd knows it's true.
Sheep so easily scatter
The wolves know what to do.

He calls the sheep by their own names
He sheers them of their dross
He tends them all so tenderly
They lose their fear of loss.

The judgments of a shepherd
Must be wiser than a king
The shepherd must remain alert
Prepared for anything.

When to use the shepherd's crook
Or let the stray roam free?
When to pass through death's dark vale
And when to let them be?

When to prod and when to poke
When to praise and then reward
When to scold or then rebuke
When to ignore or to record?

When to leave the 99
And pay a dreadful cost
When to risk one's livelihood
To seek and save the lost?

Who is sufficient for these things
Who'll keep the freezing warm?
Who lays down his life for silly sheep
Or shelters them from storm?

So persevere good shepherd
Don't give way to dark despair.
Guide, and guard and goad again
This is pastoral care.

*Kingdomtide*

Lead us in paths of righteousness
For his own dear namesake,
We're bound for greener pastures now
Lead on until daybreak.

## THEOLOGICAL MUSINGS

I've had occasion to watch shepherds and sheep from time to time. One thought constantly recurs. Sheep are not notably bright. A flock of them require both a good shepherd and a good sheep dog to keep them on the right path and moving in the right direction. Yes, it's easier than herding cats, but no, it is not easy to shepherd sheep. Sheep do have one endearing quality however. They do know how to play follow the leader. Dale Carnegie tells the story of growing up on a sheep farm. He used to love the end of the day when the sheep dog would drive the sheep into their pen. Carnegie said he would open the sheep pen gate and then place a stick in the way of the opening. The first sheep would jump over it, then the second, then the third. Then Carnegie would withdraw the stick. But those sheep just kept jumping over the now non-existent barrier. They knew how to follow and imitate the leader. Somehow it is not all that reassuring when Jesus likens his followers to sheep, and himself to a Shepherd, though he adds the comforting reminder that he is the *Good* Shepherd. The image suggests that there is never a time when his followers will not need his pastoral skills.

Much then depends on the quality of leadership in a church. Of course now we have all sorts of high tech aids meant to help us be better shepherds. We even have Leadership Magazine to help us adopt and adapt the latest techniques from the business world. This is forgetting however that directing employees is one thing, guiding and guarding sheep quite another. I'm not sure such secular leadership models really transfer all that well to the pastoral work.

As the poem suggests, much depends on the judgments of the leader. If the followers are looking to the leader for guidance, then he had best be ready to guide, not merely to take an opinion poll of the congregation. His or her cues for leadership should be taken from good models that are already out there. Models of previous excellent ministers, and of course Biblical models we find in the NT, with Jesus being the pre-imminent one.

Being a shepherd can be a thankless task. Very few persons really like to be prodded or poked or goaded into going the right way, and doing the right thing. Sheep would much prefer just to be fed, not to be forced in any particular direction. Yet all of this is the task of the shepherd.

There are times when one needs to realize that as a shepherd one must do the right thing, and do it for God's name sake not for one's own, much less for the plaudits one receives for the effort. One more thing. While the sheep do know the sound of the shepherd's voice and will follow it, sheep are not much given to listening to long speeches. They have a short attention span, and their feet and minds wander. This is why discipline and tough love are often necessary. The miracle is, they will follow you if you lead them where they need to go and where God wants them to go, even if you don't exactly have the best pastoral skills.

## Spiritual Meditations

### "The Shepherd"

- Lectio Divina: John 10:1–18; Psalm 23
- Christian leadership demands humility and mercy, both with oneself and others. The surest way to this is through confession. As we confess our own sins to God, we are enabled to walk with others in theirs. Seeing where we have sinned and strayed will grow in us deep, abiding humility and a capacity for mercy toward others that we cannot know without confession.
- To be an effective Christian leader (or shepherd as this poem puts it), a person must first allow themselves to be led. This being led involved the leadership of Christ and others. "Leadership," writes Henri Nouwen in his book *In the Name of Jesus*, "for a large part, means to be led." We must always place ourselves in an attitude of learning if we are to teach, of being led if we are to lead. Consider finding a spiritual guide to help lead you as you seek to lead others. You might contact a friend in the faith who you see as spiritually strong or even consider consulting one of the great saints of the ages for wisdom.

*Kingdomtide*

### Thoughts for Further Reflection

*"Being a Shepherd can be a thankless task. Very few persons really like to be prodded or poked or goaded into going the right way and doing the right thing. Sheep would much prefer just to be fed, not to be forced in any particular direction. Yet all of this is the task of the shepherd."*

Ben Witherington III

*"[S]heep will follow you if you lead them where they need to go and where God wants them to go . . . "*

Ben Witherington III

*"[W]hen Jesus speaks about shepherding, he does not want us to think about a brave, lonely shepherd who takes care of a large flock of obedient sheep. In many ways, he makes it clear that the ministry is a communal and mutual experience . . . We cannot bring good news on our own. We are called to proclaim the Gospel together, in community."*

Henri Nouwen

### Personal Ponderings on "The Shepherd"

Not many of us have had the opportunity to watch a shepherd herd sheep. Yet it is to this biblical image that many of us are drawn when we think of God. The Lectio Divina passages for this selection are beloved passages. We love them because they paint a vivid picture for us of a God who is tender and attentive, gentle and trustworthy. We enjoy these images because they give us the sense that we are provided for and protected. We know that the "great Shepherd of the sheep" will give us everything we need (Hebrews 13:20).

It is to this sort of leading that we are called as leaders or shepherds of others. We are all called to lead as God leads, like a shepherd with his sheep. The most important thing we can do as Christian leaders, as Henri Nouwen has said in his book *In the Name of Jesus*, is to make ourselves like a shepherd and come in "powerlessness and humility." A leadership of littleness and love is what those in our care need. This is the task of the shepherd and our task as well.[39]

Christian leadership, like shepherding, is not for the weak. Shepherding and leadership alike demand a deep well of inner strength and confidence. To be a humble and powerless leader does not imply weakness, but strength. The true Christian leader is first led by Christ and "so deeply in love with Jesus that they are ready to follow him wherever he guides them, always trusting that, with him, they will find life and find it abundantly." As Nouwen writes, "If there is any hope for the church in the future it will be hope for a poor church in which its leaders are willing to be led."[40]

(JNH)

---

39. Nouwen, Henri J. M. *In the Name of Jesus*. New York: The Crossroad Publishing Company, 1989, 82.

40. Ibid., p. 84.

*Kingdomtide*

## BRAIN FOOD

I've got a genuine replica brain,
It's a collectible rendition,
I grant it's not the latest model,
But it's in good condition.

It still processes data well
Though there are some memory lapses
It knows the difference between good and evil,
And even between knaves and apses.

There's minimal start up time (with the help
    of good coffee)
And it can multi-task
But if you want infallible or word perfect
You'd best not ask.

This brain is not for sale,
Nor is it on permanent loan
But what with our new technology
I understand it can be cloned.

If you're looking for help with the Bible,
Or music and good books,
I've got a lot of things stuffed into the cortex
That deserve a second look.

If you find someone to clone it,
Please do make it known,
I would like a backup copy
Of my very own.

I've got a genuine replica brain,
Though some synapses are misfiring
This accounts for the forgetfulness,
Just blame it on the wiring.

I was thinking of advertising this on eBay
But then remembered I had a blog,
If you would like a data dump download
Then reply to my data log.

## The Living Legacy

## THEOLOGICAL MUSINGS

This rather whimsical self parody is meant to make us think about some more serious issues, like cloning. Cloning of course, and the use of embryonic stem cells for regenerating organs and the like, is a hot topic to say the least. The problem of course for Christians is that few know enough about the science of what we are talking about to really know whether we should see it as a blessing or a bane, and good thing or a wicked one. My wife the biologist tells me that we don't need embryonic stem cells from fetuses to use stem cells for medical purposes. We can harvest them from other sources.

But there is something else going on in this poem that took me a while to realize, namely I am describing the brain as if it were a computer of sorts. Whether we are happy about it or not, living in the computer age affects our thinking about everything, even our thinking about thinking. But is there more to the brain than just wiring and synapses firing? What is implicitly being asked in this poem is whether the hardware should simply be identified with the software, or put more clearly, is the mind the same thing as the brain, or does the brain just house the mind?

While this is a question perhaps primarily for philosophy of science, it is also a theological question since we now know that the brain alone, (and not our internal organs such as that pump called the heart), is the seat of all thought, feeling, will, and the like. The Israelites spoke of the heart being the control center of the personality, even referred to the 'thoughts of the heart' but in fact all that we are seems to be processed through the brain itself, or at least the mind. But clearly the mind is so much more than just the physiological brain.

Take for instance the story of Ezraf, a Turkish artist. I blogged about his remarkable story in February 2008. He is a man not merely born blind, but born without eyeballs. And yet, and yet he is able to paint three dimension landscapes and objects. His story is remarkable too in that scientists have hooked up his brain and studied it while he is painting, and the eye area of the brain lights up when he visualizes things in his mind's eye. When I posted this story on my blog, various other contributors, including one blind girl, contributed their own stories of similar realities. In Ezraf's minds eye, he sees many things, even though he has never physically seen anything. And this involves more than just one part of the brain compensating for another that is damaged, though that is part of the truth. There is more going on than even a heightened sense of touch compensating, though that is true. Ezraf's abilities are bordering on the miraculous. Could it be that rather than the mind being in the brain, perhaps the mind only uses the brain to access the world? Could it be that the mind is what the ancients called the human spirit, which they believed was a gift of God's Spirit. What is most interesting to me about the story of Ezraf is that it raises the question—whose running his brain? By this I mean, who's doing the thinking on behalf of Ezraf's damaged system so that it knows to over-compensate in other areas, and it knows to stimulate the sight areas in the brain when he imagines a landscape even though Ezraf isn't physically looking at anything? I am not buying that this is just a chemical process in the brain. Chemicals can't think and make rational decisions about compensation, and changing a system so it still functions. And please don't tell me 'it's because of evolution' because that explains nothing. A brain cannot think by itself without being connected to a person who does the thinking.

What this whole story of Ezraf reminds me of is what the psalmist said so long ago—'We are fearfully and wonderfully made' for God has woven us together. Perhaps, he keeps giving input and tinkering with the wires, as life goes on. Whatever may be the empirical truth about all this I have confidence that when we get to the bottom of the human brain we will discover that we are far less god-like than we might have thought, someone else's running the show, and as it turns out, God is far more God-like in our lives than we ever realized, constantly being involved in our daily existence.

## Spiritual Meditations

### "Brain Food"

- Lectio Divina: Psalm 139
- The discipline of study has the power to renew and transform the mind so that it might resist being conformed to the world. Failure to study prevents us from becoming whole and holy. "The discipline of individual and corporate study keeps us aware of our growth needs,

alert to the vital issues of the world around us, and sensitized to what God is doing to grow us up into Christ and call us forth to be agents of grace in the midst of the world's issues," writes M. Robert Mulholland.[41] In order to be "transformed by the renewing of our mind," we must engage in the discipline of study (Romans 12:2). If you are not already involved in a small group study, consider forming one around a book of the Bible or a Christian classic. The group and individual time will help keep your mind on the things of God and provide encouragement and strength when you need it most.

- Worship is another means by which we orient ourselves, more specifically our minds, to God. The act of worship should by no means be limited to a weekly church service. Worship can and should be entered into the entire week through. As you go about your week, take time out to worship God. The Book of Psalms is always a great guide for this, reminding us of God's greatness and calling us to praise and singing. Spend at least part of your worship times this week asking God to surprise you in your everyday, that you might worship Him spontaneously even amidst the mundane tasks of life.

### Thoughts for Further Reflection

*"Could it be that rather than the mind being in the brain, perhaps the mind only uses the brain to access the world? Could it be that the mind is what the ancients called the human spirit, which they believed was a gift of God's Spirit?"*

Ben Witherington III

*"God is far more God-like in our lives than we ever realized, constantly being involved in our daily existence."*

Ben Witherington III

*"In the final analysis, there is nothing we can do to transform ourselves into persons who love and serve as Jesus did except to make ourselves available to God to do that work of transforming grace in our lives."*

M. Robert Mulholland

---

41. Mulholland, M. Robert. *Invitation to a Journey: A Road Map for Spiritual Formation.* Downer's Grove: InterVarsity Press, 1993, 118.

## Kingdomtide

*"My God, here I am, all Yours; Lord make me according to your heart."*

Brother Lawrence

### Personal Ponderings on "Brain Food"

While it is not within our power to transform ourselves, we can make ourselves available to God through spiritual discipline. This is where Brother Lawrence of the Resurrection provides unmatched guidance and help. In that classic collection of his letters and thoughts called *The Practice of the Presence of God* are the tools we need to be faithful and available people of God. Lawrence encourages that the real business of being a Christian is simply to think of and adore God with our lives.

In order to give ourselves and our minds over to God, we must "devote ourselves entirely to knowing God." Brother Lawrence writes that "the more we know Him the more we want to know Him; knowledge is commonly the measure of love, the deeper and wider our knowledge, the greater will be our love."[42] Redeeming our minds for the purposes of God and the fulfillment of our calling as Christians demands that we "seek Him often by faith" and banish "from our hearts and minds all else." God alone should inhabit our minds and this is something we cannot accomplish on our own. We must, as Lawrence put it, "ask this grace of Him." If we do this and "on our part we do the best we can, we will soon see in ourselves the changes that we are hoping for."[43]

(JNH)

---

42. Lawrence of the Resurrection, Brother. *The Practice of the Presence of God.* New York: Image Books, 1977, p. 82.

43. Ibid.

## CHANGED

"Changed.
I say I'm changed.
Ironing out one's deepest wrinkles
Isn't strange."

"Gone.
Perhaps gone on.
Those wanderlusting feelings
Once so strong."

"Clear.
Horizon's clear.
I see where I must go
While standing here."

"Hope.
That helps me cope.
Even though I've started down
The dark and dusty slope."

"Resolved.
To not look back.
In longing or in anger
And get off track."

"Possessed.
Not a possessor.
By a Spirit not my own
I'm made confessor."

"Consumed.
Not a consumer.
There's room for growth
In a late bloomer."

"Changed.
But for the better.
The Giver is no more
A greedy getter."

*Kingdomtide*

In short—
Spotless leopards can adapt
Old dog saying isn't apt.

For my Father on his 90th birthday
May 31, 2006

## THEOLOGICAL MUSINGS

THE CONCEPT OF CONVERSION seemed a strange one to most ancients. Most of them believed that a leopard could not change its spots, nor an old dog learn new tricks. In societies that highly valued the static and unchanging, the notion of a person changing made him seem quixotic, unreliable, chameleon-like. Most ancients believed that a person was born with a certain personality and stuck with it. It did not develop or change over time, it was simply revealed over time. Needless to say the ancients were innocent of Freudian and Jungian theories about developmental personality issues and early childhood influences.

It thus comes as something of a surprise, if you know the character of ancient culture, that there is so much emphasis in the New Testament on 'turning' 'turning around' 'turning back' or just plain changing. In Acts alone we have a plethora of accounts of people converting to Christianity from all sorts of different backgrounds. Clearly Luke did not subscribe to the ancient notion that geography, gender, and generation determined who one was and could be. He even recounts the story of Paul's conversion three times, and we may compare the repetition of the Cornelius story as well. Doubtless Luke felt he had to be emphatic about the change in these person's lives lest the idea be dismissed as improbable.

We by contrast are all too ready to believe that people can and do change. I have a colleague who says that he responded to the altar call to be 'born again' so many times when he was a youth that he came to have stretch-marks on his soul! The poem above comes out of that sort of environment, as I am the child of a revivalist tradition known as Methodism. Of course there can also be changes for the worse, as well as changes for the better. We can all think of persons who have converted to some cult like Scientology, and it has ruined their family's lives and unity. I am not talking about what might be called a negative or retrograde conversion, much less of outright apostasy. I am talking about a work of grace in the soul of a person that changes them for the better. This of course presupposes that they needed such a change.

It is often the case that many people don't accept change in their life until they are either forced to do so, or at least until they realize that they profoundly need to do so. I once had a parishioner who could be called a really independent stubborn farmer's wife. She had major health issues but wouldn't do anything about it. This finally landed her in the hospital. As I walked in the room to visit her she boomed out "Howdy preacher, I guess God had to lay me flat on my back before I would look up to him." St. Paul could relate.

What I am especially focusing on in this poem is how a real conversion makes a person a more hopeful, future oriented, and more selfless person. The most primal of all sins can be said to be narcissism, "coeur in curvatus in se"—'the heart turned in upon itself', or as we would call it, self-centeredness. Notice the story of Adam and how he became not merely self- aware, but profoundly self-conscious, and in the process not focused on God, once he had sinned. Thank goodness grace can do something about this, but it takes more than a one time conversion for a person to live a self-sacrificial life.

Here is where I must make a confession. Self-absorption is something I have really had to battle in the last decade or so of my life. I love what I do, and love to use my gifts and graces, and I have had an enormous amount of positive feedback to my preaching, teaching, and writing. But that can lead to a person becoming far too self-centered. I have learned that the conversion of the will must be an ongoing thing, even if the conversion of the mind or imagination has long been in place. John Wesley speaks of the need to depend on God's grace day by day, and sometimes even hour by hour so one will be one's best self on an ongoing basis. You see what we do with a change in our lives is in large measure up to the individuals in question. How will we respond to what God has wrought in our souls? This poem attempts to articulate what some of the positive responses could be to such 'change', so that one becomes 'better' not 'bitter.' While it may be true that 'there is nothing so inevitable as change', the sort of change I am talking about is neither inevitable nor automatic in a person's life. It must be sought and embraced, and its impact must be felt and then lived out.

Conversion is not merely ordinary mundane change in another disguise. It is a change only God can bring about, and which humans can only request, not create or engineer. I wish sometimes that some revivalists would realize this. Revivalists sometimes seem to think that with the right music, preaching, and importuning we can make God an offer he can't refuse, and conversion will inevitably happen at such a worship service. We would do better to pray "Spirit of the living God, fall afresh on me" and leave it in God's hands and with God's timing.

George Mueller was a remarkable man of prayer, and he prayed for the conversion of two men he had known since youth with great regularity for twenty-nine years. When asked whether he still expected God to do something in their lives, after so long a time, his response was words to the effect of "Yes. For I cannot believe God would put such a burden on my heart for so long, were he not planning to intervene." In due course the desired change happened in both men's lives, one converted only weeks before his death. God is the change agent, and the sooner we realize he is, and we are not, the sooner we will know the source of our help and strength. It does not lie ultimately in self-help plans or programs or New Year's resolutions or small group therapy, it lies in God, and more particularly in Christ.

## Spiritual Meditations

### "Changed"

- Lectio Divina: 1 Corinthians 2:1–5
- The discipline of silence grows in us an inner stillness that is in tune with God's work within us. Jesus himself required times of silence and solitude to center Himself. Silence and solitude can bring us back to the place where we remember that it is God who works in and through us and that he is the source of our strength and power. Take advantage of the little silences that fill your day however they come and reflect upon God's constant help in your own life. Journal your thoughts that you might return to them in times of pride or weakness.
- Pray through the divine reading passage for this selection. Ask God to grow in you an attitude like Paul's. Consider rewriting his words as a prayer for your own life.

# The Living Legacy

## Thoughts for Further Reflection

*"Conversion is not merely ordinary mundane change in another disguise. It is a change only God can bring about, and which humans can only request, not create or engineer."*

Ben Witherington III

*"God is the change agent, and the sooner we realize he is, and we are not, the sooner we will know the source of our help and strength."*

Ben Witherington III

*"The call of God is the expression of God's nature, not of our nature... The majority of us have no ear for anything but ourselves, we cannot hear a thing God says. To be brought into the zone of the call of God is to be profoundly altered."*

Oswald Chambers

*"[I]f you want to make some great strides toward spiritual maturity, then do not trust in your own power or your own knowledge. Humility before God and distrust of your old self, with an open simplicity are fundamental virtues for you."*

Fénelon

### Personal Ponderings on "Changed"

Since being introduced to the life and works of E. Stanley Jones, I have wished that I had been given the opportunity to know him personally in his lifetime. I feel I have had the opportunity to converse with him through his books, but would have reveled in the chance to sit at his feet and listen to his life. A remarkable man of faith and action, Jones "devoted his whole life to the subject of conversion" as a missionary and a writer.[44] While he was a man of many accomplishments, the greatest was his "keen understanding of the spiritual life and the means of spiritual renewal."

---

44. Foster, Richard and James Bryan Smith, eds. *Devotional Classics*. San Francisco: HarperCollins Publishers, 2005, p. 281.

"Conversion," Jones reflects, "is a gift and an achievement. It is the act of a moment and the work of a lifetime."[45] It is a gift of God and not something we can earn. Yet the paradox is that "you cannot retain it without disciplines." We can do nothing to earn salvation, but "when the self is surrendered to Christ and a new center formed, then you can discipline your life around that new center—Christ," writes Jones. "Discipline is the fruit of conversion—not the source of it."[46]

Our converted life will "fade out" unless we engage in daily "receptivity and response" through what Jones calls "simple habits." He writes that these habits are found first in Jesus Christ himself and ought always be found in us as well. "No converted person," Jones states, "can live without [these] habits at work vitally in his life."[47] These habits are simply "reading the Word of God daily, preferably in the morning," speak to God daily through prayer, and "pass along to others what you have found."

As we engage ourselves in these habits and virtues, we will grow in our conversion. As Jones puts it, the area of our conversion will be enlarged and we will take "in fresh territory everyday." Conversion is a growth process and all "growth in Christian living is growth in love."[48]

---

45. Ibid.
46. Ibid.
47. Ibid., p. 282.
48. Ibid., p. 285.

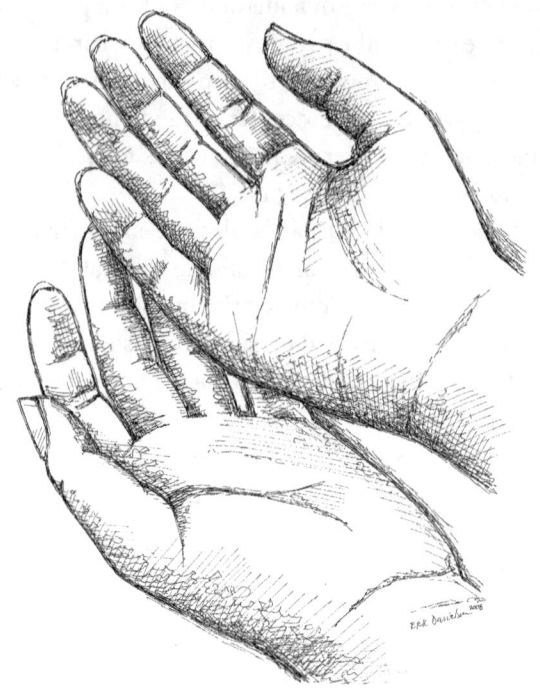

## CLOSURE

"My life closed twice, before its close"
Said Emily in her prime,
But closure happens many ways,
And comes at many times.

At birth the cord is severed,
The start requires an end,
Cut off, a form of closure,
Allows you to begin.

But how to shut the mental door,
And close out endless sound?
Or is the whispered still small voice
Heard through the noise around?

## *Kingdomtide*

How do you close a painful wound,
Caused by friends on edge
Whose jagged way of loving
Has pushed you to the ledge?

How do you finish efforts
Abandoned by those you trust,
Your heart's no longer in it
But finishing's a must?

How do you turn the page,
And let bygones be gone,
And realize moving forward,
Requires your moving on?

Completion, finished, ending
The longing for the goal,
But what if its perfection,
That finally makes us whole?

The letting go, the giving in,
The learning to release,
Is half the key to living,
And half the key to peace.

A person can be measured
By closures on the way,
And by the One who carried her
Upon her dying day.

The Alpha and Omega Man
Is where all endings lead
If we're enclosed within his grasp,
It's all the end we need.

    July 22, 2004

# The Living Legacy

## THEOLOGICAL MUSINGS

THIS POEM IS AN appropriate one with which to end this collection. It is also a good one to end the Christian year with as well. The Christian year, it will be remembered begins at the end of November with Advent. It is the Roman calendar which begins with January, the month celebrating Janus, the god who looked both ways. The Christian calendar differs both from the Roman one which is generally observed in the world today, and the Jewish calendar when begins in the early fall with Rosh Hashannah, the head of the year. The Christian calendar, like the Jewish calendar is lunar, not solar, which is why we have some 'moveable' feasts, like Easter and Pentecost which parallels moveable Jewish feasts like Passover.

I have found as I have gone through life that for me it helps the rhythms of life to think not so much in terms of the calendar as the Romans bequeathed it to us, nor to think in terms of the natural seasons (and of course many Christians live where there aren't four proper seasons anyway), but to think in terms of the Christian calendar which begins with celebration of a second coming (the first Sunday in Advent) then a first one and ends with thanksgiving and praise for all the year and harvest home.

'Closure' is a poem intended to speaking about bringing to orderly conclusion certain cycles of life, and doing it in a Christian manner. It is of course true that in a world full of broken relationships of all sorts, most of us are longing for some closure and resolution of the lose ends in our lives. Many relationships, even Christian ones, end badly and without closure, which is another way of saying many end in non-Christian fashion. But there is something to be learned both from the natural and supernatural closures in our lives, and this poem reflects that conception. Closure is not just something that happens at the end of life, but as the poem says comes in many ways and at many times.

For example, birth itself is an ending. No more hiding in the womb, its time to face the real world. And in fact, this can be a metaphor for a lot of transitions in life. While you can live your life as an ostrich, continually sticking your head in the sand when trouble arises, not only is the view boring but it rarely solves anything, and meanwhile everyone else is getting a front row view of your posterior! Facing life means knowing how to bring things to good closures, even when the transition is very painful. When someone wounds you deeply, the character of your faith has an opportunity to shine forth. Will you be proactive or will you merely be reactive, either licking your wounds and looking for sympathy or lashing out against the one who hurt you? What would Jesus do in such a situation? Well actually we know what he did do. He forgave even his executioners from the cross! Obviously this took a lot of grace and was not a normal human response. But then followers of Christ are not called to 'normal human responses.' They are called to Christ-likeness.

Or consider what happens when you are given a task in life which is challenging, and you have every reason for your heart not to be in it any more. How do you finish? Do you finish strong, or do you simply limp to the finish line, perhaps because of how you are treated in the execution of the task?

I learned a real life lesson when I saw how my father responded to the way North Carolina National Bank treated him at the end of his career. First they froze his salary for some years, I suppose hoping he would quit. But Dad had a ministry to the younger workers there. Those Harvard MBAs kept showing up and he kept training them with grace and kindness to be good employees of the bank, even though they were much younger and already making way more money than Dad made. Then the bank, instead of adding to his pension fund or the like, had a farewell to my father in which they gave him a few golf clubs instead of a nest egg to help him through the rest of his life and thank him for decades of service. He smiled nicely and thanked them. My father at that point was the only remaining employee from High Point N.C. who had moved to Charlotte in 1971 when the Bank bought out a factoring firm in High Point and incorporated it into the bank itself (though they had initially said they would not move everyone). The others who made the move fell by the wayside or moved on, but my father stuck to his job right to the end, and did it well, even when he wasn't treated well and appropriately. He kept his word and he worked hard to the end. This is finishing strong and in a Christian manner. I learned a lot about closure from watching that whole life scenario unfold.

Sometimes closure means knowing how to let go of some things as well. This includes knowing how to let go of some relationships, which is hard. Since you cannot and should not try and control other people's every moves, you have to release them into God's hands and plans. I find that I have to do this repeatedly. I love my children, but I have to resist the temptation to orchestrate their lives now that they are also grown ups. I can advise, but they must decide whether they will take the advice. I can assist, but I must resist the tendency to do it for them. As that pop philosopher Sting once said "if you love somebody, set them free." What he did not say is how excruciatingly hard it is to do that when you really love someone. There is always a deep urge to possess that person or to control that person or to make sure nothing goes wrong for that person. This is a natural parental instinct, but it has to be overcome when your children grow up. Closure sometimes means letting go and letting God take over.

Lastly, closure means releasing your death grip on your own life and placing it back into the hands of God. It means unclenching your fists as Henri Nouwen liked to say. Human beings have a propensity to want to take back what they lay on the altar, especially when it is themselves! Yet there is wisdom in recognizing that all the while we thought we were running our own lives, in fact Christ was carrying us especially through the crises. Closure involves recognizing, accepting and submitting to the fact that we are not the masters of our own fates, nor the captains of our own souls. Christ is Lord of our life, and so we need to do less micromanaging of it. In the end, the closure we most need is knowing that Christ has a firm grip on us right to the end, and he will be with us always, right through death and on to the other side preparing a nice afterlife for us. In short, closures are God's way of prompting us to ask "What's Next?" because for the person who has everlasting life, there is always something more coming soon.

## Spiritual Meditations

### "Closure"

- Lectio Divina: Psalm 31:1–5; Jude 24–25
- Confess to God those areas of your life that you have failed to fully surrender to him. Releasing and relaxing your grip through daily confession of your own need to control your life will allow God to break in and do new and powerful things in and through you. Ask God to help you unclench your fists, as Henri Nouwen, puts it, and take his hand.
- For Christ to truly be Lord of our life, we must learn to let go. Part of letting go is remembering where God has met you and sustained you in the past. Spend some time reflecting on how God has shown

himself faithful and capable of guiding your life. Journal through this or use another medium to express your gratitude for this. Regularly reflecting on God's goodness to you and provision for you in the past will help you to let go in the present and the future.

### Thoughts for Further Reflection

*"[C]losure means releasing your death grip on your own life and placing it back into the hands of God."*

Ben Witherington III

*"Closure involves recognizing, accepting and submitting to the fact that we are not the masters of our own fates, nor the captains of our own souls. Christ is Lord of our life, and so we need to do less micro-managing of it."*

Ben Witherington III

*"Self is emptied into God, and God in-fills it."*

Thomas Kelly

*"Our strength and energy for work increase when we have prayed to God to give us the strength we need for our daily work."*

Dietrich Bonhoeffer

*"We are not ourselves by ourselves."*

Eugene Peterson

### Personal Ponderings on "Closure"

I have come to the realization in my own life that faith is best understood as a process of constantly holding on and letting go. We hold onto Jesus and we let go of ourselves. We lean into God's sovereignty, embrace all the mystery, and trust God instead of self. One of the greatest descriptions of faith I have found is in Frederick Buechner's *Wishful Thinking*:

*A Theological ABC*, which I have referenced before in this collection. His thoughts on faith encourage and inspire.

> "Faith is better understood as a verb than as a noun, as a process than as a possession. It is on-again-off-again rather than once-and-for-all. Faith is not being sure where you are going but going anyway. A journey without maps."[49]

This to me is what the poem "Closure" is all about. It is not a once-and-for-all thing, but a course in letting go that is repeated throughout our lives. We must choose to submit and surrender again and again in this life. We must constantly choose to follow God on this "journey without maps," because he has shown it to be the only worthwhile journey in the end.

(JNH)

---

49. Buechner, Frederick. *Wishful Thinking: A Theological ABC*. New York: Harper and Row Publishers, 1973, p. 25.

# Kingdomtide

www.ingramcontent.com/pod-product-compliance
Lightning Source LLC
Chambersburg PA
CBHW071233230426
43668CB00011B/1424